Marianne M. V...

Financial Success in Mental Health Practice

Financial Success in Mental Health Practice

Essential Tools and Strategies for Practitioners

Steven Walfish and Jeffrey E. Barnett

American Psychological Association

Washington, DC

Second Printing December, 2010

Published by
American Psychological Association
750 First Street, NE
Washington, DC 20002
www.apa.org

To order
APA Order Department
P.O. Box 92984
Washington, DC 20090-2984
Tel: (800) 374-2721; Direct: (202) 336-5510
Fax: (202) 336-5502; TDD/TTY: (202) 336-6123
Online: www.apa.org/books/
E-mail: order@apa.org

In the U.K., Europe, Africa, and the Middle East, copies may be ordered from
American Psychological Association
3 Henrietta Street
Covent Garden, London
WC2E 8LU England

Typeset in Meridien by Circle Graphics, Inc., Columbia, MD

Printer: Sheridan Books, Ann Arbor, MI
Cover Designer: Minker Design, Bethesda, MD
Technical/Production Editor: Tiffany L. Klaff

The opinions and statements published are the responsibility of the authors, and such opinions and statements do not necessarily represent the policies of the American Psychological Association.

Library of Congress Cataloging-in-Publication Data

Walfish, Steven.
  Financial success in mental health practice : essential tools and strategies for
practitioners / Steven Walfish and Jeffrey E. Barnett. — 1st ed.
      p. ; cm.
  Includes bibliographical references and index.
  ISBN-13: 978-1-4338-0374-1
  ISBN-10: 1-4338-0374-7
  1. Mental health services—Practice. 2. Mental health services—Administration. 3.
Mental health services—Finance. I. Barnett, Jeffrey E. II. Title.
  [DNLM: 1. Mental Health Services—organization & administration. 2. Practice
Management, Medical—economics. 3. Financial Management—methods. 4. Private Practice—
organization & administration. WM 30 W174f 2009]
  RA790.75.W35 2009
  616.890068—dc22   2008005954

British Library Cataloguing-in-Publication Data
A CIP record is available from the British Library.

Printed in the United States of America
First Edition

To David E. Stenmark, who would have grinned from ear to ear seeing this book published, and to Mary, who always helped and always will help to fill my life with warmth, love, and purpose.
—Steven Walfish

I express my deepest thanks to my wife, Stephanie, and to my children, Stuart and Maddie.
Their ongoing love, support, and encouragement throughout my career have enabled me to achieve much of what I have accomplished thus far. They make it all meaningful to me.
—Jeffrey E. Barnett

Contents

III

IV

Preface

Between the two of us we have been in full-time practice for 45 years. During this time we have completed an estimated 4,500 psychological evaluations and participated in 49,000 psychotherapy sessions.

This level of experience has allowed us the opportunity to make mistakes too numerous to count. These mistakes have cost us money that we will never see again. Our goal in presenting the material in this volume is to help the reader learn from our experiences and mistakes and to optimize income and minimize financial mistakes. In our opinion people can learn things the hard way (through their own hit-or-miss experiences) or the easy way (through the benefit of others' experiences and hard-learned lessons). One of the reasons we had to learn the hard way was because this type of information and training was not available when we were (a) in graduate school or (b) establishing and building our practices. We are now able to share much of what we have learned, including what to do to be successful in the business of practice and what not to do so as to avoid costly mistakes.

We must emphasize that this volume is not solely about business. We assume that to be financially successful in private practice the mental health professional has to be clinically competent. However, we believe that performing at a clinically competent, if not superior, level is a necessary but not sufficient condition for financial success. We know of many gifted clinicians who have not been able to develop a successful private practice because of attitudes and skills related to business. For many clinicians, earning money and being a kind, caring, and empathic clinician are mutually exclusive. This belief, one that we do not endorse, is based on both individual attitudes and societal and social pressures. One goal of this volume is to help the private practitioner (or future private practitioner) overcome this attitude so he or she may be both emotionally satisfied and well compensated for being the owner of a small business.

Clinicians spend a great deal of time in graduate school, practicum settings, internships, postgraduate training, peer supervision, and continuing education workshops working toward the goal of becoming excellent in practicing their craft of assessment and psychotherapy. They learn, refine, and master their skills so they can deliver the best clinical services to clients. However, little, if any, emphasis is placed on learning, refining, and mastering the business aspects of private practice. In this volume we highlight the business skills to be mastered to complement the private practitioner's excellent clinical acumen. The combination is a recipe for success.

Organization of the Book

The first part of the volume is related to the private practitioner's attitude about money and being a small-business owner. We present issues to consider when deciding whether private practice is the correct career path, because it is not for everybody. We discuss the satisfactions and stresses involved with owning a private practice and highlight economic conflicts involved with this choice. We believe it is important for the private practitioner to understand concepts of both entrepreneurship and customer service to achieve optimum success.

The second part of the volume focuses on the "how to" of private practice. We address deciding on the model that best fits how you want to practice, assembling the consultants you need to have on board, billing and collecting fees, keeping track of your earnings, paying the appropriate taxes, and making sure you have in place the loss-prevention tools most appropriate for you and your practice situation.

The third part of the volume is related to issues of practicing (or not practicing) within a managed care system and income opportunities that are available for mental health professionals. Some practitioners are completely dependent on managed care, some avoid it like the plague, and others have developed a hybrid model, as this best fits their practice style and values. We discuss aspects of each of these models. We have found the creativity of mental health professionals to be awe inspiring in terms of the ways they use their knowledge and skill base to earn a living. There are numerous ways to provide services to those who are in need of our skill set and willing to pay for our expertise.

The final part of the volume addresses financial management and retirement planning. At no time in graduate school were we offered a course titled "Money 101." Therefore, it is essential for the private practitioner to take the time and energy to learn these concepts to ensure a comfortable lifestyle and retirement.

At the beginning of the volume is a set of 20 principles of private practice that we believe are overarching concepts related to success in private practice. These principles are integrated into the relevant sections of chapters in the volume.

We are knowledgeable about many areas of private practice. However, in some areas we are not. Throughout the volume we plea for practitioners to use outside consultants in areas beyond their expertise. We have done the same in this volume and include tip sheets and interviews with individuals with important experiences and knowledge to share with our readers.

Acknowledgments

We first thank Lansing Hays, acquisitions editor at the American Psychological Association (APA), for seeing the value in a volume like this and for believing that we were the right people to bring his vision to fruition. Linda McCarter assumed editorial responsibility for the book when Lansing left APA. We thank her for her patience and support of our work.

We also thank the many individuals who contributed interviews or tip sheets to the book. These include Barrie Alexander, Amy E. Brown, Darlene DiGorio-Hevner, Henry Harlow, Jennifer Kelly, Thomas B. Lewis, Tammy Martin-Causey, Nancy McGarrah, Barry Melancon, Lauren Miller, Don Osterfelt, Sidney J. Strong, Jean Thoensen, Jody L. Woodward, and Robert H. Woody. Their generosity has enriched what we have been able to present in this work. Finally, we thank Aubree Lundie for her valuable assistance in conducting interviews with individuals attempting to sell their practice and to the anonymous individuals who graciously agreed to share their experiences with our readers.

STEVE'S TURN

I have had the privilege of being in private practice with a number of fine clinical practitioners. I have been fortunate to be able to practice with Alan Saunders, John Schinka, R. Bob Smith, John Cobean, Yvette Canals, Bob Fink, Dave McConnell, Mary Anne Godfrey, Ed Brown, Amy Clark, Kristin Schaaf, Stephanie Kutler, Mark Gilson, Jane Yates, Ann Brown, Derek O'Brien, John Watkins, Nancy McGarrah, and Barrie Alexander. I have learned from each of them. I would like to thank my mentors Bill Kinder, Tony Broskowski, and David Stenmark. Bill taught me the value of psychological assessment, and this skill set has helped me to be successful through the many phases of my career. Tony taught me about mental health administration and community systems. David helped to instill in me the spirit of an entrepreneur. I thank Merry Shaurette for supporting me in my practice with her fine skills and dedication for more than 2 decades.

I thank Jeff Barnett for agreeing to work with me on this project and for his collaborative and easy working style. His knowledge of the ins and outs and ethics of private practice is most impressive. He is an awesome writer and editor who has improved my writing tremendously and helped me to say with clarity what I had previously said with murkiness.

On a personal note I thank my parents for helping to instill in me a strong work ethic and a compassion for people. Finally, I thank my wife, Mary O'Horo. As my partner she has encouraged me, continues to encourage me, and I have no doubt will always encourage me.

JEFF'S TURN

I feel deeply indebted to all the mentors who have taught me, supervised me, served as role models for me, encouraged and supported me, and inspired me. Some of these mentors include Sue and Bob Brown, Dorothy Cantor, Pat DeLeon, Helanine Gold, Tim Jeffrey, Elaine Rodino, Jack Wiggins, and Tony Zold. Countless other colleagues have been excellent role models who have shown me how to be a competent, caring, and committed professional who is also a successful businessperson. I thank them all. I also am appreciative of the great support I have received from my colleagues in the Psychology Department at Loyola College. They have consistently valued my contributions as a private practitioner on an academic faculty. I also thank Steve Walfish for inviting me to participate in this project that I hope will be a valuable resource for private practitioners. Working with Steve has been an easy, enjoyable, and intellectually stimulating process.

Principles of Private Practice

1. You need to resolve the conflict between altruism and being a business owner.

2. Although others may help, you and you alone are responsible for your success and income.

3. The mental health professional with the spirit of the entrepreneur is most successful in private practice.

4. There is no shortage of clinically skilled mental health professionals capable of doing excellent work. Those clinicians with the best customer-service practices will likely be the most successful in private practice.

5. Without excellent clinical work, no amount of customer-service practices will produce success in private practice.

6. With rare exceptions, having excellent clinical skills but poor customer service will not produce success in private practice.

7. The key ingredient in cultivating and maintaining referrals from gatekeepers is understanding the needs and demands of their job and how your skill set and practice behavior can best meet these needs.

8. When joining a group practice, choose your associates wisely. These individuals can enhance or detract from your reputation and increase or decrease your liability.

9. The negotiated costs to work in a group practice are not based on a "fairness doctrine." Rather, they are based on a business model in which both prac-

tice owners and the clinician joining the practice are attempting to maximize their income.

10. It is essential for mental health professionals to have ready access to competent professionals to answer questions outside of their areas of expertise. Ignoring this principle places the clinician at ethical, legal, and financial risk.

11. If collections are less than 90% of fees charged, you should take a hard look at your fee-setting and collection process.

12. Clinicians should charge fees that the market will bear. To charge less does not make good business sense. To charge more does not make good business sense.

13. Private practitioners need to become comfortable negotiating from a position of strength. If you are desperate for the job or income, you will negotiate from a position of weakness. Strength is found in the ability to say "No, thank you" and walk away.

14. Clients often misunderstand their insurance benefits. As part of the informed consent process clinicians should have procedures in place to clarify this issue.

15. Although not to the point of having a disorder, it is helpful to have some obsessive–compulsive tendencies when dealing with insurance companies and collecting payments from clients.

16. Be sure to make accurate estimated tax payments. We have known too many clinicians who have had an "oh my goodness, what am I going to do now" experience on April 14 when they learned of their tax liability.

17. Whether you see one client per year or 1,000 clients per year, it is imperative that you purchase malpractice insurance. It takes just one lawsuit to create havoc in your financial life.

18. Participation in a managed care plan is not a requirement for being in private practice. If you choose to participate, you must clearly understand and emotionally accept all of the financial and clinical ramifications and limitations beforehand. If you do not, you will set yourself up for a great deal of frustration during your participation.

19. There are only so many hours in the week during which a private practitioner can earn income. Therefore, it is financially advantageous to develop revenue streams of passive income.

passive income

20. Although you may receive consultation from others, the responsibility for your retirement planning remains with you, the private practitioner.

MENTAL HEALTH PROFESSIONALS' ATTITUDES TOWARD MONEY AND BUSINESS

I

The Mindset of the Psychotherapist

Being a Caring Professional and Earning a Living Are Not Mutually Exclusive

1

W orking in a private practice is a goal for many people who enter graduate training in the mental health professions. Numerous data confirm that this is the primary career path for many individuals training to be mental health professionals (MHPs), including psychologists, clinical social workers, marriage and family therapists, and professional counselors. In fact, within the American Psychological Association (APA), Division 42 (Psychologists in Independent Practice) is the largest of the 56 APA divisions. In a longitudinal study of psychotherapists, Norcross, Hedges, and Castle (2002) found that the proportion of psychologists in private practice rose over 20 years, whereas the proportion of those working for institutions declined. Barker and Kohout (2003) reported that now more psychologists are in private practice than in all educational settings combined. In addition, significant numbers of psychologists who are employed in community settings also maintain a part-time private practice (Norcross et al., 2002; Norcross, Prochaska, & Farber, 1993). In a national study, Whitaker, Weismiller, and Clark (2006) found that 56.8% of licensed social workers either have their own solo practice (44.9%) or are part of a group practice (11.9%).

And why not choose private practice as a career path? Several studies with psychologists found this choice to be related to the greatest level of career satisfaction. Boice and

Myers (1987) compared the satisfaction level of a sample of psychologists in private practice with that of a sample of those in a university academic setting. Private practitioners tended to experience fewer job-related stressors, more positive physical health, and more positive mental health. Many psychologists in academia felt "bogged down" in paperwork and committees and were unhappy with the low salaries. Those individuals planning to leave a university counseling center position were most often leaving for private practice. The main reasons other individuals cited for leaving were lack of personal growth and poor pay (Simono & Wachiowiak, 1983). Rupert and Morgan (2005) examined the relationship between work setting and burnout among a large sample of professional psychologists. They found that both solo and group independent practitioners reported a greater sense of personal accomplishment than did those psychologists working in agencies. In a sample of marriage and family therapists, Rosenberg and Pace (2006) similarly examined the relationship between work setting and burnout. They found that clinicians in private practice experienced less burnout compared with those working in agencies. Those clinicians reported the highest levels of personal accomplishment and lowest levels of depersonalization and emotional exhaustion.

Prochaska and Norcross (1983a, 1983b) presented data from a study they conducted with a national sample of psychotherapists. Ninety percent of the sample was either "quite satisfied" or "very satisfied" with his or her choice of psychology as a career. Compared with public-sector clinicians, independent practitioners appeared to be more satisfied with their career choice. Nash, Norcross, and Prochaska (1984) identified the most satisfying components of this career path in a sample of private practitioners. These components included professional independence, promotion of patient growth, autonomy, professional success, and enjoyment of the work. "High income" was surprisingly not considered one of the primary satisfactions. Walfish and Walraven (2005) sampled psychologists in private practice regarding career satisfaction. They found these psychologists' highest ratings to be in satisfaction with level of success closely followed by flexibility, intellectual stimulation, and relationships with colleagues. Once again they found the lowest rating to be in satisfaction with income. In terms of their earnings, only 69% of those sampled indicated some level of satisfaction and 30% some level of dissatisfaction.

These findings are not limited to psychologists. Bogo, Michalsk, Raphael, and Roberts (1995) cited data indicating that a certain segment of social work graduate students aspire to careers in private practice. Gibelman and Schervish (1996) noted an upward trend in the proportion of social workers engaged in private practice. Using a sample of clinical social workers, Koeske, Lichtenwalter, and Koeske (2005) found that those who were most highly involved in working with the poor but desired less involvement (because they felt demoralized) had aspirations of working in private practice.

Walfish and O'Donnell (in press) conducted a national survey of psychiatrists, psychologists, clinical social workers, and professional counselors regarding satisfaction with their work in private practice. This study found the highest levels of satisfaction to be in degree of professional independence and autonomy, flexibility of hours, and level of success with clients. It is interesting that the second lowest satisfaction rating was attributed to income.

Is it the Right Choice for You?

Barnett and Henshaw (2003) pointed out that a career as a private practitioner is not for everyone in the mental health professions. Although the data presented earlier suggest that the highest level of career satisfaction comes from this choice of a career path, it is important to remember that these conclusions are based on group data. Differences in professional values, personal preferences for lifestyle, and risk tolerance come into play in deciding whether this choice is right at the individual level. Individuals need to carefully assess their goals, preferences, and needs so that they may make an informed decision about entering private practice.

Barnett and Henshaw (2003) presented issues related to the pros and cons of developing a career in private practice. The pros included being one's own boss; ability to decide practice location, hours, and area of specialization; unlimited earnings potential; flexibility; control over business decisions; and full responsibility for the success of the practice. The cons included financial uncertainty and the risk of possible periods of low earnings; responsibility for all expenses and overhead; possible professional isolation for solo practitioners; and responsibility for billing, collections, insurance, and employee and staff decisions.

J. Young and Weishaar (1997) believed that successful private practitioners must have three important attributes. First and foremost, they must have good clinical skills. Second, they must have good financial management skills. Finally, because of the nature of the work, they must be emotionally stable and well adjusted and have an adequate social support system.

Walfish and Coovert (1990) suggested that for many people in the mental health professions, the development of a full-time private practice is the culmination of a long-term dream. However, those individuals considering entering private practice must have realistic expectations and be sure that the realities of independent practice fit their interests, needs, and temperament. Tryon (1983) identified several potential challenges of private practice that include isolation, time pressures, and economic uncertainty. Nash et al. (1984) identified time pressures, economic uncertainty, caseload uncertainty, business aspects, and excessive workloads as the five dominant stressors in the private-practice setting.

Walfish and O'Donnell's (in press) previously mentioned national survey of MHPs also examined the stresses associated with working in private practice. This study found the highest levels of stress to be with relationships with managed care companies, emotional demands associated with this type of work, and economic uncertainty. Yet, as we highlighted, for many entering independent practice, the pros significantly outweigh the cons. Furthermore, with appropriate expectations and needed business training, private practitioners can achieve great success and fulfillment.

Economic Conflicts in Being a Private Practitioner

The financial aspects of clinical practice are often downplayed during graduate school. As Trachtman (1999) pointed out, issues relating to money are seldom addressed in clinicians' education and training. He further suggested that in Western culture the very nature of money can make it a source of anxiety and add to the taboo against thinking or talking about it. Because many enter the mental health professions primarily out of a desire to help others during times of distress, it may be very uncomfortable to focus on the financial aspects of this professional relationship.

We believe the anxiety about money manifests itself in issues related to charging fees, negotiating fees, collecting fees, and how much money one "should" make or allows oneself to make as a private practitioner. During training and supervision, much is made of issues of transference (clients' reactions to psychotherapists) and countertransference (psychotherapists' reactions to clients). Gelso and Hayes (2001) summarized research on countertransference and therapeutic outcome. They indicated that "for both experienced and inexperienced therapists unmanaged countertransference can seriously impede treatment, including bringing therapy to a halt. At the same time, countertransference that is managed effectively can positively affect outcomes" (p. 420). To this we add that poor countertransference as it relates to money will likewise interfere with the therapeutic relationship. It is our further contention that poor countertransference management regarding the economics of practice may significantly interfere with the satisfaction derived from private practice as a career choice.

Trachtman (1999) also suggested that the psychological meaning of money is rarely discussed because of the taboo regarding the subject of money. Psychotherapists are not immune to the damaging nature of this situation. Trachtman believed that what causes practitioners to be so concerned about money is largely their beliefs about the attitudes and behaviors of others toward them as well as about how they treat themselves. Barth (2001) noted that it is often difficult for both the psychotherapist and the client to become comfortable with the business side of the therapeutic relationship and to reconcile the wish to be genuinely caring or cared about with the reality of paying for the psychotherapy. She further elaborated that some issues are particularly salient for social workers. As individuals and as members of a field of practice, social workers commit to providing service for those who cannot afford high-priced private-practice fees. Furthermore, because social workers are more often women, gender issues often influence people's attitudes toward money and their comfort in discussing it. These issues may also become more common among psychologists because the majority of those entering PhD and PsyD training programs are now women.

Rodino (2005) opined that people are more likely to discuss very private sexual issues than to disclose their income. She stressed that MHPs may have the same hang-ups about dealing with money as others do. Furthermore, when consulting about practice development, the professional should begin with self-examination about money issues. Important issues to examine include family history; role models; ambivalence about success; feelings of unworthiness; and conflict with religious, ethical, and moral upbringing. She wrote,

> The thought of success and wealth may conflict with religious, ethical and moral upbringing that stressed values of altruism, sacrifice and selflessness. For some there is a conflict between earning money and altruism. Because psychology is a caring profession, some people feel that it is incongruous to be paid for this, or at least it may be wrong to be paid well. (p. 54)

Rodino further added that "it is important to separate one's altruism from the need to earn money and more importantly to see the two values as non-conflicting" (pp. 54–55). Grodzki (2004), also a practice management consultant, urged the MHP to make peace with money. She wrote,

> You need to identify and resolve any childhood-based, negative beliefs that may be influencing the way you conduct business. For example, maybe you grew up with money deprivation. There was never enough money for your basic needs as a child. You still believe money is in short supply, watch every penny, and fail to give your business the resources it needs to flourish. Or perhaps

you grew up believing money was mysterious because no one in your family understood how to make it or save it. You ride an emotional money roller coaster. . . . Or you may have been taught that money is inherently wicked. You saw anxiety on your parents' faces when they talked about money, so you feel scared or impure when you have to deal with it, too. . . . You find all aspects regarding money unpleasant and suspect. The solution? Resolve any negative beliefs and irrational behaviors that impede your business growth. Reconcile money and service. Separate the caring you have for your clients from your skills, recognizing that you charge solely for the skills; the caring is free. (p. 18)

Many years ago Steve Walfish was talking with a friend from graduate school. Instead of choosing the private-practice path, she had gone into public mental health, designing programs for those who are homeless and those who are chronically mentally ill. In a moment of guilt (because he was originally going to be a community psychologist) he shared with her his belief that what she was doing was really important work and far more important than his own. She kindly replied, "Don't forget that what you do is prosocial as well. You just happen to be better paid than I am for your prosocial behavior." These words assuaged his guilt for choosing to follow a career path in the private sector.

Bernay (1983) pointed out that philosophically we, as health care professionals and healers, hold the notion that altruism, service, and poverty are synonymous. As Steven's friend pointed out, this does not have to be the case. Bernay suggested that these attitudes lead some people to conduct their practices more in the manner of a mom-and-pop store rather than as established professional practices. Cantor (1983) contended that anyone who decides to enter private practice has to be able to generate a self-image of an entrepreneur that is both acceptable and gratifying. The problem, as Cantor viewed it, is that because psychotherapy is perceived as being helpful and nurturing, accepting money directly from clients may lead to guilt engendered by role conflict. Furthermore, R. Barker (1982) contended that many people in the helping professions are ambivalent about business, if not overtly apathetic about it. He further suggested that MHPs sometimes talk about business pejoratively and use terms such as *profit motive, capitalism,* and *free enterprise* rather derisively.

Private Practice Principle Number 1: You need to resolve the conflict between altruism and being a business owner.

Many MHPs have an elitist attitude about being in a profession in which the primary objective is helping others and not making money. Being in the caretaker role places a clinician in a difficult position that creates great ambivalence, and conflicted feelings can emerge at times when one begins thinking about making more money. After all, how can you focus on money when you're dealing with helping others? How can you use others' distress and suffering to your advantage? How do you reconcile your caregiving, altruistic mentality with being in business and working hard to earn a living? Much of the professional work in clinicians' practices is founded on caring relationships with others. A focus on making money seems to be in conflict with the emphasis on caring, empathy, and concern. How do you reconcile this? Can you be a caring, empathic helper who provides high-quality clinical services in the context of a caregiving relationship and at the same time be a business owner who is focused on making as much money (to provide for yourself, your family, and your future) as is reasonably possible? You don't want to take advantage of others, but do need to be sure you are compensated fairly for the services you provide and the significant differences you can make in people's lives. If you can help save someone's marriage, help someone live free of depression, identify the nature of a learning disability so a child may become successful in school, or help someone overcome anxiety so he or she can achieve his or her own life goals, how much is that worth?

It is important to see the value of the services you provide and realize how much they are worth despite the blocks to doing so as discussed by Rodino (2005) earlier. If you are helpful to most people, you need not feel guilty for making money and being successful. Indeed, the more successful you are in helping other people, the more money you are likely to earn because word of mouth from satisfied clients best builds stable long-term practices. If you are therapeutically successful, then you are not becoming financially successful as a result of others' misery. MHPs need to get comfortable with this concept or they will burn out quickly. They need to become comfortable with the fact that our clients provide our income, which allows us to have the staples in life such as a roof over our head, food on the table, and health insurance, not to mention luxuries that they might like to indulge in such as having a nice home, owning a reliable car, and occasionally going on vacation. Clients also pay for our children's education and fund our retirement. To have such luxuries while feeling guilty for having them only leads to dissatisfaction with the nature of clinicians' work and dissatisfaction with themselves as people and thus adversely affects their ability to successfully assist others.

Grodzki (2004) advised MHPs to differentiate themselves from their businesses. She suggested that a major reason that social workers dislike business is because they overidentify with the business. Professionals need to separate themselves from their businesses and see them as distinct entities, even if they exist only as the result of their efforts.

Kase (2005) suggested that it is possible to help people and earn a great living at the same time. She stressed the importance of values exploration and values clarification for the MHP in designing a career path. She further elaborated that these values can help guide a vision for a career that will allow for business and practice decision making that is consistent with what is really important to the private practitioner. We encourage those of you considering private practice as a career path to develop your own vision as suggested and outlined by Kase to help keep yourself focused and on course to shape a practice that is both financially and personally satisfying.

In their book, *How to Survive and Thrive as a Therapist: Information, Ideas, and Resources for Psychologists in Practice,* Pope and Vasquez (2005) emphasized two points that are essential for success in private practice. First, you must find out what you really enjoy doing, what is most meaningful and important to you, and pursue that dream. Second, create a business plan that addresses your financial goals, the type of practice you plan to have, your financial needs, and the likely expenses you will have. Although selecting work that is enjoyable and meaningful is essential for success, perhaps of tantamount importance is developing your private practice as a business. Knowledge of the likely expenses associated with opening and running a practice, how to advertise and market your practice, whether you will hire staff or other MHPs, whether you will participate in managed care or insurance, and the like are important issues to address. In addition, consultation with other professionals such as an accountant and an attorney will prove invaluable when addressing incorporation and business tax structure, payroll and tax issues, insurance issues, and legal issues.

The overarching goal of this volume is to help aspiring private practitioners develop the knowledge, skills, attitudes, and mindset needed for success in independent practice. We strongly believe that private practitioners who are competent clinicians can be successful in the business of practice and also have an enjoyable and rewarding career. This volume provides the essentials for establishing and successfully running a private practice. This guidance should serve as an excellent starting point for achieving financial success in mental health practice.

You Are a Small-Business Owner
Think Like an Entrepreneur

G raduate training in the mental health professions almost uniformly skips over (or at best gives a passing glance to) the business aspects of being an independent practitioner. Although practice models may vary, we think it important that practitioners understand that they are the owner of their own small business. The success of this business depends on their ability to provide a service that people want and to make a profit while doing so. Owning such a small business is different from practicing in an institution in which a set paycheck is received every 2 weeks and there are no concerns about paying rent, making payroll, or planning for how the practice will grow over the next year or 2 or 5 years. It has been our experience that mental health professionals (MHPs) can make a good living in independent practice. However, the ones that make the best living are those who are willing to adopt the spirit of an entrepreneur. In other words, they are creative, able to predict market trends and adapt to them rather than fight against them, and take calculated risks. Owning this small business is not typically a 9-to-5 job, and hard work (e.g., long and flexible hours) is necessary to develop a successful practice. Once established, the practitioner will have more control over scheduling (e.g., may not have to work evenings or weekends) or the types of clients seen. However, hard work and competent work will always be necessary as there will always be competition in the marketplace.

This Is Your Business

Walfish and Coovert (1990), in tracing dictionary roots of the word *business*, suggested the word refers to the establishment and maintenance of a functional legal and social entity for the purpose of generating income. These authors believed that for MHPs, private practice is the business of mental health provision. Although MHPs call the people that seek out their services *clients* or *patients*, in the true sense they are their customers. MHPs in private practice are in a service business. Although they are not making widgets for sale in the marketplace or restoring cell phones or computers, they offer products: psychotherapy, assessment, and consulting. Broadly defined, these skills are ones that people want to purchase and by filling that need in the marketplace MHPs are able to generate income. Generally speaking, the higher the quality of product that the clinician can deliver in a market that highly desires these products, the higher the profit that will be generated for the business. Walfish and Coovert indicated that many MHPs may view such an attitude as mercenary but as outlined in chapter 1 of this volume, earning a living in private practice and being a kind and caring person are not mutually exclusive.

Private Practice Principle Number 2: Although others may help, you and you alone are responsible for your success and income.

What are the implications of owning a small business? Both macro issues and micro issues are involved. First, it is important to understand that the owner of this business is the "chief cook and bottlewasher." In other words, the ultimate responsibility for the success or failure of the practice lies with the MHP. This does not mean that some of the tasks involved in operating this business cannot be delegated to others (e.g., reception, typing, billing and collecting, bookkeeping) but they must be planned for and consistently monitored and evaluated. The following are but a few examples of pitfalls:

- If the receptionist for the practice has poor social skills, then potential clients (e.g., customers) will be turned off and choose to purchase their mental health services elsewhere in the marketplace.
- If monies billed and collected are not appropriately monitored, then the business will have large amounts of uncollected receivables.
- If monies collected are not tracked by the MHP and this task is solely delegated to others, then there is a potential this employee will embezzle funds (an example of embezzlement is provided in chap. 6, this volume).

Second, the mental health marketplace is always evolving. How MHPs practiced 20 years ago is different from how MHPs practiced 10 years ago, which is different from how they practice today. The one thing we are sure of is that it is likely to be different 10 years from now. In this regard Walfish (2001a) pointed to the need to recognize the evolving public policy and market forces that affect the delivery of mental health services (e.g., MHPs' businesses) rather than resist and become stagnant and bitter. For example, some clinicians can operate a successful full-time business of providing psychoanalysis to those desiring this therapeutic approach. However, because of cutbacks in insurance funding for mental health care and the advent of managed care determining "medical necessity," it is difficult for all of those wanting to have this type of practice to do so and be financially viable. For those who are steadfast in wanting to have only this type of practice and are unwilling to adapt to other avenues for providing mental health services, we would predict frustration, bitterness, and burnout. Changes in public policy, in terms of either grants for payment of mental health services or laws regarding the mandating of mental health or human services, can affect the marketplace. For example, an increase or decrease in federal funding for Head Start may affect the monies available for independent contractors to complete learning disability or school-readiness evaluations with this population. If a state legislature mandates couples therapy for those considering divorce or substance abuse treatment for those arrested a second time for driving while intoxicated, the need for these types of services would be significantly affected.

Third, individual referral sources cannot be counted on to remain constant, for a wide variety of reasons. Referral sources can become dissatisfied with you for either legitimate (e.g., a mistake on your part) or illegitimate (e.g., their own quirks or psychopathology) reasons and then send their business to another provider. They are under no obligation to continue to refer to you. Referral sources can stop working. For example, physicians or attorneys who refer patients can become ill, disabled, or impaired as a result of alcohol or drugs; leave private practice to work for an organization; relocate out of the area, or retire. If referral sources work for an agency sometimes they move into another position and may no longer be in a position to refer. They may also leave the agency for another opportunity or be terminated or laid off. Thus, for a range of reasons, referral sources should not be counted on to continue indefinitely. The care of current referral sources and the development of new ones are an integral part of running a successful practice.

Fourth, in private practice there is no such thing as a paid vacation, a paid holiday, sick leave, paid maternity leave, continuing education leave, or a paid snow day. The Family Medical Leave Act does not apply to private practitioners. If you do not work (e.g., deliver a service), you do not generate income. Consider the clinician in private practice who sees 20 clients each week. Assume this clinician collects $50 from each client for individual psychotherapy. If he or she takes a 1-week vacation, before spending any money on plane fare, hotel, restaurants, or souvenirs, he or she will have lost $1,000 of income for that week (and this number is an underestimate, as private practice fees are usually twice this amount). The same is true for attending conferences or workshops. Not only do you have to pay for the course, but there is also a lost opportunity for income. In addition, clinicians may become ill, snowstorms may cause clients to cancel appointments, and family obligations may keep clinicians from working at times. A colleague shared with us that she lost $1,700 in fees because she could not see clients for 2 days during a recent snowstorm. Business owners should plan for and factor in these expenses and lost opportunities for income in their yearly business plan. Thus, private practitioners should plan in advance for vacations, continuing education, weather-related cancellations, and so forth, rather than count on someone else to take care of these for them or simply hope that everything will work out.

Fifth, in private practice the clinician has to pay for all professional expenses. If you want to join a professional association, you have to pay the dues. If you want to attend a conference or workshop, you have to pay for the registration and any travel and accommodation fees. There is no such thing as agency or organizational reimbursement. If you want to subscribe to your favorite journal or read the latest book that has come out in your field of interest, you have to make the purchase. In private practice there is no such thing as an educational advancement fund. You have to pay your own licensure fees and malpractice insurance. Steve Walfish recently consulted with an attorney regarding a request for records from the estate of a deceased client and had to write a check for $400 to the attorney. He did not have the luxury of consulting with the agency or university attorney to answer his question at no cost. Although these expenses are tax deductible (see chap. 7, this volume), it is important to understand that all of these costs are borne by the small-business owner and must be planned for in the practice business plan.

Sixth, in private practice the clinician has to pay for insurance premiums. If you work for a university, health clinic, or organization or agency, most likely the position comes with benefits. These benefits could include partial or full payment of health insurance for the clinician and his or her family, life insurance, and disability insurance.

Seventh, in private practice clinicians are totally responsible for funding their own retirement. There was a day when a MHP could work 25 years for a university, nonprofit agency, or for-profit corporation and then be able to retire with a gold watch and a predetermined pension. Although this arrangement still exists, the movement is more toward employer-sponsored retirement plans in which the employee and the employer each contribute amounts of money each pay period to a stock market fund. This amount (one hopes) compounds over time and the accumulated amount is then given to the employee on retirement. In private practice there is no defined pension plan and no one will match contributions to a 401(k) plan. The responsibility of saving for retirement lies solely with the private practitioner. If the private practitioner wants a comfortable retirement, he or she must make it happen.

Eighth, on a micro level it is the responsibility of the private practitioner to ensure a smooth-running business operation. The clinician must make decisions regarding office space, furniture, office amenities, and hiring (or not hiring) personnel, as well as perform the mundane tasks of supplying the office with pens, pencils, and paper clips.

Mistakes of Small-Business Owners

Hendricks (2004) interviewed businessman John Osher to discover common mistakes that entrepreneurs make when starting a new business. Hendricks contended that these are mistakes the small-business owner cannot afford to make if he or she wants to be profitable. Several of these mistakes are applicable to the business of delivering mental health services in private practice.

MISTAKE 1: FAILING TO SPEND ENOUGH TIME RESEARCHING THE BUSINESS IDEA TO SEE IF IT'S VIABLE

The MHP cannot wake up one day and say, "I think it's time to go into private practice" and the next day be open for business. This complex decision should be well thought out. Barnett and Henshaw (2003) pointed out the following:

> Preparation for entering and succeeding in private practice is one vital area that graduate programs typically can not give adequate attention [to], due to the long list of "academic" courses that must be offered. The preparation specific to having a career as a private practitioner is an important aspect of career growth and planning. . . . Rather than just learning as you go along, it is best if you prepare to enter private practice well in advance. (p. 145)

Many people like the concept of "hanging out a shingle" and having the freedom, income, and independence that they feel are missing in the job they have with an organization. They may possess superb clinical skills and excellent conceptual ideas for operating a successful private practice. However, without laying the groundwork, doing the appropriate background research, and developing the skill set necessary for success in private practice, they may launch the business venture prematurely or ineffectively.

MISTAKE 2: MISCALCULATING MARKET SIZE, TIMING, EASE OF ENTRY, AND POTENTIAL MARKET SHARE

We have a colleague whose wife is a podiatrist. She contracted with a high-quality direct mail company, and before her first day of practice her entire schedule was filled with new patients for the first 2 weeks. The odds of this happening for a MHP is somewhere between slim and none, and Slim is likely out of town! Deciding where and when to open a practice and predicting how quickly one can grow the practice and how long it will take for the practice to be financially viable are difficult. How many MHPs are needed in one area? What is the need (incidence of mental health problems) and demand (people who will actually seek out and pay for mental health services) in the area? What effect will the competition (e.g., current private practitioners) have on the ability to grow a practice? How will the new practitioners convince the gatekeepers of mental health services (e.g., physicians, attorneys, employee assistance programs [EAPs]) to refer clients for treatment? These questions must be carefully considered but are often overlooked or miscalculated.

MISTAKE 3: UNDERESTIMATING FINANCIAL REQUIREMENTS AND TIMING

In private practice, unless one is paid at time of service (which is not possible if one is a provider for a preferred provider panel of an insurance company or a member of a managed care panel), collection of fees may be sporadic and unpredictable. If the clinician files insurance on behalf of a client then payment is received anywhere from 2 to 6 weeks after submission of the claim. Also, payment is dependent on the clinician completing the form correctly and sending it to the correct place for processing and the insurer not making any mistakes in processing the claim. Furthermore, organizations may wait 30 to 60 days before paying for services rendered. At the same time, practice expenses (e.g., rent) and life expenses (e.g., food, shelter) remain due on certain dates. Cash flow can be a significant problem for the private practitioner because of the unpredictability of payments.

MISTAKE 4: MAKING COST PROJECTIONS THAT ARE TOO LOW

Many new to operating a practice are unaware of all of the costs involved in this endeavor. There are the obvious costs of obtaining space, furniture, telephone, malpractice insurance, and basic office supplies. However, there are also other incidental costs such as having a pager or cell phone to be accessible for emergencies, office insurance in case of a slip and fall by a client on your premises, and leasing a photocopier. Then there are the costs of taking potential referral sources out to lunch or dinner, continuing education activities, credit card fees for those choosing to pay with this method, bank charges for the occasional bounced check written by one of your clients, and gasoline and parking fees to make presentations to community groups. If you are a psychologist, then there are costs for testing materials. With the advent of the new millennium one of our practices had to pay $1,000 to upgrade a computer chip for the telephone system so the system could continue to function after Y2K. Practice overheads generally vary between 25% of collected revenues on the low end to 50% to 60% on the high end, depending on the nature of the practice and contractual agreements.

MISTAKE 5: HIRING TOO MANY PEOPLE AND SPENDING TOO MUCH ON OFFICES AND FACILITIES

The overhead needed to operate a practice can run anywhere from bare bones to the Top of the Ritz. The practitioner must decide important questions about overhead for operating the practice. There are several models for entering practice (see chap. 4, this volume), and the amount of money needed for each model ranges from a minimal amount to a significant amount. Because the new practitioner cannot be sure of the amount of income that the practice will generate, considerable forethought must be given to these issues. If the practitioner overestimates income, he or she may make large investments in office overhead (e.g., renting expensive office space, purchasing computer systems and furniture, hiring support staff). The practitioner may thereby at best feel financially squeezed or at worst run out of money. However, significantly underestimating income may lead the practitioner to do things on the cheap and present an impression that may not be professional (e.g., rent space in an insurance agent's office, purchase furniture from Goodwill or the Salvation Army).

The advantages of having support personnel such as a receptionist or secretary and a billing person on premises are clear. However, this benefit must be weighed against the cost of such services. For example, hiring a full-time employee at the rate of $10 per hour translates to an annual cost of approximately $25,000 including indirect costs of payroll taxes, unemployment charges, and workers' compensation benefits and this may not even include health insurance.

MISTAKE 6: FOCUSING TOO MUCH ON VOLUME RATHER THAN PROFIT

Often private practitioners focus on the number of clients they are seeing per week to determine their level of success. Consider the clinician who sees 20 clients per week referred by a managed care company. With a reimbursement of $75 per session, weekly income would be $1,500. Compare this with the clinician who develops a niche practice and sees 10 workers' compensation clients (reimbursement of $120 per session) and 10 Social Security Disability applicants for evaluation (reimbursement of $145 per evaluation). Such a niche practice would yield a weekly income of $2,650. With 4 weeks of vacation each year, the annual income in the managed care model would be $72,000 and in the niche model, $127,200. The annualized difference is $55,200. Do this for 20 years and the income difference is more than $1 million. However, there are pros and cons to developing a niche practice. The pros include having a specialty that others don't and therefore one may be the preferred provider for those wanting the service. On the con side, the need for the specialty may disappear or someone else may enter the market and deliver a similar service.

MISTAKE 7: SEEKING CONFIRMATION OF YOUR ACTIONS RATHER THAN SEEKING THE TRUTH

Everybody wants to believe that he or she is doing a good job. Everybody wants to believe that he or she is excellent at what he or she does. However, MHPs are just as subject to the effects of self-assessment bias as anyone else. How do you know your skills are good? How do you know your clients are improving? How do you know your clients are not regressing? Research by Walfish, McAllister, O'Connell, and Lambert (2007) found the average private practitioner self-rated his or her own skill level at the 80th percentile compared with peers in private practice. In this sample, 91.6% self-rated their skill level above the 75th percentile. Almost half of the sample believed that none of their clients regressed as a result of psychotherapy with them, despite evidence that a small portion of clients do indeed regress in psychotherapy (Lambert & Ogles, 2004). It is important to seek out opinions of those who will validate what you are doing. However, it is just as important to consider the opinions of those who will serve as external critics. It is important, especially in the beginning phases of private practice, to develop a relationship with someone that you respect and who will be willing to review clinical data with you (e.g., psychotherapy cases, assessment reports) as well as business data (e.g., billing and collection procedures, marketing efforts, personnel issues).

MISTAKE 8: LACKING FOCUS AND IDENTITY

Osher (c.f. Hendricks, 2004) suggested that too many companies try to go after too many targets at once and end up with a potpourri rather than a focused business entity with an identity. MHPs may also have this problem. Beware clinicians who indicate they are expert at working with all ages (infant to geriatric) and with any problem that may enter the door. Although we think it is important for clinicians to have general skills, their business benefits when they develop a specialty area for which they can become known in the community. It is too difficult to be "all things to all people." As Osher suggested, when a business becomes a potpourri, it loses its power, but when a company is focused, its power can build from that. We believe this is true for the private practice clinician as well.

MISTAKE 9: LACKING AN EXIT STRATEGY

For how long will you own your private practice? What will you do with it when you decide that you want to retire? Will you just close your doors or will you try to sell the practice? These are important questions to ask because the answers may determine the type of practice that you want to build in the long run, whether you want to stay small as a "solo shop," take on a few junior associates, or build a large practice. We have colleagues who formed a partnership with the goal of building the practice and then later finding a buyer. All of their business decisions were based on this goal. They developed an EAP that was marketed to corporations, developed capitation agreements with insurers (which meant that all of their subscribers were referred to their practice), and hired top-rate clinicians and provided them with incentives to remain in the practice. Eventually a health company listed on the New York Stock Exchange purchased the practice from the partners for a "handsome sum." Our colleagues had their exit strategy mapped out well in advance. Needless to say, we believe few private practitioners share the vision of these colleagues. However, we also believe that most make the mistake of not considering what will happen when they are ready to retire and not developing an exit strategy other than closing their doors.

The Spirit of an Entrepreneur

Social psychologist Robert Baron and his colleagues have studied entrepreneurs and the entrepreneurial process. Their work has implications for the development of a successful private practice. The development of the skill set and attitude of an entrepreneur will help the private practitioner to see opportunities where others do not and provide the know-how to make these opportunities come to fruition.

> **Private Practice Principle Number 3:** The mental health professional with the spirit of the entrepreneur is most successful in private practice.

If you want to learn more about this area, we would highly recommend Baron and Shane's (2008) textbook *Entrepreneurship: A Process Perspective*. In this book the authors presented scientific and applied information regarding this complex area of study and practice. According to these authors, entrepreneurship is a process that includes (a) the generation of an idea or the recognition of an opportunity, (b) the gathering of resources to help bring the idea or opportunity to fruition, and (c) launching the opportunity and helping it to grow. They suggested that at each phase of the process, individual-level variables, group- or interpersonal-level variables, and community- or societal-level variables all play a role and intersect with each other. An individual may have a great idea to develop in private practice but if the resources (e.g., money to buy necessary supplies, necessary skill level to apply the idea) are not available to develop the idea, or if social policy factors (e.g., no insurance reimbursement available, community opposition to the idea) are not favorable, the excellent idea will not come to fruition. Here are two hypothetical examples: An astute clinician reads the empirically validated research for treating obesity, one of the nation's leading health problems, and decides to offer this service in his practice. The clinician becomes trained in the appropriate techniques (develops "resources") to provide this service. However, the clinician then learns that because of insurance laws, most policies written in his state specifically exclude reimbursement for treatment for obesity. Therefore, this excellent concept would likely fail. As a second example, a clinician reading the latest issue of a journal notes that eye movement desensitization and reprocessing (EMDR) is an effective technique for treating certain types of trauma (the "idea"). She also has been told by many referral sources that they would gladly send the clinician many cases if the clinician were skilled in this technique (the "community support"). However, the clinician then explores becoming trained in EMDR and discovers that the cost for becoming certified in this specialty area is prohibitive (please note that we are not singling out EMDR here; certification in most specialty areas within the mental health field takes a significant investment of funds and time). Therefore, this excellent idea will not come to fruition.

Baron and Shane (2008) presented a checklist to help individuals to examine the question, "Is becoming an entrepreneur right for you?" We discuss these thought-provoking questions here.

CAN YOU HANDLE UNCERTAINTY?

There is no such thing as certainty in a private practice. No aspect of the practice, whether on the community and social policy level, interpersonal level, or intrapersonal level, can be counted on to remain constant. As changes occur in societal attitudes and needs as well as in which services are covered by insurance, these changes will affect the nature, and possible success, of private practice. This small business operates not in a vacuum but in the context of the community in which the services are being delivered. The people whom you deal with to help support your practice can change (e.g., may no longer be in a position to support your practice) or decide that they no longer want to help you. As noted earlier, referral sources may not be referral sources forever. This aspect of your practice will always be in flux. The support personnel (e.g., secretary, billing person, attorney, accountant) whom you hire or contract with when you begin your practice are not likely to be the same people supporting you 10, 20, or 30 years into your practice. People change, grow, and move on as part of their natural life cycles. If you join a group practice it is unlikely that the composition of this group of clinicians will remain the same over time. People will join the practice, and people will leave the practice.

On an intrapersonal level, you have to be able to cope with the possibility that one day the phone will stop ringing with referrals. There will be times when referrals slow down. For example, psychologists who conduct psychoeducational evaluations for children not doing well in school can count on not getting many referrals at the beginning of the school year. However, once the first report card comes out they may then get swamped with calls to complete such evaluations. The financial insecurity that comes with the ebb and flow of practice may be too nerve-racking to cope with for someone who needs the certainty of a certain amount of steady and predictable income.

ARE YOU ENERGETIC?

Baron and Shane (2008) quoted a speech by an award-winning entrepreneur:

> Luck definitely plays a role. You have to be in the right place at the right time and know the right people who can help you. But after that, it's largely a matter of hard, mind-bending work; if you're not willing to put in the hours and give up lots of things in your life, you won't succeed—you won't make it happen. (p. 18)

We couldn't agree with this entrepreneur more. Although at some point the amount of time and energy required to run an effective and profitable practice may decrease, this is certainly not the case in the beginning. We know of no successful private practitioner who did not work really hard building his or her small business, including working long hours delivering services, spending administrative time running the business, writing reports and corresponding with referral sources, and engaging in activities to help maintain and grow the business. Although we later discuss some passive ways to earn income, the math is simple. For the most part MHPs get paid by the clinical or consulting hour (or day). If they don't work, there is no income. The more hours (days) MHPs work, the more income they generate. (We have always found it interesting that individuals working in an agency feel "maxed out" at 25 clients per week, whereas in private practice they feel "maxed out" at 30 to 35 hours per week. There is nothing like working for oneself, and reaping the fruits of one's labor, to energize the practitioner.) Both of us are actively involved in professional activities that do not directly increase our incomes. We conduct research and publish our findings in journals, serve on editorial boards, participate on professional e-mail lists, and (in the case of Jeff Barnett) provide service to state and national organizations related to psychology. Each activity bolsters our reputations, increases our visibility with other professionals, and enhances our credibility, which in turn translates into a solidified practice and higher income. However, we are also spending parts of evenings, early mornings, and weekends engaged in these practice-building activities while others may be reading a good book. A postdoctoral fellow whom one of us supervises aspires to having a hospital-based job doing work that pays well and is professionally meaningful but in which it is expected that all work stops at 5:00 p.m. She is aware that a full-time private practice would not be a good career route for her on the basis of her particular goals and needs.

DO YOU BELIEVE IN YOURSELF AND YOUR ABILITIES?

Most states provide licensure to qualified psychologists, clinical social workers, marriage and family therapists, and professional counselors to practice independently. To practice independently without the umbrella protection of an agency or organization, MHPs must have confidence that they have the ability to practice both competently and ethically. They have to believe that their skills merit being reimbursed at a level of private practice fees and that people will be willing to pay them for their ability to positively improve their quality of life.

CAN YOU HANDLE REVERSALS AND FAILURES WELL?

You will seek out other professionals or gatekeepers to send you referrals. Some will be impressed with you and send you a lot of business. Some will be impressed with you and promise to send you business, and then you will never hear from them again. Some will not be impressed with you at all. It is important that the private practitioner have the resiliency to attempt to earn business without being rewarded or reinforced for these efforts. If not, these efforts will cease or be half-hearted. The resulting pessimism will surely result in a failed practice. Markman, Baron, and Balkin (2005) found that although entrepreneurs had intense regrets when ventures did not turn out well, they scored higher on measures of personal perseverance and self-efficacy than did nonentrepreneurs. It is our experience that quantity of attempts to generate income results is directly related to the amount of income generated. One never knows what marketing effort will pay off, and when. For example, when Steve Walfish was first developing his practice he was trying to do as many talks as possible for local community groups. Many said no; some said, "Yes, by all means please come and talk with us." One alcohol treatment center responded, "No, we don't need anyone to do a talk for us, but we do need a psychologist." This phone call led directly to 3,000 referrals for psychological evaluations. Had he given up when he heard several *no's* his entire career would have been different.

It is important to remember that the successful long-term entrepreneur or private practitioner is going to have to adapt to changes in his or her practice and setbacks. In this regard the book *Great Failures of the Extremely Successful: Mistakes, Adversity, Failure and Other Stepping Stones to Success* by S. Young (2002) should be considered important reading.

ARE YOU PASSIONATE ABOUT YOUR GOALS AND VISION?

Owning a small business and developing it into a successful venture is not for the ambivalent. Baron and Shane (2008) suggested that entrepreneurs ask themselves whether they are passionate enough about what they are doing to sacrifice almost everything to get there. Successful private practitioners must be committed to the type of work they are doing and not just to earning money. The work of the MHP is emotionally demanding, and if earning money is the sole motivator, then perhaps banking and finance would be a more appropriate outlet. It is difficult to imagine someone committing to making a practice successful in terms of excellent client care and attending to the numerous business details without a passion for the work. Burnout would surely follow quickly.

ARE YOU GOOD WITH OTHER PEOPLE?

Most people naturally assume that MHPs have good people skills. However, we know many who are painfully shy, avoid conflict at all costs, cannot give presentations in front of groups, and are too uncomfortable to meet a potential referral source for lunch. It is possible to have a successful private practice by sitting in your office and waiting for the telephone to ring. However, it is highly unlikely to happen unless there is something spectacularly special about your skill level or specialty. Or, it is possible to achieve this if one is involved in a group practice of people who are highly successful at generating referrals for the entire practice. However, having a successful practice means meeting with gatekeepers of referrals (e.g., physicians, EAPs, teachers, probation officers) and earning their confidence in your skill level. Being a skilled clinician is rarely enough to ensure a very successful practice.

Possessing the skills that usually fall under the rubric of emotional intelligence will greatly enhance the likelihood of success. Salovey and Grewal (2005) defined the four branches of emotional intelligence as

- *Perceiving emotions:* The ability to perceive emotions in oneself and others as well as in objects, art, stories, music, and other stimuli.
- *Facilitating thought:* The ability to generate, use, and feel emotion as necessary to communicate feelings or use them in other cognitive processes.
- *Understanding emotions:* The ability to understand and to appreciate such emotional meanings. The ability to understand emotional information, to understand how emotions combine, and to progress through relationship transitions.
- *Managing emotions:* The ability to be open to feelings and to modulate them in oneself and others so as to promote personal understanding and growth.

It is easy to see how possessing high levels of each characteristic contributes to success for the private practitioner. In addition to being helpful for interacting with referral sources, this skill set is helpful for dealing with support staff, colleagues within and outside of the practice, and the frustrations of being put on hold by insurance companies or clients not paying their bills. Baron (2002) suggested that social competence is an influencing factor in the ability of the entrepreneur to succeed. The ability to get along with one's partners and deal with those outside the business (e.g., bankers, potential customers, and perspective employees) increases the likelihood of success. We think it would be helpful for those aspiring to private practice as a career path to self-assess their own development on these dimensions of emotional intelligence. Where strengths are noted, play to them in developing the practice. Where weaknesses are noted, take steps to enhance these areas through reading, skill training, or personal psychotherapy.

ARE YOU ADAPTABLE?

Not every idea that you have in private practice will be a successful one. Our colleague, R. Bob Smith III, president of Psychological Assessment

Resources, a psychological testing company, once told one of us, "There are lots of good ideas that for some reason don't make any money." Baron and Shane (2008) suggested that entrepreneurs ask themselves if they can make midcourse corrections easily. They view being able to recognize a mistake, admit that a mistake was made, and then take action to correct the mistake or to set sail on a different course as being important. An amazing number of decisions to be made by the private practitioner fall outside of clinical work. Where to practice? Whom to practice with? How should the office be decorated? What phone system should be bought? What is the most efficient way to do photocopying? How do I optimize collections? How to best market or advertise my practice? What type of insurance do I need? How do I fund my retirement? The list goes on and on. The successful private practitioner will make decisions, evaluate them, and choose a new course of action when appropriate. Otherwise, periodically continued mistakes will affect the bottom line.

ARE YOU WILLING TO TAKE RISKS OR LEAPS OF FAITH?

Owning a small business is not for the fainthearted. Nor is it for those who have a style of reckless abandonment. For the MHP who is completely risk-averse we suggest a government-funded position as a career choice. Although these jobs carry some risk, the likelihood of being laid off is minimal. Baron and Shane (2008) suggested that entrepreneurs need to ask themselves whether, once the goal is set, they are willing to take reasonable risks to achieve it. We would not advise anyone to immediately start a private practice right out of graduate training with student loans to pay and little or no money in the bank. There are ways (to be discussed later) of entering practice so that the risks are minimized, but they still exist. If one has zero tolerance for risk, then private practice is not appropriate.

More Tidbits on Entrepreneurship

Baron and Shane (2008) suggested that ideas for new products or services do not just appear out of nowhere. Rather, they emerge when individuals use existing knowledge they have gained from a previous experience to develop something new, spurred on by new knowledge or a new experience. They suggested that concepts can be stretched by either combining concepts together or expanding current concepts, or be expanded by analogy (taking a similar product and placing it in a new but similar situation). They further suggested that opportunity recognition is central to this process. Baron and Shane elaborated that some people are more likely than others to recognize opportunities because they have access to specialized information and are able to use information in a way to create opportunity. Information may be accessed through work experience, through a social network, or by actively searching for information. For example, a MHP working in an agency may learn a special skill (e.g., parent training) and if allowable then take this skill and apply it to a revenue-generating opportunity outside of the agency. Through networking with other professionals, clinicians may learn of opportunities to apply their specialized skills and training. State professional associations, peer consultation groups, local chambers of commerce, and a variety of other interest groups provide a rich source of networking opportunities for the enterprising MHP. By reading data-based research, clinicians may generate ideas that may be turned into a service not previously provided in their local community. For example, while "journal cruising" one day, Steve Walfish came across an article titled "Psychological Morbidity Associated With Motor Vehicle Accidents" by Blanchard, Hickling, Taylor, Loos, and Gerald (1994). These authors found an incidence of posttraumatic stress disorder of 46% for individuals who had been involved in a motor vehicle accident and sought out medical attention within 1 week. When he read this report he immediately thought of the size of the market this might represent given the number of accidents that occur annually. This idea spurred him on to read more of the research in this area and to develop an evaluation service for physicians, attorneys, and chiropractors. They are the gatekeepers of individuals likely to be experiencing emotional difficulties as a result of their accident, and they indeed did refer a steady flow of their patients for evaluation.

Baron and Shane (2008) indicated that the individuals who actively search for opportunities are the ones most likely to find them. They cited the work of Gaglio and Katz (2001) regarding the mental framework or cognitive schema of "entrepreneurial alertness." With such a schema some individuals can create valuable opportunities "where there once were none." Baron and Shane presented six practical techniques for increasing opportunity recognition. The first is to build a rich knowledge base. The more you know, the more likely the knowledge can be put to creative use. The second is to organize your knowledge. The organizational system may be as complex as a computerized management information system or as simple as a well-organized box with index cards. If you cannot access the information, it cannot be put to creative use. The third is to increase your access to information. You could do this through reading, social networking, finding a mentor or practice development consultant, or participating in professional e-mail lists. Baron (2002) suggested that some entrepreneurs begin new opportunities as a result of having been exposed to successful entrepreneurs who served as mentors to them. The fourth is to create connections between the pieces of knowledge that you possess. For example, if you know how to do psychological assessment for one health problem, would this generalize to other health problems that might also benefit from psychological assessment? The fifth is to build your practical intelligence. This type of mental brainstorming is useful when traditional solutions to the problem may not fit. Sarason (1981) and O'Neill (2005) suggested that how you define the problem will in turn determine how you go about solving the problem. Redefining the problem may then lead to an alternative mindset to go about solving a seemingly insurmountable obstacle. Furthermore, Ames and Runco (2005) found that successful entrepreneurs produced many ideas to solve problems and relied on their own thought processes rather than on routine and rote solutions to problems. The sixth is to be aware of potential false alarms. At times, seeming opportunities are actually mirages and should not be pursued.

Conclusion

In this chapter we pointed out that the private practitioner is the owner and operator of his or her own small business. Therefore, the MHP is responsible for the success or failure of that small business. Avoiding the pitfalls associated with having a small business and adopting the spirit of an entrepreneur will not guarantee success but will greatly increase its likelihood in the free market system. Cultivating a cognitive schema of "entrepreneurial alertness" allows the private practitioner to see opportunity where others do not and to be alert to alternative ways to deliver professional services.

Customer Service and Competence

3

The Keys to Financial Success in Independent Practice

A former student recently contacted Steve Walfish. She had battled with a blood phobia for several years and she finally mustered up the courage to ask for help. She asked whether he knew the name of a psychotherapist whom she could see to tackle this problem. Steve gave her the name of a trusted colleague, and a couple of weeks later he followed up with an e-mail to see how it was going. She replied with the following,

> I did not make an appointment with Dr. X; however, I am still thinking about it. I did send him an e-mail and his response was not what I expected . . . but the only responses I have to compare it to are the ones from my psychology college professors who always exceed my expectations. I sent him a detailed message of my issue and I thought that he would have at least introduced himself and given me his credentials but he simply gave me the name of his secretary and asked me to call her to set up an appointment. I am a little skeptical. Is this something I should expect from most psychologists?

Steve explained to the former student that not all mental health professionals have the same practice styles or office policies and guidelines. He suggested that she still contact this person because of the psychotherapist's skill as a clinician but also gave her the names of other resources with which she might feel more comfortable.

> **Private Practice Principle Number 4:** There is no shortage of clinically skilled mental health professionals capable of doing excellent work. Those clinicians with the best customer-service practices will likely be the most successful in private practice.

This principle was conveyed to Steve when he first entered private practice. One of the senior practice associates was R. Bob Smith III, current president of Psychological Assessment Resources (PAR), a psychological testing company. Steve asked Bob why he put such an emphasis on seeing clients for evaluation in the morning and sending the report in the mail the next day. Bob explained,

> There are plenty of people who want these Vocational Rehabilitation and Social Security Disability evaluations as part of their practice. As long as I do a good job in my reports and send them in a timely manner, the referrals will keep coming my way instead of going to one of these other excellent clinicians.

Bob subsequently left private practice to start a company, and by no coincidence its emphasis on customer service (orders filled and shipped the same day) has helped it to stand out over other test companies. The product development staff at PAR also regularly consults with the users of their products to determine in what other ways the company can be helpful to them. This feedback then helps to shape the development of new psychological tests and practice support products.

Regarding the student with the blood phobia, we believe that most people have ambivalent feelings about seeing a mental health professional in the first place. Indeed, Vogel, Wade, and Haake (2006) summarized research to suggest that 40% of people with mental health problems will never seek out any type of mental health treatment. These authors surmised that people do not seek help because of self-stigma or the perceived stigma from others for seeking such help. Cowen (1982) found that people talked about moderate to serious problems with their bartenders, industrial supervisors, family law attorneys, and hairdressers (especially the latter two). The point is that anything done from a customer-service perspective may help to reduce clients' ambivalence in their help-seeking behavior.

Psychotherapists as Providers and Clients as Customers

Mental health professionals do not like to think of themselves as providers of services nor do they like to think of their clients as customers. Clinicians do psychotherapy or counseling and have clients or patients. There is something distasteful (too commercial perhaps? Too demeaning to be thought of as providers because mental health professionals have advanced degrees?) in thinking of themselves as providers of services. However, whatever the verbiage or title there is no getting around the fact that mental health professionals provide a product or service (e.g., assessment, treatment, consulting) to consumers or purchasers of their skill sets. A *customer* is "a person who purchases goods or services from another" (Customer, n.d.-a) or "one that purchases a commodity or service" (Customer, n.d.-b).

Despite the fact that clinicians provide services to customers, you do not have to think of clients in a financially mercenary manner. Nor do you have to think of them in an impersonal manner. Nor is customer service a replacement for excellent clinical skill. However, there is no getting around the fact that clients (or third parties on their behalf) purchase services from you, and fees for these services are how you earn your livelihood. A mindset of optimizing client (customer) experience will not only enhance the client's experience (and impression) of you and your practice but also ultimately contribute to the bottom line of your small business.

In discussing this issue Glazer and Merris (2004) warned against the total transfer of a business model of customer service to the practice of medicine. The same may be true for mental health services. They warned that the maxim "The customer is always right" may not fit when delivering health care services. It would be poor psychotherapy to always agree with clients and tell them what they want to hear as opposed to providing helpful feedback that sometimes could make them defensive or angry. It would reflect poor assessment skills to indicate that a client was a good candidate for a surgery when he or she was actually a poor candidate, just to make him or her happy. Glazer and Merris pointed to the distinction between the care the patients want versus the care they need, and at times patients have to be told news they don't want to hear to improve their health status. In a similar way, mental health professionals cannot offer a money-back guarantee for the assessment and therapy services they provide. You should, however, actively work with clients to help them establish realistic expectations of you and should demonstrate flexibility in your interactions with them including accepting cancellations and requests to reschedule appointments, being available for telephone consultations in between appointments, and scheduling your time flexibly.

A Customer-Service Framework

Mental health providers have two groups of "customers." The first are the clients who come to you for assessment, treatment, or consulting services. They are the people who seek out your expertise because you can help alleviate some of their emotional pain or improve the quality of their life in some way. The second are gatekeepers or referral sources who believe you can be helpful to their clients or organizations because of the skills you have to offer. Your success in pleasing each source, both clinically and from a service perspective, will help determine how filled your schedule becomes with revenue-generating activities.

Ask any mental health professional in private practice whether he or she has excellent customer-service skills and behaviors and we are positive he or she will reply, "Yes." Crosby and Johnson (2006) reviewed data on customer experiences and how customers remember the company. They indicated that the vast majority of companies believe they provide superior customer experiences. However, only 8% of their customers agreed with this belief. A similar study has not been completed with mental health professionals, but there is no reason to believe they are immune from a similar self-assessment bias. Crosby and Johnson indicated that extremely positive or extremely negative impressions of the customer experience will create strong memories. We believe these memories will determine whether clients will continue to do business with you or not and what they will tell their friends, family, coworkers, and referral source (e.g., their physician, employee assistance program [EAP], insurance company).

Ralston (2003) stated that the value a customer places on the services they purchase affects their loyalty and is the driving force behind customer attraction, retention, and repurchase. If customers encounter a helpful and sincere problem resolution process they tend to form a favorable impression of the service. Furthermore, customers are affected by the values manifested by the procedures and interpersonal interactions during the service encounter. When customers perceive themselves of lower social status as an outcome of a transaction, they will attribute negative traits to the organization and its products or services.

Ford (2003) suggested that research has demonstrated that customers have high expectations for personalized communication practices from professionals. She further suggested that these expectations are raised even higher with health care providers. No study to date has examined client satisfaction with mental health providers in private practice. She cited data from several studies to indicate that quality of the interaction, information sharing, and affiliation behavior (e.g., involvement, immediacy, and affective orientation) were strong predictors of patient satisfaction. Ford concluded that customer satisfaction with health care providers is a consistent predictor of loyalty.

Berman (2005) went beyond the concept of customer satisfaction to one of "customer delight." He suggested that delight requires a mixture of joy and surprise and is an emotional response that commits a customer to the product. Citing Kano (1984), Berman further expounded that customers expect a quality product and therefore do not become delighted unless they experience something that they believe goes above and beyond the delivery of this quality product. Berman noted differences between customer satisfaction and customer delight:

- Satisfaction is cognitive and based on perceptions; delight is affective and more emotional.
- Satisfaction is based on meeting or exceeding expectations; delight requires out-of-the-ordinary experience.
- Satisfaction has a weak memory trace; delight experiences are more memorable.

Berman cited research to indicate that delighted customers develop loyalty and ignore competing brands in favor of the brand that has delighted them in the past. In addition to loyalty Berman indicated that delighted customers provide positive feedback on their positive experience to others, including by word-of-mouth and the Internet. According to Berman, the opposite of customer delight is customer outrage. As positive as customer delight can be to a clinician's reputation and referral flow, at times customer outrage can have just as negative an effect in closing down referral sources. In an editorial in a trade publication, Finlay (1999) discussed the issue of customer satisfaction in car dealerships. He stated that a customer has the capability of becoming either "an apostle" or "a terrorist" for the dealership. He suggested that those dealerships that focus on surprising and delighting customers are likely to turn their customers into apostles.

If for some reason you believe that Finlay's (1999) analogy applies only to car dealerships and not to psychotherapy offices, this would be short-sighted. From where do mental health professionals receive their referrals (or customers)? They come from physicians, EAPs, attorneys, clergy, school counselors, probation officers, other mental health professionals, and a handful of other sources. However, once the clinician has been established in practice for a few years we believe a significant portion of referrals come from former clients. We have worked with these clients to reduce their depression or anxiety, improve their marital situation, maintain their recovery from alcohol, or diagnose a learning disability that had previously been undetected. Because of the potential stigma, a portion of people will never talk about their mental health treatment. However, there is also a portion who will tell everybody what a wonderful psychotherapist they have and how their marriage had been saved by Dr. Smith or Mr. Jones. They will tell friends, family, coworkers, their physicians, and other participants in self-help meetings. This positive word-of-mouth advertising from your "apostles" is key to building and maintaining a profitable small business. However, if these individuals weren't helped by the services or felt treated unfairly or unjustly in some manner, know that these individuals may be just as vocal, if not more vocal, in your community about their displeasure with your services.

As another example, take the case of presurgical psychological evaluations for weight-loss surgery. This is a specialty area for Steve Walfish. Surgeons may require their patients to obtain such an evaluation before they will perform the procedure (and some insurance carriers require the evaluation). They may refer to a specific psychologist or allow the patient to choose one on his or her own. One glance at http://www.obesityhelp.com (an online community related to weight-loss surgery) will demonstrate that patients talk. On this site are reviews of hundreds of mental health professionals with ratings on politeness, expertise, whether they are surgery supportive, how good a listener they are, whether they were an effective helper, and overall value of the evaluation. In addition, there is a comment section. Patients can be praiseworthy or brutal and terroristic in this section. With enough laudatory comments the provider may have more referrals come their way. If the provider garners enough vicious, brutal comments, patients may stay clear, especially if they have a choice of evaluators.

These concepts work for gatekeepers as well. EAPs typically have several counselors working in their program. These counselors consult with each other on a regular basis. They will ask, "Who do you know who is good working with adolescents? Who knows about traumatic brain injury? Know a good marital therapist?" In a similar way, school counselors also talk among themselves. Certain mental health professionals develop positive reputations with one or two counselors and then soon after start receiving referrals from other school counselors. These counselors will tell the clinician, "Jane Doe told me you were really good working with acting-out boys and I've got three on my caseload who really need help. Do you have room in your schedule to take on some tough cases?" However, be late with a report, do not follow up with a counselor who needs to know how his or her client is doing (or whether the client is even still in treatment), write reports in jargon that only mental health professionals can understand, or develop an elitist attitude toward the person referring clients to you, and this information will also spread and the referral well will run dry. As noted earlier, Ralston (2003) believed customers will attribute negative traits to the organization and its products or services if they perceive themselves to be of lower social status than the professional. We believe it essential to remember this concept especially as it relates to the development of elitist attitudes about your skills, level of education and training, and status as a mental health professional.

Very few people have the insight to know or believe they are presenting themselves as elitist, but you all know mental health professionals who present themselves in this manner. We suggest—actually, we urge—that private practitioners adopt and actively strive for a genuine attitude of appreciation and humility in your work so this may be communicated to the people you serve. You are not entitled to receive referrals or make a living at this work. It is an honor and a privilege to work for individuals who open up their hearts and vulnerabilities and deepest darkest secrets in hopes of removing suffering and improving the quality of their lives.

Value of a Lost Customer

Hogan, Lemon, and Libai (2003) discussed the value of a lost customer; this concept has direct implications for the mental health practice provider. A large number of lost customers will seriously impair the income of the private practitioner. Take the example of the referral described at the beginning of the chapter, for the student with the blood phobia. Hellstrom, Fellenius, and Ost (1996) presented data that this condition can be successfully treated in five sessions of behavior therapy. Suppose she did go see the psychotherapist. At a fee of $100 per session, the clinician would earn $500 for treating her. Now imagine that she told two of her friends what a great psychologist she went to for help with this lifelong problem. Imagine that when one of these friends is discussing her boyfriend difficulties, the client suggests seeking out the services of Dr. X because he had been so helpful with the blood phobia. As the average course in psychotherapy is six sessions, this would then be another $600 of income for Dr. X. This friend may also tell other friends. One can see how losing this one referral could easily add up to a few thousand dollars of lost income. However, the loss of income is even greater: Imagine if the client had been successfully treated and she went back and told her physician of the success she had overcoming this problem area working with that wonderful Dr. X. In light of the high incidence of blood phobia and needle phobia that physicians encounter, Dr. X would likely have received numerous referrals. In addition, had Dr. X been successful with most of these patients, then the physician would likely have been willing to refer patients with other mental health problems such as anxiety or depression. This "lost customer" may have resulted in the loss of tens of thousands of dollars in revenue for Dr. X.

We believe that mental health professionals lose customers all the time because of lax customer-service practices. Sometimes clients are given the name of one and only one mental health professional as "the person to see." However, when insurance companies, EAPs, or school counselors refer a client for assessment or counseling they usually provide the name of three mental health professionals for the client to contact (or the client may consult an entire list of clinicians posted on the insurance company's Web site). If the person has a general problem (e.g., depression, anxiety, adjustment reaction), most mental health professionals are competent to successfully address such problems with the client. Therefore, it does not usually matter to the client which of the three he or she sees for help (the situation is different if it is a specialized problem area and only one or two people in the area have the requisite training and skill set to treat the problem area). Who the person makes the appointment with will depend on a few things. First, the potential client goes down the list and will usually make an appointment with the clinician who calls back first. If psychotherapist number one on the list is unavailable to talk to Mr. Doe when he calls, Mr. Doe will then call therapist number two. If therapist number two is unavailable, the client will then call psychotherapist number three. If psychotherapists check their messages only once per day and then return calls in the evening, they are likely to lose referrals. Losing one referral every other week because of not returning calls promptly will add up to 25 per year. Do this for 5 years and this will be 125 referrals and probably $100,000 in revenue not generated, if one uses the multiplicative example of the client with the blood phobia. The moral of the story is to check your messages often (e.g., three or four times per day). Plenty of other competent mental health professionals would love to have this same referral. Want to create "customer delight"? Check your messages every hour and call the client back promptly. We cannot tell you how often we hear the words, "Thank you for calling back so quickly." Clients generally are calling because they are in crisis. It is comforting to them to know that help is on the way.

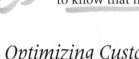

Optimizing Customer Service on an Individual Basis

Dwore (1993) took the position that quality performance comprises the complementary services of patient care and customer service. In this chapter we focus on customer-service attitudes and behaviors of the private practitioner. However, we do not for a second undervalue or underemphasize Dwore's emphasis on quality patient care.

Private Practice Principle Number 5: Without excellent clinical work, no amount of customer-service practices will produce success in private practice.

In a Delphi study, highly regarded private practitioners (Fellows of the American Psychological Association Division of Independent Practice) were asked to provide advice on the best strategies for developing and maintaining an independent practice (Walfish & Coovert, 1989). Performing at a superior level, not practicing beyond one's level of competence, and establishing a specific area of competence were highly rated strategies for the development of a practice. Knowing your limits, cutting no corners in the quality of your work, and getting peer supervision with candid feedback and genuine support were viewed as strategies for successfully maintaining a practice. If you want to create customer delight, help a family eliminate enuresis in their child with an empirically validated treatment (Houts, Berman, & Abramson, 1994) or help an adult overcome a lifelong fear of public speaking (P. Anderson, Zimand, Hodges, & Rothbaum, 2005). This Delphi panel also provided tips for graduate students who want to pursue private practice as a career path. Developing competence through diversified training and experiences was at the top of their list. As we noted earlier, clinical competence is a necessary component of success in private practice. However, with that being said we also believe that clinical competence alone is not enough.

> **Private Practice Principle Number 6:** With rare exceptions, having excellent clinical skills but poor customer service will not produce success in private practice.

As Dwore (1993) pointed out, both clinical excellence and customer-service practices are essential ingredients for success in this service business. Regarding the latter, we think it is important for the clinician to pay attention to a number of areas to improve customer service. These are presented in random order.

ENHANCE AVAILABILITY OF APPOINTMENTS

Although this is not always the case, our experience is that most people wait a long time between having the thought of calling a mental health professional and actually making the call to schedule an appointment. They think about seeing a psychotherapist, they think some more about seeing a psychotherapist, and then they think even more about seeing a psychotherapist. Then, something happens in their life (usually a crisis) and voilà! They actually do pick up the telephone and make the call. At that point, there is nothing more deflating than being told, "Yes, I can fit you in a week from Friday." We think it important that new clients be seen within 1 week; otherwise, they are likely to look elsewhere. To create customer delight, try to see them the next day even if it means working an extra hour that day.

In addition to providing new appointments in a timely manner, we also believe it is important that appointment times be provided during nontraditional hours. This flexibility may not be necessary for someone who has an established practice and has no desire to work nontraditional hours. However, we think having nontraditional hours is essential when building a practice and also a helpful behavior in maintaining one's practice. It is not that difficult for clients to make appointments between the hours of 9:00 a.m. and 4:00 p.m., Monday through Friday for a limited number of weeks. They may have sick leave that will accommodate such appointments. However, it becomes a hardship for most to have to take off from work on a continuing basis if they are involved in long-term psychotherapy. In a similar way, it can be a hardship to take children out of school during the week on a continuing basis to attend counseling sessions. It is our experience that the hardships created by having only traditional office times available for appointments will result in the client

having a shorter course of psychotherapy or parents ending counseling prematurely because of this obstacle. For this reason we think it is important for mental health professionals to offer early morning and evening appointments. If you want to create customer delight, offer appointments on Saturdays. Steve Walfish does this in his practice, and he finds that this offers him a competitive advantage, especially when completing presurgical psychological evaluations for gastric bypass surgery. These evaluations take 4 hours for the client to complete (3 hours of psychometric testing and 1 hour of interview). One surgeon specifically tells his patients that Steve sees patients on Saturdays, and for this reason they choose him over two other psychologists on their referral list. This service results in his receiving an additional 50 evaluations each year that likely would have gone to the competition. Clients are thrilled not to have to take time off from work to complete the evaluation because they also have other medical appointments related to the surgery and will also be out of work for 2 weeks following the surgery.

Jeff Barnett provides comprehensive psychoeducational evaluations in his practice that involve two separate 3-hour testing sessions during the evaluation process. He regularly works on days when children are out of school, including school holidays and Saturdays. In addition, he regularly meets with psychotherapy clients before school or work in the early morning or in the evening after school and work.

It is also of vital importance to understand the effect of a potential client's first contact with your office, whether it be with office staff or you personally. Staff should be trained to answer the telephone right away and not let calls turn over to voicemail. They should also have a courteous and friendly manner that is welcoming to potential clients without being overly chummy or intrusive. Staff should be provided with training on just what information to share with potential clients. Jeff Barnett accepts all telephone calls personally whenever possible and if not, returns all calls within several hours. He takes the time to provide information about his practice and to listen to their concerns. Although

he doesn't conduct the intake interview over the telephone, that call involves much more than just setting up an appointment. The point is that the personalized service, caring, and commitment to excellence and to meeting clients' needs come through in the first contact. These attitudes are then backed up with actions throughout the assessment and treatment relationship.

BE AVAILABLE FOR EMERGENCIES

Mental health professionals have a responsibility to their clients on a 24-hour, 7-day-a-week basis for emergencies. This is just part of the territory. This does not mean that clinicians cannot go out of town or take a break from this responsibility, but they must arrange coverage by another appropriate clinician when they do so. Clients are comforted knowing they may call their psychotherapist if life becomes overwhelming for them, they are feeling suicidal, or they feel like they are having a nervous breakdown. Some clients clearly abuse this part of the therapeutic relationship. However, this abuse then becomes a treatment issue, and the skilled clinician will know how to set firm but appropriate limits. It is also important for the clinician to respond quickly to the emergency call. Wait a day to return the call and you will have an angry client. Call back within 30 minutes and you will create customer delight.

An important recommendation is to schedule brief breaks throughout your workday and regularly check for telephone messages. At a minimum, schedule a mid-day break to check for messages and to return telephone calls. Do this again at the end of the day before leaving for home.

SIMPLIFY OFFICE FORMS

Clients are used to coming to medical offices and having to complete forms at the time of their first appointment. These forms may request contact information, insurance information, and health history information. Some states require disclosure forms that serve as a contract between the mental health professional and the client. Snyder and Barnett (2006) indicated that these forms are an important element of the informed consent process. We think it important for mental health professionals to provide forms that are clearly written and easy to understand. Snyder and Barnett suggested that such consent forms may help decrease the occurrence of surprises, disappointments, and false expectations (e.g., "What do you mean I have to pay for no-show appointments?" "I thought you guaranteed I would get better if I did this cognitive therapy with you"). Despite an ethical mandate, mental health professionals have a difficult time developing forms that are written in simple language. For example, Handelsman et al. (1995) found that the informed consent forms psychotherapists presented to their clients were written on average at the reading level of a college junior, and almost two thirds were written beyond college level. Walfish and

Ducey (2007) evaluated Health Insurance Portability and Accountability Act notices of privacy practices of psychologists in private practice and found similar results. The vast majority was written beyond a high school reading level, and most could be classified as being in the difficult range of reading ease. There is no reason why these forms have to be so complicated. Paasche-Orlow, Taylor, and Brancati (2003) found that complicated medical consent forms could be written at the eighth-grade level or below. Walfish and Ducey presented examples of how to improve readability of informed consent forms, and Snyder and Barnett advocated that the forms used by mental health professionals be written at a fifth- to eighth-grade reading level. Having an appropriate reading level is important because 50% of the adult population reads below a ninth-grade level (Doak, Doak, & Root, 1996).

In addition, most clients expect to arrive 10 to 15 minutes early to complete the necessary paperwork. To create customer delight, consider placing these forms on your Web site, if you have one, or offer to mail or e-mail them to clients with their permission. Including written directions to your office will also contribute to customer delight.

VERIFY INSURANCE BENEFITS

In chapter 6 (this volume) we discuss issues of billing and collecting and procedures for verifying benefits. Suffice to say, most clients often have limited knowledge about their insurance benefits and how the insurance system works. Many assume they can just arrive at the clinician's office; show their BlueCross BlueShield, UnitedHealthcare, or CIGNA card; and receive services and have them paid for as if they were having an office visit with their primary care physician. In this day and age this is simply not the case given that some plans have (a) no mental health benefits at all, (b) "carved out" their mental health benefits to a managed care company such as Magellan or ValueOptions, (c) a limit on the number of sessions that may be used during a calendar year, (d) different reimbursement rates in terms of percentage of copay due from the client, (e) restrictions on which clinicians can be reimbursed and which cannot, (f) different deductibles and copays depending on whether or not the clinician is part of their network of preferred providers, and (g) requirements for preauthorization that must be met before coverage for mental health services will be provided. The reason for verifying benefits on behalf of the client is twofold. First, clients cannot be trusted to always call their insurance company ahead of time to determine these benefits. We cannot tell you how many times clients have arrived for their first appointment and when asked if they had called their insurer the reply was, "I meant to but I got real busy this week. I'll call tomorrow and get it all straightened out." If a managed care company is involved with this case the company may choose to or may choose not to reimburse for this session. In this case, noncompliance with the contract is the reason for denial; medical necessity has nothing to do with it. In these cases, even if it is client error, by contract the clinician may not bill the managed care company or insurer for the session if it is not preauthorized. Second, clients cannot be trusted to get this complicated information correct and then be able to accurately relate this information to the therapist. Any inaccuracies may result in misunderstandings and unhappy clients who owe a larger amount of money than they had anticipated or believed they were promised. It is difficult to create customer delight when it comes to billing but most clients are grateful that they don't have to deal with their insurance company, that that aspect of the treatment process will be taken care of for them, and that they will not be surprised with a significant bill at a later date.

PROVIDE FOR A CONVENIENT AND UNDERSTANDABLE BILLING SYSTEM

If you accept insurance, file on behalf of the client and wait to be reimbursed. This will create customer delight. This way clients do not have to pay up front and wait to be reimbursed. If treatment is a financial hardship clients will be especially appreciative as they will not have to defer payment on another life expense. If you do not accept insurance, present clients with a *super bill* (a detailed bill that includes all information typically needed by insurance companies to process claims; discussed in chap. 6, this volume) at the time of service so they may immediately submit it to their carrier for reimbursement.

Make arrangements to accept credit card payments from your clients (see chap. 6, this volume). We have found this to be especially appreciated when clients are paying several hundred dollars at one time for an evaluation for themselves or their child. Having this payment method available may mean the difference between the client entering psychotherapy, continuing psychotherapy, or undergoing what is for him or her an expensive evaluation.

Hochhauser (2005) discussed one aspect of customer service that is often overlooked by providers: the billing process. Let's face it, no one, including clients (and yourself), looks forward to receiving bills in the mail or dealing with insurance companies. The smoother the clinician can make this for clients, the happier they will be with the overall service being provided for them. Hochhauser, a psychologist and readability expert, suggested that receiving a bill may produce unpleasant emotions and thus clients may avoid opening the bill, which will result in either late payment or even nonpayment. What upsets clients even more is not understanding the billing process or receiving a bill they cannot understand. We think it is important for clinicians to provide bills that are timely as no one likes receiving a bill several months or a year after services were delivered. It is imperative the bills are easily understood so clients understand all of the charges and their portion due (see chap. 6, this volume). In addition, a preaddressed envelope to return payment is also appreciated by clients. Some psychotherapists actually include a stamp on that envelope with the belief clients will appreciate the thought and the payment will be received sooner.

PROVIDE A COMFORTABLE AND PROFESSIONAL-LOOKING OFFICE SPACE

Clients are coming to see a professional for help. In private practice they are usually paying significant fees for this help. Clients are aware of the fees regardless of whether they are paying the entire fee or a portion of it. They would likely not feel comfortable knowing these fees are going to the mental health professional when the space provided does not look and feel professional. They should not expect the Ritz, but they are not necessarily going to be happy with bargain basement either. For this reason the mental health professional is expected to practice in an office building and not the upstairs of a grocery store, back room of an insurance agency, or the basement of a YMCA where the sounds of a basketball bouncing can be heard from above. The space does not have to be a traditional office building but it at least has to look like a professional space. For example, many mental health professionals (as well as physicians and attorneys) buy a house in a neighborhood that is zoned for commercial purposes and renovate the property so it feels like a home but looks like an office space.

The space should be kept up and the furniture comfortable. Most traditional medical buildings provide a cleaning service. The service will not do deep cleaning but at least will vacuum and empty the wastebaskets. As part of normal upkeep, the office should be painted every few years. Furniture should be comfortable and not look worn. Couches left over from graduate school (that were likely purchased from Salvation Army in the first place) will leave a negative impression and be uncomfortable for the client. Artwork or posters on the wall should be tasteful and noncontroversial. The space should be furnished and presented in such a way that the client will feel comfortable coming in and discuss issues of importance. The office should also be handicapped accessible so clients with physical challenges will not find the office difficult to navigate. One excellent resource for information and resources related to disability and accessibility is Kenneth Pope's Web site (http://www.kspope.com).

PROVIDE AMENITIES IN THE OFFICE

In creating a comfortable office space it is helpful to have a waiting room to which clients will look forward to coming and where they will feel comfortable. Have coffee, tea, and water available. Keep in your office a variety of (noncontroversial) magazines that clients will enjoy reading while they wait. If children are seen in the practice, provide an area for them with an assortment of play or educational materials that are age-appropriate.

HAVE HELPFUL AND PLEASANT OFFICE STAFF

This recommendation may sound like a "no-brainer" but it takes a special person to be able to meet all of the demands of working as a support staff member in a mental health practice. In a group practice the support staff has to meet all of the demands of a variety of mental health professionals, answer the phone for several clinicians, and provide reception services to a large number of clients. These individuals have no formal training in mental health but have to deal with clients who have a wide spectrum of mental health problems. Being a receptionist in a mental health practice is different from being one in an accounting firm. A percentage of clients (with poor boundaries) will readily pour their hearts out to a receptionist while waiting for their appointment. Clients will routinely interact with reception staff when scheduling their appointments or paying their bill. If the receptionist is having a bad day and has difficulty containing a bad mood, clients' perception of the practice can be negatively affected. However, having strong support staff can help create customer delight. "Sherry was so helpful in clearing up this thing with my insurance company," "Marcus is such a polite young man. It's a pleasure to talk with him," and "Caron was really helpful when I had to reschedule my appointment" are all remarks that we have heard. We urge you to remember that the front-office staff reflects on the mental health professional even though they have nothing to do with the clinical services being provided.

Optimizing Customer Service With Referral Sources

As noted earlier, the second group of customers for private practitioners comprises gatekeepers or referral sources who believe you can be helpful to their clients or organizations. You have assessment and treatment skills, and their clients need such services. These referral sources may be helping clients with their health (e.g., physicians, chiropractors, workers' compensation case managers) or their education (e.g., teachers, school counselor), overseeing their employment (e.g., human resources section of a company, EAP), or monitoring some aspect of their life (e.g., probation officer, state licensing board) on behalf of the government. These individuals have the capability of filling your practices. Their clients have needs and they are interested in finding mental health professionals (a) in whom they can have confidence in their abilities to provide such a service and (b) who can provide the service in a timely and professional manner. Finding such a relationship is a "win–win" for all involved and the relationship should be cultivated by the private practitioner. In this section we turn our focus to physicians, the largest gatekeeper and referral source to mental health professionals. Although some of these principles apply solely to working with medical professionals, several of the concepts generalize to other gatekeepers of mental health services.

An insightful study by Kainz (2002) examined psychologist–physician relationships to determine how to develop a positive referral arrangement. As gatekeepers of mental health services for their patients, physicians (assuming they are not in a rural area) have their choice of where to refer their patients. Kainz identified several barriers but two are specifically worthy of mention because they relate to customer service. The first barrier is not being able to see the psychologist quickly, especially in an emergency. The second is related to insurance: Physicians believe that if coverage is not available, the patient will not go to psychotherapy.

Kainz (2002) was also able to identify several factors that encouraged physicians to refer to psychotherapists:

- Having a good rapport with the psychotherapist. This factor relates to the concept of emotional intelligence discussed in chapter 2 (this volume). Physicians must be comfortable with the mental health professional as a person. After all, physicians have a responsibility to their patients. If physicians are not comfortable with the clinician, why would they expect their patient to feel comfortable talking about their personal and private issues? Tovian (2006) noted that successful collaborative relationships between physicians and mental health professionals depend on excellent interpersonal skills, not unlike those skills necessary to make a therapeutic difference with a client. Tovian also stressed the importance of empathic understanding of the roles and demands of the physician. Physicians do not think or practice in the same manner or style as do mental health professionals. However, clinicians have to adapt to their preferences rather than the other way around.

- The reputation of the psychotherapist. How do most physicians decide who to refer to for assessment or psychotherapy? They ask their colleagues. They want to refer their patients to someone who has a track record of being effective with medical patients, especially difficult ones. So they ask their colleagues questions such as, "Whom do you refer your depressed patients to for psychotherapy?" "My patient has stress headaches. Know anyone good with somatisizing patients?" "My patient was in my office crying today because she and her husband are having difficulties. Know any good marriage counselors?" "My patient's kid just got his report card and he flunked four subjects. Who does a good learning disabilities workup?"

- The clinical competence of the psychologist. Physicians have a finite set of skills with which to address their patients' psychosocial problems. They can listen, give light advice, order laboratory tests to determine if a biological condition is the cause of anxiety or depression, and write prescriptions (most prescriptions for antidepressant and antianxiety medications are written by primary care physicians). They want their patients to get better and see their symptoms dissipate. Although prescriptions can help people, physicians are aware that (a) they do not work for all patients and (b) some patients also need the skills of a psychotherapist in conjunction with medication management to make optimal gains. They do not like it when their patients come into their consultation rooms complaining of anxiety, depression, and anger. When a patient is referred by a physician to a mental health professional you can bet the physician will ask at the follow-up appointment, "So is your psychotherapist being helpful? How are your symptoms?" If physicians consistently hear positive feedback from their patients, you have two satisfied consumers of your services. More referrals will surely follow.

- The timeliness of the feedback to the clinician. When physicians refer a patient for psychotherapy or assessment, the next time they see the patient and open up their chart they expect to see correspondence from the mental health professional. If it is not there, they will be left wondering what the patient's mental health diagnosis might be and what treatment plan is being carried out. Because they referred the patient for these reasons in the first place, they will be unsatisfied consumers of your services. Physicians especially want to be made aware of any emergencies that may be taking place in the patient's life. Examples might include significant suicidal ideation, previously undetected substance abuse, an impending psychiatric or substance abuse hospitalization, or decompensation headed toward a psychotic break. They generally have two reasons for wanting to be informed of such events. First, they genuinely care about the welfare of their patients and want to know if they can be helpful. Second, as their physician they are likely to receive a phone call from a hospital emergency room or a distraught family member. They need to be prepared so they may respond in an appropriate manner should they receive such calls.

▪ Confidence that the patient will be comfortable and dealt with in a sensitive manner. Let's face it, mental health professionals have reputations of being somewhat "out there" in their thinking, their treatment approaches, and sometimes their behavior. Indeed, mental health professionals are often stigmatized as being "a bunch of quacks." By nature most physicians are conservative. They prefer empirically based treatment approaches delivered by people who practice in professional office space. This is how they typically practice and this is what their patients expect. If a patient reports to the physician that the person he or she was referred to was easy to talk to, future referrals will likely result. If the patient reports, "He was weird and nuttier than a fruitcake" then the referral well from this physician may dry up, especially if the physician hears this type of feedback more than once.

Kainz (2002) also identified those factors related to the physician's decision to refer for mental health treatment. Three of the factors receiving the majority of "great importance" responses included (a) insurance coverage, (b) summary of treatment sent, and (c) short-term treatment approach. Kainz also noted that in terms of correspondence from mental health professionals, physicians indicated they wanted an intake report that included primary complaints and diagnosis. A significant percentage of the physicians indicated that the ideal length of the intake report was one full page. We suggest clinicians obtain permission from their clients to correspond with their physicians for the purpose of integrated care. The physician should then be sent a letter within a few days indicating the patient has been seen, the nature of the problems assessed, a treatment plan, and any other concerns, especially those of a medical nature (e.g., medication, medical problem that may have a behavioral or emotional manifestation). A sample letter is provided in Exhibit 3.1. When treatment is over the physician would appreciate knowing that it has been completed, what success has been accomplished, and what, if any, problems remain. A sample follow-up letter to referral sources at the end of treatment is included in Exhibit 3.2.

Tovian (2006) identified effective communication parameters and necessary skills for successful collaboration with medical professionals. Effective communication parameters include being aware of differing physician styles and needs, avoiding jargon, being brief and concise, and keeping the physician in the communication loop. Necessary skills include focused assessments, flexibility in practice style, decisive decision making with limited data, enhancing patient motivation to change behavior, and understanding medical conditions, procedures, and medications. The mental health professional does not have to become a "junior physician" but rather should understand that the patient is often being referred in the context of treatment for a medical condition. Many illnesses have behavioral implications. For example, medical treatment

EXHIBIT 3.1

Sample Initial Letter to a Physician

Jeffrey E. Barnett, PsyD, ABPP
1511 Ritchie Highway, Suite 201
Arnold, MD 21012

March 1, 2007

Mary Johnson, MD
22 Ritchie Highway, Suite 3
Arnold, MD 21012

Dear Dr. Johnson:

Thank you for your recent referral of Mr. William Smith for evaluation and treatment in outpatient psychotherapy. I had the opportunity to meet with Mr. Smith earlier today. As you know, Mr. Smith presents with a longstanding history of depression that has troubled him since the breakup of his marriage. When I discussed these issues with Mr. Smith, it became clear that in addition to symptoms of depression he also suffers from a number of stress-related difficulties. Mr. Smith denies any suicidal ideation, intent, or plan, past or present, but does report diminished sleep and appetite over the past 2 months with a reported weight loss of 12 pounds during that time.

Mr. Smith informs me of his current use of Paxil under your care, which he reported being prescribed earlier this week. As would be anticipated, he denies any benefit from this medication yet, but I am glad to report that he denies any side effects either. I will continue to monitor for any effects and side effects of this medication and inform you immediately if any are experienced. Mr. Smith denies use of any other substances and understands the importance of following your recommendation to avoid all alcohol use while taking his prescribed medication.

My initial assessment indicates Mr. Smith to presently be overwhelmed by a number of ongoing stressors in his life and that he lacks the needed coping skills and resources. He also presents with a pattern of negative thinking and avoidant behavior that contribute to his ongoing depression. Our plan at present is to work together in outpatient psychotherapy using a cognitive–behavioral approach that should be most appropriate for his treatment needs. Mr. Smith is amenable to this plan and we have already begun work to assist him to develop needed coping skills and to overcome his current negative patterns of thought and behavior.

As treatment progresses I will keep you informed of all significant changes in Mr. Smith's functioning as they occur. Once again, thank you for this timely and appropriate referral. I will do all I can to be of assistance to Mr. Smith.

Sincerely yours,

Jeffrey E. Barnett, PsyD, ABPP
Licensed Psychologist

---

for hepatitis C is typically accompanied by a severe depression that is biologically induced. A physician may want to have a mental health professional monitor the severity of the depression to ensure the patient does not become actively suicidal. However, although counseling may help to slightly minimize the depth of the depression, no course of cognitive therapy is going to eliminate this depression completely.

EXHIBIT 3.2

Sample Follow-Up Letter to a Physician

Jeffrey E. Barnett, PsyD, ABPP
1511 Ritchie Highway, Suite 201
Arnold, MD 21012

March 1, 2007

Mary Johnson, MD
22 Ritchie Highway, Suite 3
Arnold, MD 21012

Dear Dr. Johnson:

I am writing to provide you with follow-up on my work in outpatient cognitive–behavioral psychotherapy with Mr. William Smith. As I mentioned to you in my recent treatment update, Mr. Smith has made ongoing progress in treatment. I am pleased to report that now after 12 treatment sessions Mr. Smith and I have agreed to end our regular ongoing work together.

Mr. Smith has developed a number of coping skills, he is using friends and family much more effectively for support, he has changed his previous patterns of negative thinking and avoidant behavior, and he has continued the exercise program you recommended for him. He has been relatively free of symptoms of depression for the past month and continues to make ongoing progress. Though we will not be meeting together regularly from this point forward, Mr. Smith understands he can contact me at any time should he experience any additional difficulties. We have scheduled a follow-up appointment for 6 weeks from now to help ensure he continues applying all he has learned and to assist him to keep moving forward.

Mr. Smith understands the importance of maintaining close contact with you regarding his use of Paxil and knows to take it only as prescribed.

I will keep you informed of all future contacts I have with Mr. Smith. Thank you for the opportunity to be of service to him.

Sincerely yours,

Jeffrey E. Barnett, PsyD, ABPP
Licensed Psychologist

Earlier in our careers when developing our practices when dealing with physicians, we felt as if we were beggars hoping they would reward us with morsels of food (e.g., referrals). As we became experienced clinicians we realized that a significant portion (though not all) of physicians view mental health professionals as specialists who are valuable resources in the overall treatment of their patients. In her study Kainz (2002) concluded that physicians look to psychologists for help in treating their patients and may feel abandoned or resentful if this help is not received. For those wanting to collaborate with physicians we suggest following the advice of Tovian (2006) who implored the mental health professional to "build the relationship, build the relationship, and build the relationship" (p. 271).

Other "customers" of mental health professionals are in a position to refer clients for assessment and treatment. In an interesting avenue of study, McMinn and his colleagues (Lish, McMinn, Fitzsimmons, & Root, 2003; McMinn, Aikins, & Lish, 2003; McMinn, Runner, Fairchild, Lefler, & Suntay, 2005) examined collaborative relationships between clergy and psychologists. Those wanting to be of service to clergy will find these papers instructive. These authors found that the strongest predictor of collaboration with clergy was the strength of the individual relationship between the two. Clergy expressed an interest in consulting with mental health professionals and many refer troubled parishioners for counseling. Clergy look for mental health professionals who respect the work of clergy and who do not have animosity toward religion. As with physicians, a mental health professional's willingness to communicate with clergy is viewed as an important component of customer service for this gatekeeper.

> **Private Practice Principle Number 7:** The key ingredient in cultivating and maintaining referrals from gatekeepers is understanding the needs and demands of their job and how your skill set and practice behavior can best meet these needs.

In their excellent book on developing a private practice, Stout and Grand (2005) asked the question, "If Nordstrom's opened a counseling practice, what would it be like?" (p. 262). This is an excellent question for private practitioners to ask themselves so they can tailor their practices to meet the needs of their referral sources (e.g., customers). When Steve Walfish practiced in Everett, Washington, he was part of a multidisciplinary group with Dr. Bob Fink as the senior psychiatrist. It turned out that most of the physicians in town referred their patients to Bob both because of his excellent diagnostic and medication skills and because of his excellent customer-service skills. The director of the behavioral health section of a large multispecialty clinic in the area described Bob as "the Nordstrom's of mental health care." The director elaborated,

> He sees our routine cases in a reasonably timely manner. He will see our emergencies that day or the next day just because we are concerned about the patient as a suicide risk or they may need to be hospitalized. He will also get on the phone and consult with us about difficult cases.

This willingness to work hard (sometimes staying an extra hour or coming in an hour early to see patients) and understanding the needs of his referral sources made Bob a success.

Jeff Barnett knows a physician who regularly refers patients with challenging diagnostic and treatment needs to him. When evaluations are completed, Jeff regularly drives to this physician's office (it is on his way to work) and stops in to drop off the evaluation report personally.

If she is in, he waits until she is free and provides her with a brief verbal report on the case. This physician repeatedly tells him he doesn't need to bring in the reports personally and that the mail is fine, but she keeps providing him with referrals and her associates have begun referring to him as well.

An important question to ask yourself is why the gatekeeper should refer to you as opposed to one of the other mental health professionals in your area. If you want referrals from an EAP, make sure that you understand the needs of the EAP counselor, the culture of the company, and what can and cannot be done for an employee in the workplace. For example, an employee may have a terrible boss and develop an adjustment reaction, with anxious mood. The EAP counselor is likely to respond positively to a treatment plan of helping the employee with cognitive restructuring and stress management techniques to help make the best of a bad situation, rather than a treatment plan that includes the employee demanding a transfer to another position within the company. If you want referrals from the state department of vocational rehabilitation, understand that it is important for these claims managers to successfully close cases as quickly as possible. Thus, they would likely respond positively to a treatment plan with focused target goals of making someone employable once again, rather than one that focuses on dealing with childhood issues that resulted in the present-day personality disorder. It is not a case of the latter not being a worthwhile undertaking. However, in the context of the work of the claims manager and the goal of vocational rehabilitation, the former treatment plan would likely be welcomed. These principles apply to school counselors, workers' compensation claims managers, family law attorneys, probation and parole officers, and any other referral source.

NUTS AND BOLTS OF THE FINANCES OF PRACTICE

II

Models of Independent Practice 4

T housands of mental health professionals (MHPs) are in independent practice. Some see one client per week in the back room of a physician's office, whereas others employ 30 psychotherapists in a multitude of satellite offices. Some are owners of their own solo practice (SP), some are partners in multidisciplinary mental health groups, some are associates in large group practices to which they pay monthly fixed amounts for space and professional services, and some are associates who pay a percentage of monies collected each month to the group practice in exchange for space and services. Some private practitioners choose to incorporate, whereas others do not. Some choose to practice with other MHPs, whereas others choose alternative practice arrangements. Each model brings with it a host of financial considerations, decision-making ability, legal liability, and professional practice options both within the current practice and after the MHP leaves the practice. In this chapter we review these issues so the individual private practitioner may make the best informed decision as to which practice model fits best.

Entering Practice

Although full-time independent practice is an oft-desired career path, new graduates entering practice typically look for existing practices that they can join to begin their careers. There are a number of reasons for this. Before a new MHP is licensed, state laws preclude his or her independent practice and a licensed professional must provide supervision. Start-up costs of renting an office and arranging for furniture and office equipment can be significant. Furthermore, the "nuts and bolts" procedures for beginning and operating a practice are just too numerous for new graduates to possibly be made fully aware of during their training.

Barnett and Henshaw (2003) pointed out several reasons why it can be impractical to begin a full-time private practice right after graduation or licensure. Their major point is that it can take time to build a viable full-time practice. Because income depends solely on the direct provision of clinical services, funds generated during the initial start-up will be minimal. For this reason individuals may prefer to begin their careers in another setting and to slowly (or, if they are fortunate, quickly) transition to the full-time private-practice setting. Barnett and Henshaw suggested one mode of doing this: Take a full-time position in an organizational setting and begin a practice in the evenings and weekends. Another option, if it is financially feasible, is to obtain a half-time position that pays salary and benefits while working to build a practice. When beginning his first practice (he has built three in three different cities), Steve Walfish had a National Institute of Mental Health–funded research grant and he saw clients in the evenings and weekends. Later in his career when he moved to Atlanta he took a full-time teaching job while he worked to build his practice. He then moved to a half-time teaching position as his practice grew and then eventually left teaching completely. Jeff Barnett joined a group practice as an associate who was paid a percentage of all fees collected. However, he quickly discovered the ups and downs of private practice and sought other options. He accepted a half-time position at a state hospital, working there four mornings each week. Because most of his practice hours were afternoons and evenings, this arrangement worked out well. In addition, he received full state employee benefits in this position, including family health insurance, and it very nicely helped combat the professional isolation of full-time independent practice. This position also included a clinical faculty appointment at a medical school. The teaching done there led to a teaching position at a local college. He eventually left the state hospital when he was offered an affiliate faculty teaching position at the college that included full benefits including family health insurance, disability insurance, life insurance, and the like. He teaches 1 day a week and works in his own private practice the other 4 days.

Another option is to venture full speed ahead into private practice. As Barnett and Henshaw (2003) pointed out, this is the "fastest route to a full-time private practice but [it] also carries with it the greatest challenges financially" (p. 147). This option may be viable for individuals who (a) have a spouse or partner who is earning a salary, (b) are willing to borrow money to finance a practice, (c) have a benefactor such as a parent or other family member who is willing to help them while they "get on their feet," or (d) have a practice situation with a relative guarantee of endless referrals. No clinician can receive from a referral source or practice a written guarantee to refer clients for evaluation or treatment. However, in some situations there may be a virtual guarantee of building a practice quickly. For example, we are aware of one psychologist, a specialist in behavioral medicine and assessment, who joined a neurology practice. In the interview this group of 12 neurologists assured him that they valued psychological services, especially neuropsychological assessment, and if he joined their practice they would refer their patients to him. He was flooded with more business than he could handle the first month that he joined the practice.

Solo Practice Versus Group Practice

Barnett and Henshaw (2003) highlighted issues to consider in making the decision to develop a solo private practice or to join or develop a group practice. One advantage of SP is level of independence. No one else is involved in making decisions about how you practice, when you practice, the type of work you do to earn a living, or the clientele you serve. For example, Steve Walfish once referred a "street kid" for psychotherapy to a colleague who worked as a psychometrist for him part time and was developing a practice. Despite this child being a full-fee non-insurance-based client paid from a trust fund, the colleague was told by the senior members of his practice that he could not see this client or clients in similar situations in their practice because it would upset their usual upper-class clientele. The child was referred to a more "tolerant" practice.

An advantage of group practice is sharing of costs. It can be expensive to rent and furnish an office, but it is not twice as expensive to rent a two-room office as it is to rent a one-room office. This same principle holds true for the costs of purchasing waiting room furniture, copy machines, computers, and telephone systems or for attorney's fees for reviewing documents. Financial savings result from the economy of scale that comes with a group practice model.

Another plus of group practice is the ready availability of colleagues to talk about cases, share ideas for practice building, and provide on-call coverage for you when you are on vacation. In a group practice setting there is also a high likelihood of cross-referral of clients. We also believe that it is helpful for clinicians to avoid practicing in isolation. Handelsman (2001) viewed group practice as one important strategy for avoiding ethical pitfalls. It is interesting to note that R. Barker (1982) found individuals returning to institutional practice from private practice because of a combination of circumstances including not liking the isolation; "they missed all the old gang at the agency" (p. 71).

One potential disadvantage of group practice lies in the issue of shared liability. In SP each clinician alone is responsible for his or her own professional behavior and decision making—and thus has sole liability for his or her decisions. This may not be the case in a group practice. In some instances the non-service-providing clinician may be held liable for the behavior or practice of the clinician in the practice who was directly providing the service. R. Woody (1988) described this situation as "vicarious liability." For example, imagine that one partner knows the other partner is actively abusing alcohol or drugs. If the partner with the substance abuse problem then commits an act of malpractice or negligence, then the fact that the other partner did not do anything to intervene may result in him or her being held accountable for this inaction. In a similar way, if the partner knows the clinician is having sex with a client and does nothing to intervene, the partner may also be held accountable for such inaction.

> **Private Practice Principle Number 8:** When joining a group practice, choose your associates wisely. These individuals can enhance or detract from your reputation and increase or decrease your liability.

Besides the liability issues already noted, the individuals in the group practice, including the support staff, can significantly affect the quality of your work experience. Some groups can be competitive and disagreeable. Some groups can be cooperative and supportive. R. Woody (1989) pointed to the concept of attraction and complementarity of group practices. It usually takes a mix of styles to achieve an optimal outcome. For example, if the practice has all "idea people," then no one would be available to actually carry the tasks to fruition. However, if the practice has all "detail people," then the big picture will be missed and large goals will not be part of the practice development landscape. Differences in style can be valued or devalued. MHPs are not immune to the group dynamics that take place in other small businesses; these dynamics must be managed in a group practice. The last thing you want to do as a clinician is to come to work every day in a setting that you dread. Such a situation will negatively affect the quality of your work life and, we believe, ultimately affect the quality of the services provided to clients.

A Mixed Model

Besides SP, a most common model of practice for mental health clinicians in private practice is to have a joint space- and expense-sharing arrangement. That is, two or more (usually more) clinicians decide they will rent an office and buy furniture together and provide clinical services. Each is a solo practitioner and is considered for tax purposes as a sole proprietor of his or her own business. They are not considered a group practice either legally or in the eyes of the community. The practice does not have a name such as the Northside Center for Psychological Services or Mental Health Associates of Elmsville. Rather, each practice is known as John Doe, LCSW, and Jane Q. Public, PsyD. In their disclosure statement to clients they let it be known that this is not a group practice but rather that both Mr. Doe and Dr. Smith are independent practitioners who are solely responsible for their own practice.

Sometimes a group of independent practitioners rent space and services together and give a title to their practice setting (e.g., Center for Mental Health Services). These practices have no formal partnership agreement or corporate structure. They have written agreements to share expenses. However, what is important is not what agreement the clinicians have with each other or what they tell their clients in their disclosure statements. What is important is the perception of the community. Even if it is not a legal entity, if the community thinks it is a group practice then it may have the shared liability of a group practice as described earlier.

Considerations in Joining a Group Practice

Barnett and Henshaw (2003) provided an excellent list of questions to consider when joining a group practice. In addition, we think it helpful to consider asking questions related to the history of the practice, the direction of the practice, and how the practice fits into the overall community. Many years ago Steve Walfish considered buying a practice in an area of the country where he wanted to move. In preparing interview questions he relied on the wisdom of Seymour Sarason (1974) in his book *The Creation of Settings and the Future Societies.* We think that the following questions, arising from Sarason's influence, the suggestions of Barnett and Henshaw (2003), and our own combined 49 years of clinical practice, are also relevant to joining a group practice. They are not presented in any specific order.

- Who owns the group and who makes business decisions?
- What are the values of the practice?
- What are the vehicles of criticism for what takes places in the practice?
- How does the practice fit into the larger community?
- What kind of reputation does the practice have in the community?
- What will the benefit be to me in joining the practice?
- What will be the benefit be to the practice by my joining?
- What is the history or evolution of the practice? What phases has it gone through? Have there been periods of growth? Periods of constriction?
- Has anyone previously left the practice? If so, when and what were the circumstances?
- If the group is multidisciplinary, is there a power difference among the different disciplines?
- How do practice associates relate to practice partners or owners?
- What is the timetable for me joining the practice?
- How quickly could I expect to develop a full-time practice and what assistance will be provided to help me get started? How much of my practice should I be expected to generate and how much help can I expect from the practice?
- What is the referral base of the practice? Are there specific contracts to the practice that provide clients?
- How will other people in the practice react to my joining? Is there competition for referrals? What has happened historically when a new member has joined the practice?
- What happens if there are perceived ethical conflicts within the practice? How are internal conflicts handled?
- What is the near-term and long-term vision for the practice? Do practice associates share in the development of this vision, or is this vision solely decided by the practice owners or partners?
- What is the process for adding new members to the practice? When do they add someone, how do they add someone, and do practice associates have a say in the process?
- What avenues are there for professional growth within the practice? What supervision or peer consultation and on-call coverage opportunities and obligations are there?
- How are resources spent in the practice? How are decisions made about spending resources? What happens when resources are tight?
- Are the fees set by the practice or do I set my own fees?
- What hours are available to see clients? What type, if any, of support staff is available after hours (e.g., weekends, evenings)?
- What type of emergency coverage is available for when I am not available or I am out of town?

- Is contribution to overhead determined on a flat-fee model or a percentage model? If the latter, what percentage of the income I generate goes to the practice and what percentage to me?
- What administrative support do I receive from the group as part of my contribution to overhead? Does this include receptionist support, secretarial, office supplies, telephone, long-distance costs related to practice activities, office supplies, photocopying, psychological tests, and so on?
- What are the billing and collection practices of the practice? What happens if someone does not pay his or her bill? Are insurance benefits verified by support staff?
- What is the success rate of collecting fees charged?
- Is everyone in the practice a provider for the same insurance companies? Do I have to take insurance? Can I be selective in which insurance I take?
- What happens to my practice and place in the practice if I go on maternity or paternity leave?
- Is a minimum number of practice hours expected of me?
- Is there a maximum number of hours that I may be allowed to practice?
- Are there limitations in how I practice? The type of work that I do? The populations that I serve? Am I allowed to decide which clients I will treat?
- How does income generated outside of direct clinical practice within the practice fit into the equation (e.g., consultations completed in hospitals, teaching, honoraria for speaking or writing, consulting to community agencies, testimony in court)?
- Are there limitations as to where else I can practice? Can I have a second office in another location?
- What is the financial solvency of the practice? Has the practice ever had difficulty meeting their financial obligations?
- How are clinicians paid? Does the practice collect all monies and then pay the clinician once or twice per month or does the clinician collect all monies and then pay the practice once per month?
- What benefits am I provided: malpractice insurance, health insurance, continuing education, etc.?
- Will I have my own office or do I have to share an office with others? Will I have to "float" to use offices that are available?
- If I have my own office, will I have to furnish the office or will it be furnished for me? If it is furnished for me, do I have a say in what it looks like?
- How does an associate become a partner in the practice? How long does it typically take to become a partner and what are the expectations of associates and partners? What are the criteria?
- If I decide to leave the practice, can I take my clients with me?

What is clear is that these questions cannot be answered in a 1-hour lunch conversation. They must be answered in multiple conversations with multiple players. We suggest you talk with the practice owners as well as other clinicians in the practice. The answers may vary on the basis of the size of the practice, how long it has been established, and the organizational tightness or looseness of the practice. It is unlikely that each question can be answered to the full satisfaction of the clinician considering joining the practice. However, we think most of these questions should be asked and the answers carefully weighed when making the decision to join or not to join a particular practice. If the practice partners or owners find the breadth and detail of these questions to be too detailed or annoying, then we strongly suggest you consider not joining the practice, or at least be aware there may be some difficulties in the practice.

Costs of Joining a Group Practice

If you are asked to join a private practice, this opportunity may take one of three shapes. First, you may be an employee paid a specific salary. Second, you may pay the practice a specific agreed-on amount monthly. Third, you may pay an agreed-on percentage of monies out of your collections. Each arrangement has its strengths and weaknesses.

Private Practice Principle Number 9: The negotiated costs to work in a group practice are not based on a "fairness doctrine." Rather, they are based on a business model in which both practice owners and the clinician joining the practice are attempting to maximize their income.

Clinicians want to join a particular group practice because they think it will be a pleasant working environment and they are confident they will be able to earn a living. Group-practice owners ask people to join their practice because they have more work than they can comfortably complete and want to reduce their overhead expenses and possibly earn a profit. Given this starting point, both parties must negotiate a deal they believe is in their best interest and that the other will accept. It is not up to one party to take care of the economic needs of the other party. For example, one psychology resident joined a successful group practice that would provide postdoctoral supervision for licensure and help her build a practice. She agreed to pay the practice 33% of monies collected to become a member of the practice. It never occurred to her that she would become successful and 2 years later be collecting $150,000 a year for her clinical work. This meant she was paying the practice $49,500 per year in overhead. At a certain point she wanted to renegotiate the financial arrangement. When the practice replied, "Well, this was the deal that you struck when you signed on," her reply was, "Well, I knew it was a great practice and I would have signed anything to join you guys." The practice did renegotiate with her because it was financially worth it (e.g., in their best interest) to retain her in the practice and it also meant she did not have to find a new practice to join (e.g., in her best interest).

As an employee joining a group practice, the clinician should receive either a set salary or a percentage of collections. As employees, clinicians are subject to the employment rules of the practice. That is, they may have to keep certain hours, see a set number of clients per week, dress in a certain way, practice clinically in a certain way, attend certain meetings, see whichever clients may be assigned to them, and follow whatever rules are set for employees of the practice. In return, especially if they are on salary, they are assured a specified income, have the practice pay the full portion of self-employment taxes, and receive free supervision or peer consultation, and they may receive health benefits, life insurance benefits, be covered by worker's compensation rules, participate in a retirement plan, and have paid vacation and paid educational leave. These benefits may vary on the basis of the setting and whatever the clinician may negotiate.

One may also join a practice by paying a set amount monthly to the practice. The amount the clinician pays monthly is negotiated between the two parties. All services provided to the clinician should be specified in writing and be part of the contract. The practice has the advantage of knowing how much it will be receiving each month. Although the amount received on a monthly basis is much less than if the practice added a successful associate using a percentage model (in this model, payment is based on percentage of monies collected for clinical services), no risk is involved for the practice. Furthermore, there are no up-front costs for having the clinician in the practice. However, a percentage-model renter is building a practice from scratch. As such, the practice may not see a significant amount of financial contribution for 6 to 12 months. The advantage to the clinician who pays a set monthly amount is knowing his or her monthly expenses and being able to plan his or her finances accordingly. Also, as in the earlier example of the successful clinician, the clinician who pays a set amount is not paying a significant portion of his or her income to the practice. However, the clinician is paying a fixed amount of monthly rent before he or she has generated any income. This potential hardship is common to start-up businesses, most of which have a waiting period (e.g., 6–12 months) before they can generate a profit. However, in the percentage model, clinicians pay only monies that are generated for direct clinical services. In the fixed-amount model, if clinicians take 4 weeks of vacation each year (which we highly recommend) they are still responsible for contributing the same amount each month (the same may hold true for maternity or paternity leave). In the percentage model no monies are paid for these 4 weeks because no direct services were provided and no monies were collected.

In this model, payment is based on percentage of monies collected for clinical services. In this model, the practice has an incentive to help the clinician build a successful practice. The more money the clinician collects, the more money goes to the practice owners. Therefore, there is an incentive to (a) maximize direct referrals, (b) assist the clinician in cultivating new referral sources, (c) help the clinician develop a specialty or niche that is of interest, and (d) maximize collections. In the fixed monthly model the practice owners want the clinician to be successful in developing his or her practice so he or she will want to remain in their practice. However, in the percentage model there are added financial incentives for the clinician to become successful as quickly as possible. One question that is often asked is, "What is a fair or reasonable percentage for me to pay to the practice for overhead?" To begin with, refer to Private Practice Principle Number 9 and note that fairness is not part of this equation. Rather, both the clinician and the group practice are trying to maximize income and the agreed-on percentage is one that both parties believe is satisfactory. Percentage splits range anywhere from 40/60 (with 40% going to the clinician and 60% going to the practice) to 70/30 (with 70% going to the clinician and 30% going to the practice). The former number is quite rare; 60/40 and 70/30 seem to be most common. As we noted earlier, if the clinician is successful, 30% or 40% of collected income can add up to a significant amount of money. For example, if a clinician sees 25 clients per week and averages a collection of $80 per session and works for 48 weeks each year, a gross amount of $96,000 will be collected. After paying 40% overhead ($38,400), the clinician will earn a salary of $57,600. With 30% paid toward overhead the clinician will earn a salary of $67,200 and the practice will collect $28,800. However, because the monthly payment is not fixed, the amounts paid toward overhead increase if the clinician works harder (e.g., sees more than 25 clients) or is able to charge and collect more money (e.g., charges higher fees). Thus arose the situation described earlier in which the successful clinician was paying almost $50,000 per year to the practice.

As noted earlier, the financial incentive in the percentage model helps the clinician build and sustain a successful practice. As shown in the example of the successful clinician, it is difficult for clinicians to believe they will build a successful practice and anticipate the financial ramifications of doing so. However, we believe that with hard work, excellent skills, an entrepreneurial spirit, and fair and ethical practices most people can become successful in private practice. Because of this we think it wise for those who enter into practice under the percentage-model arrangement to negotiate a floating percentage of payment. For example, for the first X dollars per month, 40% is paid to the practice, and for everything above this number, the percentage is reduced to 20%. Suppose that Licensed Professional Counselor A is very successful as a result of clinical acumen and a strong work ethic. She generates $10,000 a month in collections. In a percentage model in which 40% goes to the practice toward overhead, the practice would receive $4,000 per month. However, if Licensed Professional Counselor A negotiates an agreement in which she pays 40% of the first $8,000 collected and then 20% of anything over this amount, her contribution toward overhead would be reduced to $3,600 per month. Over the course of 12 months she would save $4,800. If Licensed Professional Counselor A earns more than $10,000 per month, even more would go to her, which would be an incentive to work harder and create income opportunities. Many MHPs starting out cannot imagine generating this much income. The important issue is to negotiate a contract with the best possible scenario in mind over the long run so that you do not live to regret having signed away your ability to earn more money.

The Group-Practice Contract

Stout, Levant, Reed, and Murphy (2001) pointed out that MHPs are often unfamiliar with contracts they are asked to sign. They suggested that under ideal conditions clinicians should understand every detail of the contract and then decide whether to negotiate, execute, or decline to sign the document. These authors have written an important paper, and we urge all those considering private practice to study the concepts they present.

Before you decide to join a group practice we recommend that you have the contract reviewed by two professionals: an attorney and a senior MHP with many years of private-practice experience. We suggest investing money in such consultations; they are well worth the cost, especially if these professionals recognize aspects of the contract that you do not understand. The attorney can tell you what is reasonable and standard practice and what may be "out of bounds." He or she can answer whatever questions you have regarding the contract and advise you as to what clarifications need to be requested from the practice. We suggest that you take the stance that the contract you are presented with is written with the best interests of the practice in mind. This does not mean they are trying to take advantage of you but rather that the practice has no obligation to look out for your best interests. You hire an attorney to look out for your best interests. In a similar way, a senior mental health clinician with significant private-practice experience will help you ask questions that you may not have considered because they are out of the realm of your experience. He or she may also advise you as to whether or not you are a good fit for the practice you are considering joining.

Over the years, we have reviewed copies of contracts early career professionals were asked to sign to join a practice. These professionals sought feedback on aspects to consider in evaluating the offer. Although it may not be a contract of employment, it is a legally binding agreement between the MHP and the group practice regarding the nature of their work together, the working conditions, the financial agreement, and stipulations of termination. In a format similar to that used by Stout et al. (2001), we offer the reader a checklist of issues to consider using some of their same categories.

TERM OF CONTRACT

Most contracts that are presented are open ended and do not have a specific termination or renewable date. As such, they are not reviewed on an annual or biannual basis. Thus, the contract being signed now is the same contract that the group practice has the right to keep in effect for 5, 10, 15, even 20 years. In other words, if your career intent is to stay with the practice you are joining, part of the decision-making process needs to take your own future into consideration. Although you can live with this contract now, do you think you could do so 5 to 10 years from now? Once again, consider the example of the psychologist who did not anticipate her success, was paying the practice $50,000 per year, and explained, "Well, I would have signed anything to join you guys." We have known many individuals who became resentful of the group practice and felt the practice was taking advantage of them. We recommend that MHPs carefully review the amount they will be reimbursed for the direct services they provide. Ask yourself the question, "Is this a fair wage for my professional services?" Also ask yourself, "Although this may seem fair now that I am beginning my career, will I be satisfied with this amount 5 years from now, as the amount may or may not change?" For example, in one contract reviewed, the psychologist, working as an independent contractor (IC), was to be paid $40 for a session of individual therapy. Because he paid no overhead and was at the beginning of his career and used to living on graduate school stipends, this amount of money seemed significant. If this psychologist sees 30 clients per week for 48 weeks per year the total reimbursement would be $57,600 per year. Although this amount may seem like a small fortune soon after graduate school, this same figure might not be as attractive 5 to 10 years out of school (especially when one wants to buy a home and a new car, raise children, and save for retirement). At that point in time we believe the professional would view this amount of money as paltry and become resentful. However, remember that no one is forced to sign a contract, and the group practice cannot be blamed for wanting to maximize its earnings as well.

Contracts usually contain a clause regarding how the contract will terminate if one or both parties want the relationship to end. A 60- to 90-day notification requirement is typical. Contracts will also delineate the conditions of severability and the rights and responsibilities of each party on termination and any restrictions that may be placed on the clinician leaving the practice. Note that these terms will apply whether or not the MHP voluntarily leaves the practice or is asked to leave the practice.

STATUS OF EMPLOYMENT

When you join the practice, will you be a partner, an associate, an employee, or a sole practitioner? The answer to this question has implications for your working conditions, financial limitations, tax status, and amount of control you have over what takes place in your practice. In a similar way, will this status remain the same over the course of the contract or is a change built into the contract? For example, some contracts do not allow for a change in the relationship between the principal partners of the group and those who choose to associate with them. However, some contracts outline conditions under which associates may become equity partners, similar to how one can go from an associate to a junior partner to a senior partner in a law firm.

If you are an employee, the group practice will bear certain costs such as unemployment taxes, payroll taxes, and half of your Social Security payment. However, if you are not an employee, but rather an IC, then you are responsible for these costs and the full amount due for Social Security taxes (self-employment tax). If you are an employee, you may be eligible for benefits such as health insurance, life insurance, and disability insurance, with the group practice paying a portion of these benefits, which are not available to ICs. In a similar manner, if you are an employee, you may be eligible for matching contributions from the group practice for a retirement plan, such as a 401(k). However, ICs are solely responsible for building their own retirement nest egg. The benefits provided to employees can add up to a significant amount of money. For example, in one contract that we reviewed the clinical social worker was to be considered an employee and the group practice was to pay 80% of individual health and dental insurance, provide a 50% match of up to 6%

of salary for a 401(k) plan, provide disability insurance coverage of 60% of salary, and also pay for workers' compensation coverage.

In most contracts reviewed, the MHP joining the group practice did so as an IC. Under these terms the group practice is not responsible for many costs (e.g., taxes), which then become the responsibility of the IC. However, the Internal Revenue Service (IRS) has specific guidelines on the differences between being an employee and an IC. According to IRS Publication Number 1779, *Independent Contractor or Employee* . . . (available at http://www.irs.gov/pub/irs-pdf/p1779.pdf), three general categories determine whether one is an IC or an employee: (a) behavioral control—whether there is an employer right to direct or control how the worker does the work (e.g., if you receive extensive instructions on how, where, or when to do the work; if you are told what tools or equipment to use; if the business provides you with extensive training about required methods and procedures), (b) financial control—whether the employer has a right to control the business aspect of the work (e.g., if you have made a significant financial investment in your work; if you are not reimbursed for some or all business expenses, especially if they are high), and (c) relationship of the parties—how the employer and the individual perceive their relationship (e.g., if you receive benefits). We have reviewed contracts in which the clinician is called an IC but is contractually obligated in a way that is consistent with being considered an employee by the IRS. For example, one contract we reviewed specified, "The psychologist will attend all staff meetings." This requirement could suggest behavioral control as outlined earlier. As Cheeseman (2005) described,

> Independent contractors usually work for a number of clients, have their own offices, hire employees, and control the performance of their work. Merely labeling someone as an independent contractor is not enough. The crucial factor in determining if someone is an employee or an IC is the "degree of control" that the employer has over the agent. . . . Substantial control indicates an employer-employee relationship. (pp. 382–383)

In some instances the group practice may be trying to "have it both ways." That is, they want the control that comes with having an employer–employee relationship but at the same time do not want to bear the financial obligations that come with such a relationship. We urge MHPs considering joining a practice to avoid this arrangement.

NONCOMPETITION CLAUSES

Once the contract is terminated, what restrictions, if any, are placed on your ability to practice as a MHP? Some contracts place no restrictions. That is, the clinicians are free to practice wherever they would like (including next door or across the street) and see whomever they would like to see. Most, though not all, contracts that we have reviewed include some restriction on the MHPs' ability to practice once they have left the group practice. This is usually a geographic limitation (so many miles from the practice) and a specified amount of time (e.g., 12–24 months after leaving the practice) during which the professional may not practice in the area. By including such a clause the group practice wants to protect itself from bringing new professionals into the practice, training them, and cultivating referral sources only to have these professionals leave and compete for the same contracts or referral sources. We strongly urge you to think long and hard when deciding to sign a contract that includes such a clause. Although this clause protects the practice, it may also severely restrict options should you want to leave the practice and remain a professional in the same local area. Some geographic clauses are based on mileage (e.g., 5 miles, 20 miles) or the county in which the practice is located. Whether you are practicing in a city or a rural area can make a tremendous difference. For example, in a rural area a 20-mile radius restriction may be manageable, but a 5-mile radius restriction in Manhattan is likely overly restrictive.

Some contracts we reviewed placed a mileage restriction on any clinical setting in which the group practice operates or has concrete plans to open an office. As group practices expand it is not unusual for them to develop operations in satellite clinics far from the main center where you may be practicing. This expansion in essence may exponentially increase the limitations placed on your ability to develop another practice if the group practice has an entrepreneurial spirit and is successful in its expansion efforts. For this reason we suggest requesting two modifications in the contract: first, that the geographic restriction be limited to the setting in which you are practicing; second, that the restriction be limited to currently existing settings operated by the group practice. It is impossible to make a reasonable decision about limiting your ability to practice without knowing what the geographic limitations are going to be for the duration of your contract. For example, imagine that 2 years after you begin your affiliation, the entrepreneurial practice owners decide to open clinics throughout the state. You would thereby not be able to open a practice or join another practice within the state in which you live. If you had signed a contract with such a noncompetition clause you would have unknowingly signed away this right.

Please also note that some noncompetition clauses preclude the clinician from soliciting current clients to join you in your new practice; that is, current clients remain within the domain of the current group practice. We recommend that this clause be amended so decisions are made on a case-by-case basis dependent on what is in the best interest of the client. If there is a dispute about what is in the best interest of the client then an agreed-on outside mediator will make the determination. The costs for mediation should be borne by both parties.

Furthermore, some contracts contain a clause that precludes the MHP from soliciting referrals or entering into a business relationship with a current referral source of the group practice. In signing such an agreement the clinician should understand that professional business relationships that have been cultivated while in the practice must be severed on leaving the practice.

Barnett (1997a) concluded that "noncompetition contract clauses are highly complex and fraught with potential difficulties" (p. 184). Thomas B. Lewis is an attorney with the firm of Stark and Stark in New Jersey (see http://www.stark-stark.com) who specializes in the area of noncompetition clauses for health care providers. In Exhibit 4.1 he summarizes a case regarding psychologists and a noncompetition clause in his jurisdiction and also provides advice on how to proceed if an MHP is asked to sign one as a condition of employment or joining a practice.

WHO OWNS THE RECORDS?

When you leave the practice, who is responsible for maintaining the client records? The assignment of this responsibility may vary from practice to practice but should be agreed on in the initial contract. For example, we have seen some contracts that specify that the records remain the property of the group practice. However, Steve Walfish brought 12 boxes of client records with him on the moving van when he relocated across the country because the records were considered his property and by state law his responsibility to maintain for 5 years.

WHAT YOU PROVIDE AND WHAT THEY PROVIDE

Contracts should spell out the responsibilities and benefits of signing the agreement. We highly recommend that these be spelled out in great detail to leave as little room for ambiguity as possible.

One contract we reviewed clearly stated what the MHP would provide to the practice as an IC. The IC was to contribute a specified percentage of collections to the practice; maintain her professional license; pay for malpractice coverage and all relevant license fees and taxes; and, we directly quote, "be responsible for all costs and expenses incidental to the performance of services." However, in this particular contract nothing was spelled out as to what the practice would provide to the IC.

At the very least we recommend that the responsibility for the payment of the following be covered in the contract: space, furniture,

EXHIBIT 4.1

Noncompetition and the Mental Health Professional, by Thomas B. Lewis, Attorney-at-Law

In New Jersey, a noncompete clause in a psychologist's employment agreement has been held unenforceable. In *Comprehensive Psychological System, P.C. v. Prince* (2005), the New Jersey Superior Court, Appellate Division, held that restrictive covenants between psychologists and their employers are unenforceable. In reaching this decision, the court first held determinative a New Jersey State Board of Psychological Examiners regulation, N.J.A.C. 13:42–10.16, that prohibited psychologists practicing in the state from entering into restrictive covenants. Since the case was first filed, the language of the regulation was amended to read as follows:

> A licensee shall not enter into any business agreement that interferes with or restricts the ability of a client to see or continue to see his or her therapist of choice. (*Comprehensive*, 867 A.2d at 1189)

The court concluded, however, that the amended language did nothing more than shift "the focus of the concern from the rights of the psychologist to the rights of the patient," and it did not remove the prohibition against psychologists entering into restrictive covenants (*Comprehensive*, 867 A.2d at 1189).

In addition, and regardless of any regulation promulgated by the State Board of Psychological Examiners, the court held that, because of the "uniquely personal nature of the psychologist–patient relationship," restrictive covenants between psychologists must not be enforced (*Comprehensive*, 867 A.2d at 1189). Even more than prohibiting the enforcement of restrictive covenants between psychologists, though, the court concluded that the unique nature of the psychologist–patient relationship places upon "a psychologist who changes his office location, [whether] voluntarily or involuntarily, . . . a duty to inform patients of the change and the new location and phone number" (*Comprehensive*, 867 A.2d at 1189). Failure to do so, the court noted, may amount to abandonment. Therefore, as a matter of public policy, the court held unenforceable restrictive covenants between psychologists and their employers.

The *Comprehensive* decision involving psychologists differs from a recent New Jersey Supreme Court decision involving physicians. In *Community Hospital Group, Inc. v. More* (2005), the New Jersey Supreme Court held that a restrictive covenant in a physician's employment agreement may be enforceable. However, the court did caution that "although post-employment restrictive covenants are not viewed with favor, if under the circumstances a factual determination is made that the covenant protects the legitimate interests of the hospital, imposes no undue hardship on the physician and is not injurious to the public, it *may* be enforced as written, or, if appropriate, as reduced in scope" (*Community* at p. 63).

As a practical matter, if a psychologist in New Jersey is asked to sign a contract containing a noncompete clause as a condition of employment, that psychologist should consult with an attorney to discuss the resultant implications. Although the *Comprehensive* decision is not a precedent outside of the State of New Jersey, it may be persuasive to other jurisdictions. The law continues to be refined. Therefore, before signing any employment agreement, seek legal counsel to determine the enforceability of the restrictive covenant.

telephone, long-distance calls related to doing the business of practice, stationery, utilities, photocopying, postage for mailing, answering service, and any electronic equipment such as a computer, pager, and fax machine. The nature of administrative support provided (e.g., reception, telephone answering, filing, transcription, client scheduling) as well as the hours of such support should also be specified. In addition, if supervision for licensure is being provided by the group practice, the nature and frequency of this arrangement should be made clear. Furthermore, arrangements for on-call coverage when the clinician is away from the office and the responsibilities the clinician may have when his or her colleagues are away from the office should be noted.

A CONTRACTS CONCLUSION AND A MODEST PROPOSAL

Stout et al. (2001) pointed out that a good contract can protect the MHP as well as the managed care organization with whom the professional is contracting. The same may be said in this instance for the MHP and the group practice. However, it is our experience that contracts tend to be written in a way that are "group practice friendly" rather than "practice associate friendly." As such, it is up to individual MHPs to determine whether they want to sign a certain contract as it sets the boundaries and framework for their professional practice. We suggest that the MHP considering signing the contract in the form it is offered ask him- or herself the following two questions: "What if this practice works out?" and "What if this practice doesn't work out?" If it works out, will you still be happy with the practice arrangements 5, 10, 15, or 20 years down the road? If it doesn't work out, what will the ramifications be if you leave the practice?

It is difficult to know whether joining a particular group practice is going to work out from a variety of perspectives. First, is the client flow one that will generate the income you want to earn? Second, are the business operations adequate to meet your needs? Third, are your colleagues cordial enough, professional enough, and ethical enough for you to want to continue to maintain a professional affiliation? The answers to these questions are difficult to ascertain before joining the practice. Only after you "live in the practice" for a while can the answers become clear. However, the contract must be signed before the MHP joins the practice. We have heard too many war stories in which a clinician joins a group practice and it does not work out (e.g., "They said they were going to send me referrals but they didn't"; "I'm uncomfortable with the ethics of their business practices"; "The clinical skills of my new colleagues are substandard"; "They seemed nice when I interviewed, but it turns out they are unpleasant people to work around every day"). As such, we propose that when considering a group practice, the MHP ask to join with the intent of being with the organization on a permanent basis but with a 90- to 180-day mutual probation period. In this way the new practice associate can better determine whether the fit will be good both professionally and emotionally. The group practice can also determine whether the new associate is a good fit. However, at the end of the mutual probation period there would be no restrictions on the MHP's subsequent ability to practice if either party ends the professional relationship (e.g., any signed noncompetition clause would be waived). Without such a trial period we believe MHPs are taking the unfair burden of risk by gambling that this is the right practice for them. If it is the wrong practice they, because of noncompetition clauses, may be signing away their right to practice in their area of choice. The group practice is gambling time, effort, and some expenses that the new practice associate will be a good fit for them. However, if the associate is not a good fit then the practice can recruit another one and the loss is minimal compared with losing the right to practice in one's area. By not asking for such a probation period, MHPs may be gambling more than they can afford to lose.

Legal Structures of Practice

Before we begin this section let us start off with "The Lawyers' Chorus": What follows in this section should not be construed as either professional legal advice or professional accounting or tax advice. We think it highly important, if not essential, that before you start a practice you consult these professionals to help determine the best corporate structure for your practice. Furthermore, as your practice grows and as you accumulate assets in your life, periodic consultations with these professionals are essential to determine whether you are maintaining the appropriate and optimal corporate structure for yourself. Furthermore, although we discuss general principles and types of corporate structures in this section, please be aware that individual states' own rules and restrictions will influence your ability to form a corporate structure. For example, in many states physicians and psychologists (or other professionals as well) cannot be co-owners of a business together. This law was put in place to avoid a potential conflict of interest. That means that in certain jurisdictions a psychologist (or clinical social worker, marriage and family therapist, or professional counselor) and a psychiatrist may not be able to jointly own a group practice.

In this section we briefly highlight several of the corporate structures MHPs in private practice may consider for themselves. In addition, we highly recommend more specific reading on the topic including Harrington (2002), The Company Corporation (2001), and sections of business law books by Cheeseman (2005) and Twomey and Jennings (2007). In addition, Stromberg and Schuetze (1997) wrote about this topic with MHPs in mind. Furthermore, you can find much more information on the Internet by searching on the term *small business corporate structures.* In this section we also provide interviews with MHPs who have adopted specific corporate structures for themselves.

Cheeseman (2005) noted that the selection of a corporate structure depends on many factors, including ease and cost of formation, flexibility needed to make management decisions, government restrictions, tax considerations, and risk tolerance for personal liability. We also note that similar to MHPs, attorneys or accountants may have differing opinions and recommendations when examining the same data set. For example, Steve Walfish has spoken with two separate accountants regarding incorporating his practice for tax savings and has received opposite opinions. One suggested that it would be beneficial, and the other indicated that the savings offset would not be worth the costs involved in incorporating.

SOLE PROPRIETORSHIP

This form of business entity is the simplest to create. We believe it is the most common business structure chosen by MHPs for their practices. It is the simplest to create because there is nothing to do. As Cheeseman (2005) noted, there are no formalities with this structure and no applications have to be filed, other than possibly for a local business license that may be required by the city or county in which you practice. Your practice is your name, such as John Doe, LCSW, or Jane Q. Public, LMFT.

Twomey and Jennings (2007) pointed out the advantages of a sole proprietorship (sole-prop): There are no organizational fees and the MHP controls all of the decisions and keeps all of the profits generated by his or her work. In a sole-prop, business earnings are not subject to corporate income taxes but rather are taxed as personal income.

The disadvantage, according to Cheeseman (2005) and Twomey and Jennings (2007), is that the SP may take on an unlimited amount of personal liability. The sole-prop bears the risk of loss of the business. Any capital contribution made by the sole-prop can be lost if the MHP does not have enough capital to sustain the business. Depending on the jurisdiction in which one practices, creditors may also recover claims against the business from the sole-prop's personal assets such as his or her home, car, and bank accounts. Harrington (2002) viewed the downside of a sole-prop: "There is no one to do half of the work, raise half of the money, and solve half of the problems" (p. 61).

Among the different corporate structures, sole-props have the easiest of tax returns to complete. They pay quarterly estimated taxes and file their personal return annually with the government. For their business expenses they submit a Schedule C Profit and Loss Statement with their personal return.

PARTNERSHIPS

Cheeseman (2005) explained that a partnership is a voluntary association formed for the purpose of making a profit by two or more individuals. Harrington (2002) pointed out that one can find business partnerships that have existed for 25 years and others that split up shortly after they were formed. For this reason it is prudent to have a dissolution agreement at the outset of the partnership formation. After having dealt with so many messy dissolutions, attorneys are recommending this measure. Harrington (2002) indicated that partners need to have a common mission, similar values, agreed-on strategies, and an overall direction and strategy for making the company successful. She viewed the primary advantage of a partnership as the ability to pool resources. She indicated that these resources can include money, knowledge, and skills, and to this we add energy and social support. Harrington (2002) also viewed the sharing of liabilities and responsibilities as an advantage of a partnership model.

Cheeseman (2005) pointed out that a partnership can operate under the names of the partners or under a fictitious name. For example, Barrie Alexander and Nancy McGarrah, whose interviews are presented in this chapter, practice under the name Cliff Valley Psychologists. However, Rice DiGorio Ripkin Counseling Associates, LLC, is a partnership of three mental health counselors practicing as a limited liability corporation (or LLC). There are rules and guidelines for choosing the name of a corporation. In addition, as Cheeseman (2005) indicated, the formation of a partnership creates rights and duties among partners and with third parties. These are established by agreement (e.g., contract among the parties) and by law.

Cheeseman (2005) stated that the partnership must develop an agreement. This partnership agreement, according to Cheeseman, delineates the terms according to which the partnership will be conducted. Partners can develop any agreement they would like with each other as long as it does not include anything illegal. Harrington (2002) indicated that the partnership "should carefully and clearly spell out on paper all of the details of the partnership even amongst the closest of friends, especially among close friends" (p. 59). As Stromberg and Schuetze (1997) stated, the rights and responsibilities of each partner should be described in this document. They opined that if no formal partnership agreement exists, then the individual jurisdiction's rules about business partnerships define the partnership relationship by default.

Cheeseman (2005) pointed out that partners are jointly liable for the contracts and debts of the partnership. Thus, all members of the partnership must be named in any lawsuit brought against any of the partners. If Psychologist X is sued and is a member of a partnership, then all partners are named in the suit. Harrington (2002) noted that one of the disadvantages of a partnership is that each partner is responsible for the actions of the other partner(s) and for the overall business.

CORPORATIONS

Stromberg and Schuetze (1997) suggested that corporations offer MHPs many benefits that outweigh any disadvantages that accompany their formation and maintenance. They elaborated that corporations are legal entities that must file "articles of incorporation with the State and obtain the State's approval to conduct business" (p. 7).

Harrington (2002) noted that corporations decrease potential liability for the individual when compared with the sole-prop model of practice structure. She also noted that the most significant advantage of incorporation is that it allows business responsibilities and personal responsibilities to be handled separately. A corporation can be held financially responsible without the individual professional being held personally responsible for debts. Therefore, whereas the corporation's assets can be seized in a judgment against it, the clinician's personal assets (e.g., home, car retirement account) may be protected in any judgment. R. Woody (1989) described this "corporate shield" as protecting shareholders from liability for debts of the corporation. An exception to this, according to Stromberg and Schuetze (1997), lies in "acts of negligence or misconduct, as well as for the malpractice of other employees or supervisees whom the mental health professional personally supervises. In this way the personal liability is only partially limited" (p. 7). R. Woody (1989) indicated that most malpractice judgments will attach personal assets.

Both R. Woody (1989) and Stromberg and Schuetze (1997) discussed issues related to double taxation (when monies paid in salary to the clinician are taxed at the individual rate). In addition, profits of the corporation are taxed, albeit at the corporate rate. It is our understanding that in some cases incorporation may actually reduce tax liability, and accountants can advise as to how this might be the case for an individual private practitioner. For example, as a sole proprietor the clinician is responsible for the entire portion of self-employment tax. However, as a salaried employee of a corporation, the clinician pays only half of the self-employment tax; the corporation pays the other half. This situation can be advantageous up to certain income levels. Some corporations also make sure they have no profits by either purchasing things for the practice or giving bonuses to the employees of the corporation (which are then considered income and taxed at the individual rate). This way there are no corporate taxes to pay because there were no profits.

EXHIBIT 4.2

An Interview With Lauren Miller, PsyD, LLC

Could you please briefly describe your clinical practice?

My clinical practice addresses primarily trauma, eating disorders, and life cycle challenges. I work with families, couples, and individuals and see numerous graduate students. My practice is located in Chicago.

What type of corporate structure did you choose for your practice?

I initially chose a limited liability corporation (LLC) and then recently applied to change matters so that I can be taxed as an S corporation, while retaining the LLC name. I am still the only employee, but this setup will reportedly reduce the self-employment tax burden.

How did you make the decision as to what was the best structure?

I initially consulted with an attorney whose spouse was a psychiatrist. My tax accountant recently suggested changing the taxable entity to an S-corp, and he filed the papers for me.

What was involved with forming this structure?

The attorney did the incorporation paperwork initially, and after that I filled out the yearly LLC renewal paper. If any information changes, it simply involves a fee. No lawyers are necessary for this process. As mentioned previously, my accountant organized the S-corp application, also a simple matter.

What have you found the advantages of this structure to be?

None so far for the LLC. It reportedly shields me to some extent from malpractice suits (of which I have none to date).

What disadvantages, if any, have you experienced with this structure?

Because the LLC is filed as part of a joint tax return (if you are married or file jointly for whatever reason), there appears to be no benefit in terms of saving money. The quarterly taxes are computed at 17% over and above your joint taxable rate, and that is consistently an unpleasant surprise at year's end. It is possible to keep on top of the situation by doing the math on a monthly basis to avoid said unpleasant surprises.

Any thoughts or advice for someone considering this corporate structure?

The advantage to the S corporation as a taxable entity is that you take out tax monthly instead of having to suddenly come up with quarterly payments that vary depending on income earned. However, you have to pay someone to run payroll monthly (not usually expensive), and they direct deposit an agreed-upon salary. At tax time, as an LLC taxable structure, you may have to come up with personal taxes as well as business quarterly taxes, which can be a problem.

With all you know now, what recommendations would you make to someone just starting out and selecting a practice structure?

A lot of people keep this simple and use either nothing or a personal corporation (PC). I was advised that I would have more legal protection within the LLC structure, but I can't tell you if this is completely accurate. Many psychiatrists seem to use either the PC or the S-corp, and perhaps that is worth considering as they tend to get into more litigious situations than your average therapist.

For more information about Dr. Miller's practice, go to http://www.chicagotherapynow.com.

EXHIBIT 4.3

An Interview With Barrie Alexander, PhD, and Nancy McGarrah, PhD, Cliff Valley Psychologists, Atlanta, Georgia

Could you please briefly describe your clinical practice?
    We have a practice in which we primarily see children and families. We specialize in forensic psychology where there is usually some type of trauma, including divorce, abuse, or personal injury. We complete court-ordered evaluations for custody and parental fitness and work with families to develop parenting plans and reconciliation. A lot of our work is completed in collaboration with attorneys.

What type of corporate structure did you choose for your practice?
    We are a professional association, a form of corporation. We are the two equal partners in the association. We also rent one of our offices to a mental health professional but he is an independent contractor and not part of Cliff Valley Psychologists.

How did you make the decision as to what was the best structure?
    We consulted with a certified public accountant (CPA). This decision was informed by the fact we were buying a building at the same time. We knew that we wanted a structure in which we could pay ourselves salaries rather than as independent contractors. We have found it better to have a standard income and monthly salary to count on. It also helps to structure our tax payments. As employees of the corporation we pay the Internal Revenue Service when our salaries are paid. Because our taxes are deducted as we go, we do not owe any monies on April 15.

What was involved with forming this structure?
    We met with an attorney and it was pretty easy to implement once we knew what structure we wanted. The attorney developed articles of incorporation and had to decide who would be president and who the secretary–treasurer. We also had to set up a system to meet annual record-keeping requirements. We also had to develop a good working relationship with a CPA.

What have you found the advantages of this structure to be?
    There are several advantages. We have similar practices so we can own similar equipment (e.g., psychological tests, forms, play supplies for children). There is certainty in our incomes. All monies collected go into the corporation which in turn pays us our monthly salaries. There are usually peaks and valleys in collections, and the corporation structure allows us to even out our monthly salaries. At the end of the year we then bring our corporate account down to zero by paying ourselves bonuses. The bonuses are determined proportionally based on how productive each of us have been and what individual practice expenses (e.g., continuing education) we have incurred. We also fill in each other's gaps and abilities. One of us is good with the finances, and the other is good with doing talks in the community, which broadens our visibility. We have a marketing advantage being known as Cliff Valley Psychologists and having been in practice for over 20 years. If attorneys or judges don't know one of us they do know the other and know we are in practice together and that adds to our credibility in the community. It's sort of like brand recognition.

What disadvantages, if any, have you experienced with this structure?
    We have not found many. We do have to pay attention to more corporate details of running a practice than if we were sole proprietors. We think there might be more difficulties if we had disagreements on how to spend our money or how to run our practice.

EXHIBIT 4.3 *(Continued)*

Any thoughts or advice for someone considering this corporate structure?
It is important to know your own temperament. We never wanted to be solo practitioners. We wanted colleagues and someone to consult with on cases. It helps that our practices are similar in nature. It is also important for all partners not to have strong personalities as this could lead to unnecessary conflicts. It helps to know your partner well enough to get along and to get through disagreements. We've had a few disagreements but have seen other groups break up because of them. You also need someone who is going to be vigilant about the finances. We have known more psychologists than we'd like to count who have been taken advantage of and didn't know until it was too late.

With all you know now, what recommendations would you make to someone just starting out and selecting a practice structure?
You have to know that you want to be in private practice. It is not for everybody and some-times it's good to try other practice arrangements (e.g., working for someone, being a per-centage model renter in a group practice) to see what fits you best. It is helpful to go into practice with someone who has a similar specialty. You have built-in consultation and a com-mitment to learning one area of practice really well. It is also important to respect each other's abilities and work ethic. We worked together before we started this practice. It's like dating before you get married. We both felt evenly productive and had similar goals. It is also easier to take a risk if you are sharing the risk with someone you trust. We also suggest that you develop a good working relationship with a CPA whom you know you can be with for a long time. The relationship with ours has been invaluable. If you know you are committed to private practice and you are committed to the city, we suggest buying the building in which you are going to practice. Beyond a shadow of a doubt, paying a mortgage is better than pay-ing rent, though it does come with expenses and responsibilities.

There are several types of corporations, and your tax professional will be able to inform you as to the ones that are available in your jurisdiction and which would be most advantageous. They come under the general titles of professional corporation, S corporation, C corporation, and LLC. Stromberg and Schuetze (1997) suggested that the LLC allows health care professionals greater flexibility than does a professional corporation in organizing their practices. Also, each entity offers different tax advantages as well as organizational advantages. However, these corporate structures also require more paperwork and have greater accounting fees than does a sole proprietorship or unincorporated partnership. In addition, each structure has specific rules that must be followed in the running of the corporation.

Exhibits 4.2 through 4.4 present interviews with MHPs who have chosen to incorporate their practices. These professionals describe the rationale for the choice they made, what is involved in developing and practicing within a corporate structure, and the advantages and dis-advantages of their decision, and offer advice for those considering a corporate structure for their practice.

EXHIBIT 4.4

An Interview With Darlene DiGorio-Hevner, LCSW, of Rice DiGorio Ripkin Counseling Associates, LLC, Ardmore, Pennsylvania

Could you please briefly describe your clinical practice?

My background is in social work though I also earned a master's degree in industrial–organizational psychology. I previously worked as a grief counselor for a funeral home and as a behavior specialist and mobile therapist with child welfare clients. My other two associates have a master's degree in community counseling.

What type of corporate structure did you choose for your practice?

We chose a limited liability corporation (LLC) for our practice corporate structure. Each of us sought out legal advice and there was a consensus on the individual LLCs. We also spoke to other professionals and accountants who did not believe that we needed an umbrella LLC for the business. However, we wanted to protect ourselves as much as we could. One of us used a lawyer to file for her LLC. Two of us went online to http://www.dos.state.pa.us/corps to download the LLC application. We saved several hundred dollars doing the paperwork ourselves. You have to make sure to follow up and keep in communication with the state during this process.

How did you make the decision as to what was the best structure?

We made the decision based on protecting ourselves to the best of our ability. We knew we wanted the best liability coverage that we could get at whatever the cost.

What was involved with forming this structure?

We first consulted professionals (lawyers, accountants, other business owners) to seek their advice and expertise. We then filed the paperwork. Once the individual LLCs were issued by the state, two of us filed for the umbrella LLC under the business name. I might add that other clinicians in private practice appeared unwilling to share information. They advised not to form an umbrella LLC because it was difficult and hard to build a private practice.

What have you found the advantages of this structure to be?

We share the expenses of our office needs such as rent, computer, furniture, and marketing. We keep a separate account to which we contribute monies during the year for these expenses. This money is used solely to pay expenses. The business does not take in any income derived from our practice. We also have each other for consultation on cases when needed.

What disadvantages, if any, have you experienced with this structure?

We have not found any disadvantages of the corporate structure. However, the disadvantages of a private practice are the challenges of continuing to market your business as your current clients are making progress and terminating. One of us has a strong marketing background and wants to spend more monies on advertising. The other two of us are more conservative in allotting the monies (recommended) for advertising.

Any thoughts or advice for someone considering this corporate structure?

Investigate and probe as to what you are doing. We have had disagreements along the way. However, we have been able to work them out and make sound business decisions. Two of us may agree on making a business decision and the third may need to concede.

With all you know now, what recommendations would you make to someone just starting out and selecting a practice structure?

Make sure that you investigate with other professionals. We were back and forth whether we really needed individual LLCs along with an LLC to umbrella the business. We were not aware of all of the implications of starting this business regarding insurance and liability issues. We sought the advice of professionals and other clinicians and asked multiple questions along the way.

Conclusion

In this chapter we have highlighted many of the issues to be considered when adopting a model for one's practice. These issues have nothing to do with therapeutic skill but rather have to do with the "business of practice." As we noted earlier, private practice is your small business, and these issues can be ignored only at the peril of the financial stability of your small business. For this reason we highly encourage you to put great forethought into all of these decisions and seek advice from seasoned professionals when making these business decisions.

Office Overhead and Practice Expenses

You Have to Spend Money to Make Money

5

Several months ago Jeff Barnett went to replenish his psychological test forms once again. He realized that he was writing check after check after check to do so. The payments for 1 year alone added up to over $900, and he started to ask himself, "Why am I spending so much money on tests?" Well, in less than 2 seconds he found the answer: These tests had allowed him to bill $40,000 in psychological testing fees over the past year. Although it was still not fun to put those checks in the mail, he realized that at times up-front investments in capital allow him to earn his living. Indeed, business expenses do not detract from making a living but rather facilitate financial success. This insight removed some of the sting of dropping these checks in the mailbox.

Very few small businesses have no overhead associated with their operation. However, mental health practices differ in what and how much overhead they have. The equation depends on the type of setting in which one wishes to practice, how much work one wants to do on one's own and how much one wants to contract out for services, and how high-tech a practice one wants to operate. These issues are discussed in this chapter.

Essential Consultants

Private Practice Principle Number 10: It is essential for mental health professionals to have ready access to competent professionals to answer questions outside of their areas of expertise. Ignoring this principle places the clinician at ethical, legal, and financial risk.

Barnett and Henshaw (2003) pointed out that a private practice can never be run on one's own. They elaborated that too many practitioners have learned the hard way just how costly being one's own attorney or accountant can be. We believe that mental health professionals (MHPs) like earning large fees for the services they provide. We believe that in general they have an aversion to paying other professionals for their expertise. However, avoiding paying such fees in the short run may cost clinicians much more money in the long run. Furthermore, trying to save money in this way may jeopardize their ability to maintain their practice. Steve Walfish had a recent case in which he deemed it essential to consult with an attorney regarding client care and practice issues. He had received a request for records from the husband of a patient who had undergone bariatric surgery and had passed away 1 year after the surgery. Steve had completed a presurgical psychological evaluation with the wife. The husband made the request as executor of the estate. After consultation with an attorney who specializes in health care law in Georgia, Steve discovered that mental health records are not treated in the same manner as physical health care records. A specific law precludes the release of such mental health records in Georgia. The attorney then helped Steve to craft a reply to the request explaining why he would not be releasing the records.

In such a case, the law addressing the release of mental health records to the executor of the estate varies by jurisdiction. There was no way that Steve could know all of the idiosyncratic laws that apply in his state. The attorney fees for this case were $400. Of course, he experienced a pang when he wrote the check to cover these services. However, had he mailed out these records (which intuitively appeared to be the appropriate thing to do because the request was received as a standard release-of-information form), he would have violated the law. Later he may have faced ethical complaints or a civil suit for this mistake. Besides the hassle and emotional distress that accompany such actions, he also could have faced thousands of dollars in attorney and court fees or penalties had he been found at fault.

Another case of Steve's in which he sought out the advice of an attorney occurred 11 years ago. In the only instance in Steve's 26 years in private practice, a client filed a complaint with the Examining Board of Psychology about his psychotherapy practice. Steve had seen the client only two times for psychotherapy, and he requested that she read a self-help book as an adjunct to her treatment. She wrote to the Board, stating, "I just wanted to let you know that he is not doing a good job. . . . Dr. Walfish wasted my time and money. If I had been suicidal I wouldn't be writing this letter." The letter Steve received from the board partially read as follows:

> The Examining Board of Psychology is requesting from you a written statement regarding the allegations in the complaint letter. Feel free to add any additional information which will assist the Board in understanding the issues. You may consult with an attorney at your own expense prior to preparing a written response. Any written response may be used in an adjudicative proceeding, if one is warranted.

Steve prepared his response to the Examining Board; it included a page-and-a-half-long letter, copies of chart notes, and correspondence with the referring psychiatrist and the client. However, clearly scared about such words as *complaint, allegations,* and *adjudicative proceeding,* he felt it imperative to have these materials reviewed by an attorney familiar with working with the Examining Board. In reviewing these materials, the attorney changed one word of the letter. Although this may not sound like much help, had he kept this word as originally written it may have led to further scrutiny or problems from the Board. Two weeks later Steve received a copy of a letter addressed to the client:

> After careful consideration of the accumulated information the Examining Board of Psychology reviewed your complaint regarding Dr. Walfish. The Board has decided to close this file. No further action will be taken at this time.

Of course, Steve breathed a sigh of relief. However, he never would have considered responding without consultation from an attorney. He viewed it as an investment in protecting his license and business.

Attorneys can be helpful to MHPs in private practice in a number of ways. Exhibit 5.1 presents an interview with Robert H. Woody, who is both a psychologist and an attorney. In this interview Dr. Woody provides sage advice regarding how attorneys can be helpful to private practitioners and how to choose an attorney who can be most helpful. We also encourage psychologists to explore resources similar to the Legal Consultation Plan offered by the Georgia Psychological Association. Psychologists who get their malpractice insurance through the APA Insurance Trust have access to a Risk Management Service that advises regarding legal problems or ethical dilemmas (the American Association for Marriage and Family Therapy has a similar service for its members, as does the American Counseling Association). In a similar way, the Maryland Psychological Association offers consultation on

EXHIBIT 5.1

An Interview With Robert H. Woody, PhD, JD

Why should mental health professionals consult with attorneys?

Like it or not, modern psychological practices operate within a legal framework. With the advent of licensing, the government became the "regulator" of psychology, at both the macro and micro levels. According to many mental health practitioners, their graduate training provided little or no knowledge of either legal or business fundamentals, and often there was an emphasis on professional ethics without recognition of possible conflicts with the law.

When are the services of an attorney important to use for private practitioners?

Any time there is an agreement or contract, such as with an employee or independent practitioner, it is essential that an attorney with knowledge of the laws pertaining to the jurisdiction and contract law review the matter. Depending on the competency of the particular attorney, legal advice can be helpful for dealing with problematic clinical cases, such as for lessening liability. Any licensing or ethics complaint against the psychologist should involve an attorney.

Should a private practitioner keep an attorney on retainer or just hire one when needed? What issues are involved in making this decision?

Having an attorney on retainer is unnecessary, except (of course) in the event of an actual legal action against the professional. Nevertheless, the private practitioner should establish a relationship with an attorney and make regular use of his or her legal services. There is reason to believe that some clinicians, because they are intelligent, tend to erroneously believe that they should direct the legal actions—no sensible attorney would accept this foolish notion. Certainly the attorney will collaborate with and seek the clinician's preferences and opinions, but legal strategies are best determined by an attorney well versed in the law of the particular jurisdiction(s).

How does one find a good attorney for a mental health practice?

The best source of information about the qualities of different attorneys is talking to other health care professionals about their positive and negative experiences. It is important for the attorney to be knowledgeable of the law in the jurisdiction(s) in which the clinician practices. For example, if the attorney is not admitted to practice in the professional's state, there is a risk of misinformation.

Do private practitioners need an attorney who specializes in work with mental health professionals? What should one look for in choosing an attorney to work on practice issues?

Whenever there is claim to being a "specialist," caution is in order. In fact, being knowledgeable about law in general commonly provides the greatest competency, including for the legal needs of private practitioners.

Are there differences between attorneys that one should be aware of and guided by when selecting one?

Having good interpersonal communication is mandatory. If an attorney does not promptly return telephone calls, it is usually time to find a new attorney. Also, with some exceptions, if an attorney's bill includes "research," there should be a good explanation of why the research was necessary.

We are aware that part of your professional practice is spent representing mental health professionals in cases brought before state licensing boards. How can an attorney be helpful to a mental health professional in these cases?

There is no logical alternative: Because a licensing complaint is a legal action, with state investigators and prosecuting attorneys involved, any clinician who attempts to be his or her own attorney is risking the old adage of "having a fool for a client." This is well exemplified by the fact that the savvy attorney against whom allegations are made, such as those submitted to a state bar ethics committee, will obtain the services of another attorney for legal representation. Just as in mental health services, legal representation must be objective.

ethical questions for its members. This type of service is a valuable member benefit. Similar resources may be available in other states and through other state professional organizations. In light of the complexity of private practice in terms of clinical issues, insurance issues, and practice management issues, we actively encourage private practitioners to invest the monies necessary to have access to these resources.

The second professional who has to be available for the private practitioner is a certified public accountant (CPA). In addition to preparing taxes and providing advice about tax issues, CPAs can answers questions, both big and small, that can increase the bottom line of profit for private practitioners as well as keep them out of trouble with the Internal Revenue Service. As noted in chapter 2 (this volume), CPAs can advise as to what type of corporate structure would best meet a private practitioner's income and financial planning needs.

CPAs can educate clinicians about what monies are deductible for tax reasons, a subject about which there are many misconceptions. For example, one question commonly posed on electronic discussion lists is whether bad debt can be deducted from one's total income. Believe it or not, despite promises to the contrary, all clients do not pay 100% of their bill. The amount may be small; they may say, "I forgot my checkbook, so I'll pay you the $25 copay the next session" and are never seen again. The amount may be large, such as when an insurance company "promises" to pay for a service on behalf of the client and then does not do so. In this case the client is responsible for the bill and at times does not live up to this responsibility. A practitioner can deduct only money actually spent. As such, this bad debt, whether it is a $25 copay or a $1,000 nonpayment by an insurance company, cannot be written off as a business loss. Imagine that clinicians could decide that their fees are $1,000 per session. However, the insurance company allows only $100 per session. If this discrepancy could be written off as a loss, then clinicians would be losing $900 per session. When it came time to paying taxes, their business would show a tremendous loss and they would not pay any taxes even though they may have collected over $100,000 in fees.

An additional matter in which a CPA may be of great help is the issue of the deductibility of one's home office. Knowing what qualifies as a home office and just what can be deducted is very important. Another area is the issue of employees versus independent contractors. Claiming that another professional is an independent contractor when he or she actually may be an employee under Internal Revenue Service rules has significant financial and legal consequences.

Another area in which a CPA may be of help is the tax ramifications of bartering psychotherapy services. Imagine Psychologist A wants to have the outside of his house painted but the $1,500 cost would be a financial hardship. Along comes Client B, who is a house painter and needs a learning disability evaluation for his son. However, the $1,500 cost would be a financial hardship. So the idea of bartering painting services for evaluation services occurs to Psychologist A, and it would appear to be an even swap. Although bartering for psychotherapy services may be ill advised (R. Woody, 1998), if the psychologist in this instance does accept this arrangement he must declare the $1,500 as income (and pay taxes on these earnings). CPAs can advise on such detailed issues that may not be common knowledge to the layperson. However, because financial management issues are so complex, we especially urge early career professionals to meet with a CPA on a regular basis to review every financial aspect of their private practice. Exhibit 5.2 presents an interview with Barry Melancon, CPA, who is the president and CEO of the American Institute of Certified Public Accountants. In this interview Mr. Melancon discusses how CPAs can be helpful to the clinician and advises how to choose a CPA who will best meet the needs of the person and practice.

Choosing Where to Practice

MHPs set up their practices in a wide variety of places. We have seen practices in Class A office buildings, strip malls, office parks, medical buildings, and houses renovated into office space. Several considerations go into making the choice. The question to ask is, "What is the message or image I am trying to convey to those who will come in contact with me and my office as a client or potential referral source?" We don't suggest that you try to compete with an expensive law firm and possibly intimidate clients or at least cause them to question the appropriateness of your fees. At the same time, it is important for them not to view you as a second-class operation either.

Class A office space and medical buildings are probably the most expensive to rent. However, if you want referrals from physicians it may be advantageous to be located in close proximity to them. Proximity will not guarantee that you receive referrals; however, it may be an advantage in getting to know physicians. Furthermore, some clients prefer seeing psychotherapists who are in the same building or same complex as their physicians. Also, being in the same building provides some level of professional credibility, and the client does not have to deal with finding a different office building.

Jeff Barnett and Steve Walfish have each practiced in a professional office building, a small office complex, and renovated houses. Clients have often reported liking the comfort of the house setting. They know it is a professional office, but at the same time it has a homey feeling that is conducive to discussion about deeply personal issues.

EXHIBIT 5.2

An Interview With Barry Melancon, CPA, President and CEO of the American Institute of Certified Public Accountants

---

Why should mental health professionals in private practice consult with certified public accountants (CPAs)?

In addition to performing traditional tax and accounting services, CPAs perform other valuable services for mental health professionals that help them better manage their practices. CPAs also can help them stay ahead of medical industry trends affecting their practice, such as diminishing reimbursement policies, increasing administrative costs, and a possible reduction in income.

When should mental health professionals seek out the services of a CPA?

Private mental health professionals can benefit from hiring a CPA to perform tax and financial management services. They also should decide whether they need basic services, such as preparation of financial statements and tax returns, or more elaborate services, such as conducting a comprehensive assessment of their practice and recommending business and financial strategies. Many CPA practices also can advise practitioners on business matters such as information technology, valuations of their practice, mergers and acquisitions, and succession planning.

What services do CPAs offer that may be of value to mental health professionals in private practices?

CPAs who specialize in serving the needs of health care professionals provide a range of services to help their clients maximize revenue, reduce costs, and run effective practices. Some of these services include evaluating current fee structures, assessing managed care plans and contracts, reviewing federal Medicare and state Medicaid billing practices and procedures, setting up internal controls, assisting with compliance, performing practice valuations, and assisting with strategic planning.

How does one find an experienced CPA to advise a mental health private practice?

One common method of finding an experienced CPA is to ask for referrals from colleagues or professional service providers such as bankers or attorneys. Another solution is to contact individual state CPA societies. Mental health professionals can locate state CPA societies online at http://www.aicpa.org/states/info/index.htm.

Do private mental health professionals need a CPA who specializes in this type of client work?

Private mental health professionals should seek out a CPA who is experienced in serving health care practices, though particular expertise in the mental health field is not necessary. An experienced CPA should be knowledgeable of the medical profession, health care trends, and regulations. It is a good idea to ask prospective CPAs if they participate in health-care-related conferences, attend professional education courses, and read appropriate technical journals. Also, CPAs who are dedicated to serving the health care segment may be members of health-care-related professional and industry associations such as the Healthcare Financial Management Association.

Are there differences between CPAs that one should be aware of and guided by when selecting one?

As trusted business and financial advisors, CPAs practice in a variety of disciplines. For example, some CPAs specialize in personal financial planning and wealth management, others in business valuation. Practitioners should speak candidly with prospective CPAs about their needs so that they can determine the best fit.

Is there anything else important for private practice mental health professionals to know in working with CPAs?

Mental health professionals should request the names of several of the CPA's clients in the health care or psychology industry as references.

Signing a Lease

A property owner usually wants a practice to sign a lease to rent the office space. The terms of the lease to be negotiated are related to price, build-out costs, and what is to be provided by the property owners. As a general rule, the longer the lease that is signed, the more favorable will be the costs of renting the property. Longer leases guarantee the space will not go unoccupied, which would be a loss for the property owner. The terms of the lease may also depend on the nature of the local office space market. In an area with significant unoccupied office space, terms may be developed that are favorable to the renter. In an area with little or no unoccupied office space, property owners are less willing to negotiate or provide economically favorable terms to renters.

Some offices are ready for the practice to move into and begin operations. However, we believe this is the exception rather than the rule. Most offices need to be built out in some manner for the space to be optimal for a mental health practice. The costs for this build-out are usually borne by the renters. However, as noted earlier, this is negotiable. The longer the lease, the more likely the property owner will be willing to negotiate this cost. These costs can be considerable, so they must be computed into the overall figures for renting the space.

It is essential that the lease be reviewed by an attorney familiar with this aspect of the law, so that there are no surprises for the practice. For instance, the term *triple net* is included in the lease of most Class A office buildings and medical office space. This term refers to the sharing of common area maintenance costs by all those renting in the building or property space. These costs could include (but are not limited to) utilities, cleaning, property maintenance, real estate taxes, or other tax assessments. The cost to each office is usually a pro rata share based on square footage and not on actual use by the office. These costs are not known until the end of the year. Most leases have built-in annual increases that approximate what these costs will be. However, at times there are extra assessments because of miscalculations or unexpected expenses. These costs can be significant. We know of one practice whose monthly rent increased by more than $1,000 because a major restaurant in the complex used an extraordinary amount of electric power. Because these costs are determined by pro rata square footage and not by use of the clinicians, the practice had to bear a disproportionate amount of this extra assessment. This case is obviously an extreme one, but it would be helpful to ask for a history of these extra assessments. Although past assessments are not guarantees of future assessments, such data may help provide an educated estimate of what additional costs could be expected.

Alternatives to Leasing

An alternative to leasing a traditional office is to rent executive office space. Such arrangements are available in most cities; they are less likely to be available in rural areas. To find companies in this business, perform a search on the Internet. Executive office space might work for a solo clinician rather than a group practice. In an office building, space is rented to a number of businesses, and the MHP would likely have one office in a large suite or a floor. Basic office accommodations, including a receptionist, telephone, a photocopy machine, fax machine, and Internet access, are usually provided. There is often a conference room that could be reserved if a larger meeting space is needed. Offices may come furnished or unfurnished. With executive office space the clinician does not have to purchase telephone systems, copy machines, or fax machines. Thus there is no up-front investment; the clinician walks into a turnkey operation and may begin practicing without making these purchases or hiring staff. An aspect of this model that is both an advantage and a weakness is that usually no long-term lease is involved. The clinician may leave at any time if the arrangement is not working out. However, the property owner can also raise the rent with little notice. One important issue for the clinician to consider when using this type of space is to make sure that the practice remains compliant with the Health Insurance Portability and Accountability Act (HIPAA).

Another alternative to renting space is purchasing office space. This route was chosen by Barrie Alexander and Nancy McGarrah, whose interview was highlighted in chapter 4 and by Tammy Martin-Causey whose building purchase is highlighted in chapter 11. Barrie and Nancy chose to buy and renovate a small house. As they knew they wanted to practice in the same city for their entire professional careers, they viewed this as a good long-term investment. Although buying was a financial hardship at first, the rise in the Atlanta real estate market over the past 22 years has made this an excellent long-term investment. Office condominiums could also be considered for purchase. These resemble traditional office space, but instead of paying rent the owner of the condominium may build equity.

Another alternative is practicing out of your home. We have known clinicians to do this, and the primary motivation for doing so is reducing overhead. Because office rent is likely the biggest cost center for the private practitioner (with the possible exception of office staff), a home office can offer significant savings and add tremendously to the bottom line. A second reason for working out of your home is the convenience of not having a commute. A third reason may lie in the tax advantages of doing so. However, we do not advocate using the home as a practice location because of potential safety concerns for the clinician. The overwhelming majority of clients are not violent and have no difficulty respecting the boundaries of their psychotherapist. However, violence on the part of clients is not unheard of (Gentile, Asamen, Harmell, & Weathers, 2002) and it is difficult to be 100% sure about who will become violent and who will not. Although rare, boundary violations on the part of clients do take place. The clinician must take a number of privacy concerns and issues of professionalism into consideration if practicing out of the home. Would you feel comfortable having clients see your children at play in the yard, hearing children fighting upstairs, or seeing toys scattered around the yard? Some clients may be personally uncomfortable with this potentially high level of self-disclosure on the part of the clinician. Do you feel comfortable having clients know this much about your personal life? Also, for those clinicians who are psychodynamically oriented, how would this knowledge affect the client and your relationship with the client? For those using a home office, special precautions will need to be taken with regard to soundproofing the office suite. Also, it will be important to establish family rules for contacting you at work. When you are working, it may be easier for family members to just open a door to reach you rather than paging you or leaving a voice mail for you. But, for some clinicians, the convenience of a home office is highly valued. Exhibit 5.3 presents an interview with Amy E. Brown, a psychotherapist who has chosen to practice out of her home. She describes her rationale for this practice choice as well as its advantages and disadvantages.

Marketing

We have found that *marketing* is both a dirty word and a frightful word for many MHPs, especially those beginning their career. As we discussed earlier, MHPs most often enter their profession out of a desire to help others and a desire to make a difference in their lives. If you work in an agency or a hospital setting it becomes easy to accomplish this goal. You sit in your office, clients call the intake office to schedule appointments, come to see you, and you then provide them with excellent clinical work. Unfortunately, this same model usually has a negative transfer to the world of private practice. To paraphrase a line from the movie *Field of Dreams,* in private practice "You can build it but that doesn't mean they will come."

You may be an excellent clinician, diagnostician, or consultant, but if no one knows who you are and the nature of your services, then it

Practicing Out of Your Home: An Interview With Amy E. Brown, MS, CAC, LPC, Media, Pennsylvania

Why did you decide to practice out of your home?

Fifteen years ago, when I initially started part-time private practice, I sublet space from another therapist. When my practice grew, and my son was born, it made sense to move to full-time private practice in our new home. I liked the idea of not paying rent and working close to my family. We bought this house specifically so we could build the ideal home office.

Could you describe the physical aspects of the office arrangement and how it interacts with your personal home space?

The office is a converted garage. The entrance to the office is off the driveway and clients enter into a waiting room with a powder room. My office is off of a hallway with an interior entrance through my laundry room. The only physical overlap between personal and professional space is the driveway. We use the front entrance and clients enter only through the office entrance. We installed highway-type reflectors in the driveway to help with night-time parking and installed extra outdoor lighting. The inside space is soundproofed and wheelchair accessible. I have a powder room, office, waiting room, and a nook in which to hang coats. My office has a closet in which I can hide the filing cabinet, paper, and all of my supplies. I feel some internal pressure to make sure the lawn is presentable.

In my office I have a fax and copier, shredder, locking file cabinet, cool desk toys, phone (on silent), and the usual white noise machines. I have a desk but do not sit behind it. Clients have several choices of where to sit. Some appreciate the distance of the loveseat though most choose the couch closer to me. Last, because I sometimes run late and have no way to signal waiting clients, I found it helpful to post a sign to the effect of "I sometimes run late but never forget appointments."

Were I to do it again I would install a ceiling fan (for ventilation) and extra window in my office, and an exit door (in addition to the entrance door) for extra privacy.

What are the advantages of practicing out of your home?

There is no commute and I get to practice in a comfortable setting. I have total control over the exterior and interior of house and office presentation. I designed the space and personally picked the furniture, artwork, and so on. I can set my own hours, need not worry about other folks in the building, and can schedule crisis sessions without checking office availability. When I have a no-show or a break I can "come home" and spend time with my family.

What have your client reactions been to practicing out of your home?

They have been overwhelmingly positive. Most new clients comment on how much more comfortable and personal it feels to see someone in this setting versus an office setting.

Do you have concerns for safety or privacy that might not be present for you if you practiced in a traditional office setting?

There are no privacy issues. Client confidentiality is maintained. They pull into my driveway and walk into the office. They are seen only by other clients (as they would be in an office setting). My neighbors have an awareness of what I do but show no real interest in who is coming or going. I have no signage so only my immediate neighbors know about my business (as required by zoning board notification). My clients know what my house and car look like, but that doesn't bother me. I thoroughly screen potential clients by phone and have never met a client who frightened me. I have one client who poses some potential risk. He now comes accompanied by a family member, and I let my husband know when the client is here. I am hypervigilant about not annoying the neighbors as well as maintaining my clients' privacy.

(Continued)

EXHIBIT 5.3 *(Continued)*

So, when the rare angry adolescent storms out of session I try to be sure he or she doesn't pout on the street and get him or her back into session more quickly than I might in an office setting. Along the same lines, in an agency setting I would sometimes walk and talk with clients. This is not feasible here. And the rare kid who won't get out of the car is a bit more problematic here. I've had one adolescent slam the door but nothing has been broken, damaged, or stolen. My husband worries that clients will "just show up," although I do not share his concern.

Are there tax advantages for practicing out of your home?
My office comprises 15% of the square footage of the residence. Therefore I deduct 15% of utilities, grounds maintenance, and cleaning service. I also take the amortized deduction for office equipment.

What drawbacks or difficulties have you experienced as a result of having a home office?
There have been virtually none. I do find it more difficult to leave work (both physically and emotionally) and I also think a commute home would help me transition from work to home. Clients may expect me to be more available because they perceive me as always being at work. However, I have designed pretty strict work hours and hold myself to them. One drawback: I cannot take snow days as I can *always* get to work, though pile-ups on the laundry-room floor can create a 10-second delay.

What would you advise psychotherapists to consider if they might want to practice out of their home?
Establish a very solid referral base first, screen potential clients thoroughly by phone before seeing anyone for the first time, have good supervision in place, and set clear boundaries on hours available. Purchase malpractice insurance as well as a home-business rider.
Practice aboveboard; that is, don't hide the business from neighbors or the township. It took a lot of hard work to get my business license approved, but I am relieved to know that I have nothing to hide and I'm modeling integrity. In my opinion a separate entrance is critical. I do not think clients should enter your kitchen en route to the office. A powder room for clients is critical. Wheelchair accessibility is important. Finally, private practice can be very isolating. It is critical to regularly consult with colleagues both informally and formally, as well as to obtain supervision.

---

will be difficult to reach the goal of being helpful to others and making a difference in their lives.

Marketing takes time, money, and creativity. Entire volumes (Grand, 2002; Lawless, 1997) as well as sections of books (Kase, 2005; Stout & Grand, 2005) have been dedicated to this concept for MHPs. We urge you to consult these resources as well as books on marketing professional services that do not specifically focus on the delivery of mental health services (Connor & Davidson, 2001; Kotler, Hayes, & Bloom, 2002) for ideas that may apply to your own individual situation.

Marketing may detract from time available for engaging in direct services. For example, if you attend a professional association meeting for 1 day, then that is a day for which you will have no billable hours. However, if you make one new contact who will subsequently send you referrals, this short-term loss of income will create a longer term gain in income. Doing a talk on surviving your child's adolescence for a Parents Without Partners group requires time to prepare and deliver the presentation. This time is not compensated. However, effective talks to the right target groups will often generate referrals (either then or at a later date). Barnett and Henshaw (2003) reported that some private practitioners write columns in local newspapers or appear on radio shows to discuss mental-health-related topics. There is typically no remuneration for such activities that take time and energy. However, as Barnett and Henshaw (2003) suggested, these indirect forms of marketing help one be viewed as an expert in the local community.

Marketing also costs money. Following are but a few of the activities related to marketing and to growing one's practice that require financial resources: having an open house, developing and mailing a newsletter, taking a potential referral source to lunch, doing a direct mailing to households in your zip code announcing the opening of your practice, developing and maintaining a Web site, copying and mailing journal articles that you believe referral sources will find of interest to them in their work, advertising in the Yellow Pages, developing and distributing a brochure describing your practice, advertising on referral directories (e.g., http://www.psychologytoday.com), being listed on a state professional association referral base, and giving community presentations to teachers and counselors at schools, to support groups at local hospitals, or to advocacy groups such as CHADD (Children and Adults With Attention Deficit/Hyperactivity Disorder).

Of course, the costs associated with marketing can vary greatly. Part of this variance depends on how much of the work one wants to (and has the skill set to) do oneself versus contracting out for the work. For example, many practitioners have developed an Internet presence through a Web site that describes their practice (Palmiter & Renjilian, 2003). Those clinicians who are computer savvy may be able to develop the Web site on their own. For those not as tech-savvy, some MHPs have created a specialty niche for themselves in developing Web sites for other MHPs. Although these should not be considered as endorsements, examples may be found at http://www.therapymatch.com, http://www.drcarolgoldberg.com/psychologists.htm, and http://www. counselorwebsites.com. In addition, professional organizations such as the American Psychological Association have developed the opportunity for their members to develop Web sites (e.g., http://www.apapractice. org/apo/websites.html). Some clinicians have the skill and aesthetic eye to develop their own brochures using software (e.g., Microsoft Publisher, Adobe PageMaker). Others without this skill set may prefer to have the brochure developed by a professional printer. Of course, the more you do yourself, the less expensive the product will be. However, we urge you not to do things "on the cheap" and have an inferior product just to save money. If a bad brochure costs you $50 to produce and a stellar brochure costs you $200 to produce, the $150 would be well invested in terms of presenting yourself to the viewers of the brochure.

Of course, there are limits; spending $1,000 on a brochure may not be worth the investment.

The most productive marketing that we have done is treating potential referral sources to either breakfast or lunch. Imagine the physician's reaction to this question: "I'd like to take you out to lunch so that you can better get to know me and my practice, so how about if we meet at McDonald's at 12:30 on Tuesday?" Contrast this with the question, "I'd like to take you out to lunch so that you can better get to know me and my practice, so what restaurant would you like to meet at on Tuesday at 12:30?" We always let the person choose the restaurant because we want it to be an experience we know they will like (recall "customer delight"). Their choice may also reveal information about themselves (remember, we are clinicians and interpret everything!) that will be helpful in knowing how to best interact with them. Steve Walfish can remember an instance in which a physician chose a fancy hotel for the lunchtime meeting and then proceeded to order the most expensive item on the menu. This lunch cost him $50. However, this investment resulted in referrals for 50 psychological evaluations with the physician's patients, and the physician told other physicians about Steve's assessment skills. However, another physician chose to have breakfast at a local "hole in the wall" that was convenient to her office, and this $12 breakfast also resulted in referrals for assessment and psychotherapy. There was always the possibility that these meals would have resulted in no referrals. Too many times we have had excellent "marketing calls" with potential referral sources who indicated they would be sending referrals and sending them soon and we never heard from them again. These experiences are frustrating but should be chalked up to the cost of doing business.

Some marketing efforts are inexpensive. For example, the costs of mailing a letter of introduction to potential referral sources are relatively minimal. All that is needed are stamps, envelopes, letterhead stationery, and the ink used to print the letter. Jody Woodward is a psychologist in private practice in St. Louis. When she left her position at a local hospital to open her practice, she sent a letter to pediatricians in her area. This simple letter (presented in Exhibit 5.4) resulted in more than 50 referrals to her new practice. Dr. Woodward believes that part of this success resulted from the fact that she worked in an area significantly underserved for children's mental health. Such success with this letter of introduction may be idiosyncratic to Dr. Woodward's location and skill set. Clinicians should be encouraged to do a thorough study of their local area and determine the most cost-effective way to reach potential referral sources. Jeff Barnett has sent out a letter similar to Dr. Woodward's and had similar success. He also has a specialty (child and adolescent assessment and treatment) that is in great demand in his local area.

In addition, with an entrepreneurial outlook there are always opportunities to market your practice. For example, Jeff Barnett took

EXHIBIT 5.4

Sample Letter of Introduction

Jody L. Woodward, PhD
10004 Kennerly Road, Suite 250
St. Louis, MO 63128
(314) 849-8399; Fax (636) 489-4767

September 9, 2005

Dear Colleague:

I wanted to introduce myself and make you aware of the availability of my services. As some of you may already be aware, I joined the staff of St. Anthony's Medical Center (SAMC) in March of this year as a psychologist affiliated with RehabCare Group. Although I have decided to terminate my affiliation with RehabCare Group, I am pleased to announce that I will be continuing to provide services at SAMC. As of September 1, I have opened my new private practice in Medical Building A and am readily available to accept consults and referrals.

I can provide a range of both psychological and neuropsychological services and have the capability to see both children and adults. I am happy to evaluate and treat your patients during hospitalization and am also currently accepting new outpatient referrals. Types of problems for which I typically receive inpatient consultations include history of psychiatric disorder, depression, anxiety, bereavement, medical noncompliance, dementia versus delirium, chronic pain, head injury, and stroke.

Requests for consults or referrals should be directed to my office number–(314) 849-8399. My new contact information is listed above, and I am also enclosing my new business card for your convenience. I look forward to assisting in the care of your patients for many years to come.

Sincerely,

Jody L. Woodward, PhD
Licensed Psychologist

---

one of his children to a medical appointment. The physician recognized his name and complimented him on the reports that he had written as being especially well-written and helpful. Jeff followed up with a letter with five of his business cards enclosed, which resulted in a number of additional referrals for evaluations.

Other Start-Up Costs

If you are joining an existing practice, the start-up costs will be different than if you are starting a practice from scratch. The good news is that no up-front monies will have to be spent. The bad news is that you may not be able to alter already existing systems that may not be optimal for your needs or preferences. For example, Steve Walfish joined a practice with a billing system in place. Although everyone agreed that it was a terrible system, thousands of dollars had already been invested by the group and they had no desire to pay to replace it with a new one.

TELEPHONE SYSTEMS

The private practitioner needs a way to contact and be contacted by clients and referral sources. The system that is put in place can be extraordinarily complicated or extraordinarily simple, and everything in between. Maddock (n.d.), Martini (n.d.), and Sacco (n.d.-a) offered multiple considerations related to the choice of a telephone system, including (a) developing a checklist of all the features that are needed, as well as extras that you might want to include; (b) evaluating the need for features such as voice mail, conference calling, and automated messaging systems; (c) taking a count of employees who need outside lines, and the number of extensions needed for fax machines, modems, and credit card terminals; (d) planning for future expansion; (e) not skimping on wiring; (f) talking with multiple vendors because not all suppliers are not created equal, nor are their systems; (g) considering buying secondhand or renting; (h) buying at the close of the quarter when sales reps are trying to hit quotas; (i) making sure the purchased system is compatible with current equipment; and (j) picking a reputable seller for the best customer service.

If there are multiple clinicians in the practice, the telephone system will need to support at least two (or more) phone lines. It will also be important to have a separate line available to send and receive faxes. The greater the number of features offered by a telephone system, the more expensive it will be. For this reason it is important to carefully evaluate the needs of the practice. There is nothing more frustrating than losing a referral to another practitioner and later hearing "I tried to call you but couldn't get through" or "I left you a voice-mail message and I never got a call back so I called someone else."

Some solo practitioners are forgoing traditional landline phone systems and instead using cell phones with voice message capability. However, this practice may be ethically ambiguous because cell phones may not be entirely private. Although using a cell phone for responding to pages and client calls evenings and weekends may be a great convenience, using them as the primary means of communicating with clients may be problematic. Before using a cell phone (and cordless phones as well because they transmit signals electronically) for practice-related communications, psychologists should consult with an attorney in their jurisdiction to be clear on legal issues that may be present. In addition, an attorney can advise on HIPAA requirements regarding privacy protections that may be relevant when using cell and cordless phones (Barnett & Scheetz, 2003).

ANSWERING SERVICES OR PAGERS

Clients need a way to get in touch with their psychotherapist in an emergency. As part of risk management procedures clients should be informed as to how you would like for them to do so. Most practices contract with an answering service to answer telephone calls after hours. When a call is received, the service either calls or pages the clinician to let him or her know about the emergency message. To find a reputable answering service, speak with other private practitioners or physicians to see who they purchase these services from. Paging services may be obtained from standard telephone companies (e.g., Sprint, AT&T) or through other companies in your local community. These services and the pager are typically not very expensive. Answering services usually charge a minimum amount each month for a certain number of calls. Surcharges are imposed for additional calls. One way to avoid surcharges is to provide clients with your pager number (either on your business card, disclosure papers, or voice-mail system). However, although this method is a cost saver, you will not have the buffer of the answering service to determine whether you want to return the call or not.

PSYCHOLOGICAL TESTS

In their survey of clinical psychologists, Norcross, Karpiak, and Santoro (2005) found that 72% of those in private practice engage in activities related to diagnosis and assessment. Furthermore, these activities constituted 21% of their professional activities. If the private practitioner is a psychologist and wants to conduct psychological testing as a profit center (note the business term) in his or her small business, a significant initial investment will be required. Camara, Nathan, and Puente (2000) identified the 10 most frequently used psychological tests. They are the Wechsler Adult Intelligence Scale—Third Edition (WAIS–III), Minnesota Multiphasic Personality Inventory—2 (MMPI–2), Wechsler Intelligence Scale for Children—Fourth Edition, Rorschach Inkblot Test, Bender Visual–Motor Gestalt Test—Second Edition, Thematic Apperception Test, Wide Range Achievement Test—Fourth Edition, House–Tree–Person projective test, Wechsler Memory Scale—Third Edition, and the Millon Clinical Multiaxial Inventory—Third Edition. According to 2007 catalog prices from the publishers, the costs to purchase all 10 would be $4,085 plus tax and shipping fees. This list of tests may represent a general repertoire for the psychologist. Depending on the type of assessment practice the psychologist chooses to maintain, he or she may not need to purchase all 10. For example, although testing and assessment of children, adolescents, and adults is a significant component of Jeff Barnett's practice, he does not conduct neuropsychological evaluations. Therefore, there is no reason for him to own a wide range of psychological tests that are used by neuropsychologists. However, he regularly uses additional tests for psychoeducational assessments, including the Wechsler Individual Achievement Test—Second Edition, the Gray Oral Reading Tests—Fourth Edition, and the Behavior Rating Inventory of Executive Function. All psychologists who conduct a range of different types of assessments and evaluations will have their own personalized list of assessment tools. In addition to the initial purchase of tests used, test record forms need to be purchased when the initial set provided with the starter kits is depleted.

If the psychologist specializes in certain areas of practice, specific tests may have been developed to address specific questions not included on this list. For example, researchers have conducted surveys on the most frequently used tests for those evaluating posttraumatic stress disorder (Elhai, Gray, Kashdan, & Franklin, 2005), neuropsychological problems (Rabin, Barr, & Burton, 2005), children and youth (Cashel, 2002), and forensic clients (Archer, Buffington-Vollum, Stredny, & Handel, 2006; Lally, 2003). Those choosing to practice in these areas will have to purchase many of these specific tests to competently complete these evaluations.

New psychological tests may be purchased from the publishers. Psychologists may be placed on the mailing list of each company to receive catalogs on a routine basis. We encourage psychologists to do so because it allows them to be aware of the newest tests on the market. On occasion Internet discussion lists have postings by psychologists who are closing their practices and have tests for sale. Purchasing previously owned tests this way may be a cost-effective way to build an inventory of psychological tests. If the funds are not available to purchase all of the necessary tests, psychologists are encouraged not to streamline and leave out essential data from their assessment. There may be creative ways to obtain use of assessment instruments. For example, perhaps two or three psychologists who are cooperative with each other may purchase a WAIS–III together and work out a schedule for its use, or perhaps a WAIS–III could be "rented" on a per-use basis from another psychologist who has purchased the test. Both of these examples require a cooperative (and not competitive) working relationship. If done in good faith, such arrangements could be win–win for all involved.

FURNITURE

If you are successful, you are going to spend a good portion of your waking life in your office. That is one reason to furnish it in a way that is comfortable to you. In addition, your office decor and presentation are a reflection on you as a person and as a professional to the public and to your clients. As noted earlier, for this reason it is important to not do things "on the cheap." For instance, we recommend furniture not come from secondhand stores or charitable organizations. Think of the kind of environment you would expect if you were paying $50, $100, or $150 for a 50-minute session.

At a minimum each office should include a desk and office chair for the clinician and comfortable chairs or couches for clients. It is important to have enough seating for more than one client, especially if the clinician sees couples or families. There should also be lighting separate from overhead lights in case clients cannot tolerate fluorescent lighting. Waiting room furniture should also be comfortable and adequate enough to seat plenty of people. Clients do not appreciate having to stand or wait outside in the hall because of inadequate seating. If children are seen in the practice, their needs should also be taken into consideration when purchasing office or waiting room furniture.

Capital outlay for furniture can be significant. If it is too burdensome, we suggest considering two alternatives. First, some furniture stores have responded to competitiveness in the marketplace by not charging interest for 1 year. Customers with adequate credit can use their credit card to buy the furniture; if the amount charged is paid off in 1 year, then no finance charges are added. This arrangement is essentially an interest-free loan. A second alternative, and one that may be especially viable for someone beginning a private practice, is to lease furniture. Companies that specialize in this area of the furniture market may be found through an Internet search. Although this strategy may be expensive in the long term, it may be a viable way for the new clinician to furnish an office without a significant capital outlay.

OFFICE SUPPLIES

Of course, to run a business you need basics, such as pens, pencils, paper, scissors, file folders, staplers, and so on. We suggest going to a large office supply store and browsing to see what you might need. Supplies may typically be purchased at reasonable prices at chain office supply stores (e.g., Office Max, Staples, Office Depot) or large discount retailers in bulk (Costco, Sam's Club). Companies on the Internet may also provide low-cost supplies.

You will also need business cards and stationery. Many computer programs allow for the printing of such materials, but we advise against using this modality. Once again, try not to appear to be doing things "on the cheap." These materials, especially if purchased in bulk, are not that expensive. Some Internet companies (e.g., http://www.vistaprint.com, http://www.businesscards.com) produce quality products at costs significantly lower than they would be at a local print shop. You will also need charting material, which may be found online (e.g., http://www.medicalartspress.com).

You will also need to purchase file cabinets to store your client files. These need to be fireproof and have a lock. You can purchase these new from the stores mentioned earlier or used from stores that sell used office furniture. Charitable stores such as Goodwill or the Salvation Army may also sell such items. Because these will be sitting in a closet and not in view of clients, they need not be shiny and spiffy as long as they are functional.

COPIERS

The clinician needs to have access to a photocopy machine. The need will vary depending on the size of the practice and copying needs. For example, many inkjet printers are multifunctional; they can print files from the computer, fax documents, scan, and make photocopies. Such printers will work well for copying but are financially viable only for low-volume needs and should be viewed as a convenience (e.g., copying an insurance card or a handout for a client).

In addition to these machines, most office supply stores sell copiers that are designed for light to moderate use. Sacco (n.d.-b) advised that if fewer than 700 copies per month are made, such a copier may be a viable option. Purchasing a copier that carries most functions that one would see in a machine found in a corporate office or an academic department is cost-prohibitive for most private practitioners. Sacco (n.d.-b) noted that mid-level business copiers cost $5,000 to $10,000, with the best office models going as high as $40,000. Because of these costs he suggested copier leasing as a more attractive option for many businesses than purchasing one outright.

When a copier is leased, typically a certain number of copies per month are included in the basic cost. There is a surcharge for going above the preset number. However, as Sacco (n.d.-b) indicated, most leases come with service agreements and repair agreements that are designed to keep the machine functioning smoothly. However, he advocated obtaining a comprehensive list of what is and is not covered in the service agreement so alternative plans can be accurately compared.

To reduce copying costs Steve Walfish found a local office supply store that has self-serve copies for $.02 per page (including collating and stapling). In his practice he uses intake forms that are several pages in length and in his assessment of weight-loss-surgery clients he uses a long questionnaire (19 pages). He makes bulk copies of these forms once per month at the inexpensive copy supply store rather than pay the higher costs charged for going over the limit of the lease. The rest of his routine copying is done in the office and to date the monthly limit has not been exceeded.

COMPUTERS

It is possible to have a private practice and not own a computer. One can (a) write chart notes in long hand or dictate to a transcription service, (b) keep track of appointments in a book, (c) write in a ledger all practice expenses by category, (d) keep an index card for each client noting how much money the client has been billed and how much the client has paid, (e) provide clients with a preprinted super bill they can submit to their insurance carrier for reimbursement or outsource all billing services, and (f) complete all relevant tax forms by hand or have this done by your CPA. This is how practices operated before the advent of computers. Now all of these tasks may be done with a computer quickly and efficiently with a few specialized software programs. A practice may be almost totally computerized, and the extent to which it is depends on private practitioners' comfort level with technology and amount of money they wish to invest in technology. Schlosser (1989) pointed to several reasons why clinicians may not use computers in their practice. These include difficulty in using the programs and the peripherals, not having enough time to adequately learn the programs, cost (in time or money) of training to properly use the equipment, and cost of hardware and software.

This is not an endorsement, but for those interested in automating their practice, products offered at http://www.helper.com will cover most of the computer needs of any practice. The company offers software for billing (including electronic billing and credit card collections), scheduling, keeping track of managed care authorizations, recording treatment planning and client progress notes, and doing a complete outcome assessment. Reports can be generated to collate information regarding almost any aspect of the practice that would be helpful to the clinician. Such information might include amounts billed and collected in a specific time frame, how long insurers take to pay, client balances, and from where referrals are coming to the practice. Clinicians can purchase one or several of these software programs. For example, Steve Walfish has purchased only a billing program and has chosen not to take advantage of the other offerings. In addition to the products at http://www.helper.com, other popular billing software may be found at http://www.delphipbs.com, http://www.pm2.com, http://www.shrinkrapt.com, and http://www.practicemagic.com. A list of software programs for clinical practice along with reviews of these software programs can be found at http://www.assessmentpsychology.com/practicesoftware.htm.

In addition to billing and practice management software, a basic financial tracking software package is essential. Popular software programs such as Quicken or Microsoft Money help keep track of expenses by category. This information allows clinicians to know how they are spending their hard-earned fees, whether it is for rent, consultants, or office supplies. Having such information on a software program also facilitates the completion of tax returns. If taxes are prepared by a CPA, his or her time spent working on the documents is lessened because all practice expenses will already have been categorized and totaled.

For practices that are more complex in terms of personnel, an advanced financial management software program may be necessary. Examples are QuickBooks and Peachtree Accounting. These packages also include programs to complete payroll.

If you want to dictate your reports, letters, or chart notes, software has been developed to transcribe your spoken word to a computer file. The most popular program is Dragon NaturallySpeaking. After you have trained the program to recognize your voice, you speak into the microphone and the words appear on your computer screen.

If you are a psychologist, you have the option to include psychological testing as part of your practice. Many major psychological tests may be administered directly on the computer. The programs also typically provide a printout of the scores on the tests as well as an interpretation of the test data to be considered in the overall evaluation. Although cognitive or projective testing cannot by its nature be administered on the computer (though a limited number of cognitive tests can), software has been developed for the interpretation of both cognitive tests such as the WAIS–III and projective tests such as the Rorschach. A review of the Web sites and print catalogs of the psychological testing companies previously mentioned will inform you about what is possible in the computerized assessment realm.

One software program that Steve Walfish uses in his practice may be somewhat idiosyncratic to him, but he finds it extraordinarily helpful. He is one of those private practitioners who strongly values conducting and publishing data-based research. As such, he has purchased a statistical software package (SPSS) for his computer. He places nonidentifying data on his patients for whom he has recently completed presurgical psychological evaluations. For all of his patients he logs their scores on psychological tests such as the Beck Depression Inventory, State–Trait Anxiety Inventory, and MMPI as well as information about their age, sex, body mass index, and weight-loss expectations. As of this writing this SPSS file contains data on over 1,000 patients. These data allow him to speak empirically about the psychological aspects of this patient population and have also resulted in 4 publications, with another 10 currently in process. In a similar way, if a clinician wants to develop a newsletter to send to referral sources, then software programs such as Microsoft Publisher or Art Explosion Publisher Pro may be added to the computer arsenal.

Schlosser (1993) warned that dealing with technology in a practice can take much time and energy. Furthermore, he warned that updating one piece of technology may have an adverse effect on previously well-functioning software programs. Schlosser (1990) advised that "the trick is to know when the changes are significant and when to stay with what you have. It is all too easy to become allured with new things that simply capture one's orienting response" (p. 8).

On a final note, MHPs using computers in their practice have to ensure the privacy of their client information. Even if the computer system is hacked into, the responsibility for protecting confidentiality still remains with the clinician. Therefore, the highest level of computer security is urged. Barnett and Scheetz (2003) highlighted the vital importance of password protecting all confidential client material and using virus and firewall protection. In addition, the clinician should also make sure all of his or her data are backed up either on a secure system or on discs that are stored under lock and key.

Personnel

Perhaps one of the tougher questions private practitioners face is whether to pay for personnel to operate the practice. The answer may depend on the size and nature of the practice. The answer may depend on personal preference and tolerance for attending to details of a practice that are not clinical in nature. The answer may depend on skill set. The answer may depend on values about spending money.

Adjunct nonclinical personnel may include individuals who perform tasks related to basic reception services and billing services. If the clinical practice is large, it may be necessary to hire a practice administrator to oversee the overall operation of the practice. Basic reception services include greeting clients, answering the telephone, scheduling clients for appointments, collecting fees for service, and filing. Billing services could include verifying insurance benefits before the client's first appointment, obtaining initial authorization for services from a managed care organization, filing a claim with an insurance carrier, sending out monthly statements to clients for any unpaid balances, and following up with insurance companies for any unpaid claims or to correct mistakes they have made in processing the claim. Another service frequently used by MHPs is a transcription service. This service may be especially useful for psychologists who prefer to dictate reports.

Steve Walfish has practiced with personnel to complete these tasks and without personnel to complete those tasks. He prefers the former to the latter because such assistance reduces the amount of things he has to tend to in his practice, and his primary focus may then be placed on clinical issues and practice development. However, he is also aware that these services come at a price. He also recognizes that having a receptionist answer the telephone may increase the number of referrals that come into his practice. Often clients are given the name of three possible psychotherapists to see, by either their insurance company or other clinicians. As they may have no preference for whom they see, they usually schedule an appointment with the first person to return their call. Having a receptionist answer the telephone and scheduling appointments could increase the likelihood that clients will see the first clinician they called rather than the two other clinicians on their list. However, the benefits of having personnel must be weighed against the costs of having personnel. The online edition of the *Occupational Outlook Handbook* (http://www.bls.gov/oco) indicates that the median annual earnings of executive secretaries and administrative assistants was $34,970 in May 2004. The middle 50% earned between $28,500 and $43,430 (http://www.bls.gov/oco/ocos151.htm# earnings). These figures do not include fringe benefits (e.g., health insurance, retirement plan) or necessary taxes (e.g., social security, workers' compensation, unemployment insurance) that must also be paid. With a base of $28,500 the final compensation could easily rise to anywhere from $32,775 (using a low-estimate figure of an additional 15% of basic salary) to $35,625 (using a high-estimate figure of an additional 25% of basic salary). For a clinician in solo practice, this can be expensive. If the clinician averages a collection of $100 per hour of service delivered, he or she has to work 320 hours (at the low end of compensation) to cover the costs of this salary. If the clinician averages 32 hours per week of service delivered, 10 weeks of work is devoted to paying for this service. These figures also do not take into account raises that would be expected each year or holiday bonuses to reward good work. These costs go down for the individual clinician if several clinicians in the practice are sharing the costs. We know of few clinicians (other than psychiatrists) who employ full-time office personnel for their solo practice. However, there is also an upper limit on how many clinicians one office staff person can adequately provide services for without becoming overextended. Clinicians who want to build strong practices need to be especially aware of this limit. As the practice grows or more clinicians are added, then additional staff must be hired to ensure that support services are being adequately provided on behalf of the clients and the service providers. We have known practices to take on new associates with the goal of reducing overhead without taking into consideration the increased workload of support staff. In some cases support staff left because of burnout, and in the end the increased costs of adding associates did not financially benefit the practice as anticipated.

As is described in chapter 6 (this volume), billing and the collection of fees are essential and potentially tedious and time-consuming tasks for private practitioners. This is especially the case if the clinicians are providers for insurance companies. Private practitioners can purchase computer programs to facilitate this task if they want to complete this task on their own (see chap. 6). Some practices will purchase this software and have their in-house support staff be responsible for billing and collecting. Another option is to contract out these services. Many individuals have started small medical billing companies that will take on this task for a few health care providers. Many of these individuals work part time and are looking to have a home-based business. These businesses are especially available in areas with a high concentration of health care services. Such a service does not involve hiring personnel, paying salaries or fringe benefits, or providing annual raises. The service also has an incentive to collect as much as possible on behalf of the private practitioner because the service is paid based on the amount of monies collected. Once again, however, as these fees can range anywhere from 4% to 12% of collectibles, the cost of this service can add up to a significant amount of money. Some companies offer a range of contract lengths; that is, the contract may be on a month-to-month basis or may be for a specific time frame. Some companies may have a termination fee. To find these services, simply ask colleagues in private practice the question, "Do you have a good billing service?" and you are likely to be pointed to a reputable service. Newsletters for state professional organizations often include advertisements for such services. It is essential that the service have experience with billing for a mental health practice and not just a general medical practice. This way the service will be familiar with the billing and diagnostic codes used by mental health providers as well as managed mental health care issues.

There are also national companies that specialize in billing for MHPs in private practice. Although these are not endorsements, examples of such companies may be found at http://www.psychologybiller.com, http://www.psyquel.com, http://www.billshrinkers.com, and http://www.psychadminpartners.com. These companies design procedures that will protect client confidentiality while also taking care of all aspects of the billing process. The advantage of such services is that they specialize in mental health billing. The disadvantage of such services is they are national organizations and you cannot sit down and review your billing with someone in person.

Jean Thoensen is the owner of http://www.psychologybiller.com, a national billing service. Exhibit 5.5 presents her advice for private practitioners to consider when deciding to hire an outside billing service.

Outsourcing billing services always comes with risk. First, because the account may be only one of several (or an untold number of) accounts, it may not receive the individualized attention to detail that one would like. Second, as your representative, the company is an extension of you and your practice; therefore, any ethical breaches on the part of your agent become your responsibility. Third, if you are unhappy with the services (depending on the service agreement that you sign), you may switch to another billing service. However, switching can become costly because most companies charge a setup fee for each account they have to enter into their database.

EXHIBIT 5.5

Ten Things to Consider When Choosing a Billing Service by Jean Thoensen

1. *Licensing and registration.* A handful of states (e.g., Arizona, Oregon, Washington) require billing companies to become licensed as collection agencies. New Jersey requires billing companies to register with the state. If your practice is located in any of these states, you can verify a company's status on the state's Web site. It can be quite expensive to get licensed or registered. A billing company conducting business illegally in a state may lack integrity and honesty in other aspects of its operation. Don't hesitate to report such enterprises to the appropriate state agency, and *don't* do business with them.

2. *Experience.* Choose a billing service with plenty of experience in mental health billing. A cardiology biller is going to quickly get lost in the maze of mental health carveouts, state-mandated benefits, parity laws, and so on. Smaller companies may specialize exclusively in mental health or perhaps even just one particular discipline, such as psychology. Larger companies or those that bill for many medical specialties should have specialists on staff with experience in mental health. It's best to work with a billing company that will assign a specific person to handle your account. You don't want your billing bounced from employee to employee.

3. *Industry knowledge.* A billing service should be familiar with the insurance companies you work with and how to bill for the types of services you render. The service should review the Current Procedural Terminology (CPT) codes you use to be sure they're appropriate. State and federal laws affect patient benefits, and a billing company must be knowledgeable about them to spot mistakes by insurance companies. Out-of-state billing services should be able to demonstrate how they can quickly ramp up on the nuances of billing in your state if they aren't already doing business there.

4. *References, references, references!* A reputable billing company should give you at least three references. How long have its clients been with the company? Why did the last client leave? A revolving door of clients may indicate internal problems at the billing company. Do other billing companies refer business to them?

5. *Commitment to education.* A clinician must acquire CEUs (continuing education credits) to maintain his or her professional license. In a similar way, a billing company must stay current on relevant coding and billing issues, the Health Insurance Portability and Accountability Act (HIPAA), Medicare and Medicaid regulations, and so on. Does the billing company provide continuing education for its employees? Does it subscribe to Center for Medicare & Medicaid Services electronic discussion lists and other Internet resources? How does it keep its finger on the pulse of the mental health billing world?

6. *Contracting.* A billing company should present you with a proper contract that spells out what each of you will do. HIPAA requires that the contract include a business associate agreement as an addendum or stand-alone document. Have your attorney review the contract, and ask the billing company to explain anything you don't understand.

7. *Preauthorizations and insurance verification.* Will the billing company obtain initial preauthorizations if necessary? Will it help track authorization usage? Will it verify the benefits of new patients? Are there additional charges for these services?

8. *Can your claims be submitted electronically?* Billing companies typically submit claims electronically to a clearinghouse. Can its clearinghouse handle claims for your payers? It may not be able to send claims to some of the major mental health managed care companies (e.g., CIGNA Behavioral Health, Magellan, MHN), certain BlueCross BlueShield plans, Medicare carriers, or state Medicaid programs. Give the billing company a list of your payers, and ask which ones it can submit electronically. If it can't reach your biggest payers now or find a way to do it in a reasonable amount of time, keep looking.

EXHIBIT 5.5 *(Continued)*

9. ***How often does the billing company submit claims?*** If the answer is monthly, keep look-ing. I think a billing service should submit claims at least weekly. I like to submit at least weekly to create a steadier stream of income for my clients. Timely filing deadlines of 90 days are not uncommon. If a claim isn't submitted until 45 days after services are rendered, there is too little time to react if the claim is lost, pended, or denied. Patient insurance policies may have lapsed by the time the claim is processed.

10. ***Professional affiliations.*** What are the billing company's professional affiliations? Is it a member of the Healthcare Billing and Management Association (HBMA)? HBMA is the largest professional association for the medical billing industry, offers in-depth educational opportunities, and works directly with CMS and the Office of the Inspector General on Medicare on HIPAA issues that affect billing companies and medical practices. Other organizations to which billing companies often belong are the American Medical Billing Association, the Medical Group Management Association, the American Academy of Professional Coders, and specialty societies.

If private practitioners decide to hire personnel, it is essential that they become familiar with employment law issues. As small-business owners they are subject to laws regarding hiring and firing, discrimina-tion, and family medical leave, just to name a few. We think it best to consult with an employment law attorney to become familiar with these issues and to learn of guidelines for appropriate interviewing and for developing procedures for terminating someone that fall within the guidelines of the law. With larger practices it may be necessary to develop an employee handbook with policies and procedures. An Inter-net search on the term *employment law* yields Web sites that may pro-vide a helpful overview of the issues with which MHPs should become familiar. However, private practitioners are not immune from being sued by current employees or disgruntled former employees who believe their rights have been violated. Sidney J. Strong is an experienced employment law attorney in Seattle, Washington (http://www.sidstronglaw.com). Exhibit 5.6 presents his perspective on frequent employment law mistakes made by employers. These things are not taught in graduate school but are an essential component of practice management if one plans to have employees.

How Do I Pay for All of This?

As we have pointed out, it is unlikely that right out of graduate school an MHP will jump in and open a practice. More often clinicians join existing practices and later venture out on their own or they have a full-time position with an institution and transition into practice slowly by

EXHIBIT 5.6

The 10 Mistakes Related to Employment Law Most Frequently Made by Employers by Sidney J. Strong, PS, Attorney-at-Law

1. *Asking applicants for information not related to the qualifications of the position.* Employers may not question applicants about their personal background, lifestyle, or any subject that is not a bona fide criterion for performing the requirements of the job being filled. Questions about family, personal relationships, retirement plans, personal beliefs, and others that do not determine whether an applicant is qualified should not be asked.

2. *Failing to keep employees' medical or health information confidential.* All health care information must be kept confidential and in files separate from an employee's personnel file. Employees have a right to privacy regarding their health condition and that information may be disclosed only under limited circumstances, such as to a manager or supervisor who must accommodate an employee with a disability.

3. *Routinely contesting unemployment benefits.* Unemployment benefits are normally granted unless the employee quit voluntarily or engaged in willful misconduct. Poor work performance will not disqualify. By contesting unemployment, the employer provides recorded sworn testimony, often without counsel, which most often helps the terminated employee prosecute a wrongful termination lawsuit.

4. *Terminating employees who have a record of good performance and no documented work performance problems.* Most employees work at will and can be terminated without notice and cause. However, when a good employee is arbitrarily terminated, it opens the door to proving that the termination more likely was motivated by discrimination or other unlawful motivation, because it makes no business sense to fire a good employee without reason.

5. *Refusing or failing to communicate with an employee's health care provider to determine whether or not a disability must be accommodated.* Employers with notice of a disabling medical condition must engage in an interactive process with the employee's health care provider to understand the nature and limitations of the disability and to determine an accommodation. Failure to engage in this interactive process is disability discrimination.

6. *Adopting policies and procedures that conflict with at-will employment.* Most employers have written disclaimers in employee manuals and employment applications that acknowledge employment to be at will. However, if these employers also insist that employee discipline, including termination, follow progressive steps with written justification, these policies may be found to be an exception to at-will employment.

7. *Asking older employees to commit to retirement dates or making age-related comments relating to continued or long-term employment.* Age is generally not an employment qualification. Comments about age, such as "at your age you should consider retiring" or "we think that you may be a little old to handle the requirements of a reorganization" may provide indications of an intention to discriminate because of age.

8. *Minimizing, deferring, or delaying response to employee complaints of sexual harassment, disability harassment, or other discriminatory treatment.* Managers, supervisors, and human resources personnel must respond promptly and effectively to complaints of discriminatory treatment. Under some circumstances, failure to do so may impose strict liability on the employer, may limit the defenses available to the employer, or may support a claim of constructive discharge.

9. *Taking adverse action against an employee who complained of unlawful treatment.* An employee's right to complain of unlawful treatment without fear of retaliatory action is entitled to the same protection as the employee's right to be free from discrimination. Adverse action includes any material change in the terms and conditions of employment. Retaliation may be inferred from adverse action taken within a short time after an employee complaint.

10. *Denying or restricting employment to employees with perceived mental or physical impairments.* Employers may not assume the existence of a disqualifying disability. An employer believing an employee to have an impairing health condition must take affirmative steps to determine whether or not the employee can perform the essential functions of the job.

seeing clients in the evening and on days off and weekends. When it appears viable, they then move into full-time practice. For those considering these routes, we strongly urge the development of a strong savings ethic. In this way money earned from working for someone else can be used to finance the development of your own private practice.

However, some people with both an entrepreneurial spirit and resources prefer to take the plunge right away. As has been the theme of this chapter, it takes money to make money, so the entrepreneur needs to develop a plan for being financially viable while building his or her practice.

The easiest way to finance the development of a practice is to have a spouse or partner who earns a regular income (and a healthy one at that). Furthermore, a parent or generous relative may give or loan the money at rates that are more reasonable than one could find with an open-market loan.

There are other ways to finance a practice, and qualifying for these may depend on the amount of debt that may have accrued from your education and your credit rating. Before we go any further, let us once again sing the "The Lawyers' Chorus" and remind you that we are not providing financial advice; if you are considering borrowing money, consult with financial management professionals to help determine the best options for your situation. One strategy is to establish a line of credit with either a bank or another lending company. A second strategy, if you own a home, could be to take out a home equity line of credit. A third strategy could be to borrow the money using credit card offerings that may come to you in the mail. Of course, such options are not for the risk-averse.

Some companies and institutions specialize in financing medical practices through working capital loans. An Internet search on the term *financing medical practices* yields several hits that may be an economic resource for MHPs. These companies typically serve a target market of physicians, dentists, and chiropractors. However, a few companies we contacted indicated that they would be willing to work with MHPs. Finally, one can approach a local bank regarding a loan. Schultz (n.d.) suggested that some banks shy away from lending to start-up practices because physicians often have a negative financial worth (because of educational loans) and may lack tangible collateral. However, he further elaborated that some banks look for ways to work with start-up physicians. Rather than looking at the new physician as a potential credit risk, the bank may see the new physician as a person with whom it would like to do business. Banks may offer the physician and practice checking accounts, credit card processing capabilities, payroll processing, and retirement and pension plans for both the individual physician and the practice. Don Osterfelt is a senior vice president at Wachovia Bank (http://www.wachovia.com). Exhibit 5.7 presents an interview

EXHIBIT 5.7

An Interview With Don Osterfelt, Senior Vice President at Wachovia Bank

How does a mental health professional approach a bank about borrowing money to fund the start-up of a private practice?

There are a variety of start-up profiles. The easiest situation for a bank to affirmatively respond to is a loan request from a practitioner who has established a reputation and following in the community through his or her work for others. The bank gains a sense that he or she is well thought of, has a following, is more likely to succeed in the new venture, and in addition through that job has created some semblance of capital via equity in a home, savings that provides the bank with a sense that should the venture fail, the practitioner has the wherewithal to retire the loan. On the other hand the recent college graduate, saddled with debt, possibly in possession of a deficit tangible net worth, and possessing no following in the community, is more problematic for a bank to work with. Nonetheless it's possible to provide start-up financing to that riskier profile through enhancements such as the personal guaranty of a creditworthy individual or some other enhancement such as a U.S. government guaranty.

How do banks feel about loaning money to psychologists, clinical social workers, professional counselors, or marriage and family therapists because they are not physicians?

How a bank feels about any medical professional is driven largely by the person's financial profile and not necessarily by whether or not MD or PhD follows his or her name.

What types of loan opportunities might be available to a person beginning a private practice?

I'm not sure what you are asking but there are a number of opportunities including the financing of the practice's physical location, providing term loans for leasehold improvements, construction or permanent financing for a practice's location, lines of credit both secured and unsecured, equipment financing, and permanent working capital financing.

An attractive lending opportunity available through Wachovia is known as the business equity line whereby a practitioner can tap the equity in his or her personal home, pledge it for collateral for a loan to his or her business, and in turn receive very attractive rates and terms.

What indicators might there be that the mental health professional is a bad risk to receive a loan?

The biggest predictor of an event of default is one's own credit score. The mental health professional who wishes to be successful in acquiring capital from a financial institution should focus on his or her credit score; the higher the score, the better. We find that how a mental health professional handles personal credit is an excellent indicator of how his or her practice will handle credit.

Many early career professionals have significant levels of debt from their college and professional training programs. How does this impact the loan process?

See the answer to the first question.

What other services might be available through a bank for the private practitioner?

Cash management services, card processing, leasing, Small Business Association loans, deposit products, products that combine the features of both loans and deposits such as sweep accounts, and financial consulting.

Are there differences between financial institutions that would loan money to mental health professionals that we should be aware of and are there particular things to look for?

In general, banks have a tendency to look at MHPs in the same way. They look for the same c's in assessing creditworthiness: credit, capital, collateral, capacity, and cash flow. Some financial institutions will take on more risk than others by using higher interest rates. They have a

EXHIBIT 5.7 (*Continued*)

sense of what the loss rate will be for a riskier profile and charge a premium in the way of higher interest rates to cover the expected future losses. Other financial institutions would rather not run the risk to their reputation associated with having their name attached to higher interest rate loans and seek the more creditworthy MHP who is worthy of the lower rate.

We think that the best way for MHPs to assess the financial institution that they are dealing with is to get to know their banker. Lending to businesses is all about relationship and trust. We prefer to come at these loan requests from a consultative position and many times wind up tailoring the loan request so that it fits the needs of both the bank and ourselves.

with him related to issues regarding MHPs using banks to finance their private practices.

Conclusion

In this chapter we have reinforced the concept that to be in private practice means that one is engaged in the running of a business. It is difficult to imagine that this small-business enterprise called private practice can be adequately developed and maintained without appropriate consultants, a comfortable place to meet with clients, and the outlay of capital to provide our consumers (or customers) with a quality product and experience.

Loss Prevention
Increasing the Likelihood You Get Paid by Clients and Insurance Carriers

6

T he likelihood that mental health professionals (MHPs) in independent practice will collect 100% of the fees they charge to clients is close to zero. Each time a client walks out of a clinician's office without paying the entire fee, there is a chance that this money, hard earned by the clinician providing a professional service, will not be paid in its entirety. A mental health practice may not be paid because an insurance company provided misinformation, a client was angry or irresponsible, a client ran into difficult times and was not able to pay the fee, a client provided faulty credit card information, a check paid for services rendered bounced because of insufficient funds, or the client went bankrupt.

Our practices have experienced losses due to all of the above. Yet MHPs can put policies and procedures into place to increase the likelihood they receive the monies due to them. We have done so, and the frequency with which we have not been paid by clients over the years has been significantly reduced. However, unless clients pay cash (not check or credit card) for the entire fee (not just the copay) before the beginning of the session or assessment, we can guarantee that private practitioners will not collect 100% of their fees. This is just a business reality. In this chapter we focus on the process of both charging and collecting fees.

Private Practice Principle Number 11: If collections are less than 90% of fees charged, you should take a hard look at your fee-setting and collection process.

Setting Fees

One of the most common questions on Internet discussion lists for new professionals is "How much should I charge for my services?" This question may sound simple, but the process of arriving at an answer can be complicated. We know clinicians who charge $300 for 1 hour of psychotherapy and those who charge $75 for delivering the same service. There is also no reason to believe the quality of the service provided by those charging more money is different from that provided by those charging less money. Factors that influence the setting of fees include (a) the prevailing fees in the area as well as the general level of affluence in the local area; (b) whether you provide unique or specialized services, have specialized credentials, or have many years of experience; (c) whether the fees are uniform in the practice you have joined and already set; (d) the decision to become a preferred provider for insurance companies and to participate in managed care; and (e) your values and comfort with money.

As part of the process of determining fees, Barnett and Henshaw (2003) suggested conducting an informal survey of those already practicing in your area. This survey may be done by making random telephone inquiries to a variety of providers. You may also ask colleagues informally over lunch or at professional meetings. If you make such inquiries, we suggest gathering these data from at least 10 sources, including clinicians from all of the disciplines (e.g., psychologists, clinical social workers, licensed professional counselors, marriage and family therapists). Doing so will allow you to determine the average fees in your area on the basis of enough providers and not be influenced by outliers who charge little or a lot. Another source of data on average fees charged is an annual survey conducted by the newsletter *Psychotherapy Finances*. This survey is available as part of the subscription to the newsletter (see http://www.psyfin.com). Data abstracted from the March 2006 issue of *Psychotherapy Finances* show the national averages for psychotherapy to be as follows: psychologists, $119; marriage and family therapists, $99; clinical social workers, $90; and licensed professional counselors, $89. But it is important to keep in mind that there are regional and even local differences in fees charged.

If you enter into a group practice, the fees may already be set by the practice, and there is an expectation that you will adopt the same fee schedule. Entering a group practice like this is different from joining a group of independent practitioners who share expenses. For example, Steve Walfish practiced at the Atlanta Center for Cognitive Therapy for 4 years. Along with six other clinicians, he paid a monthly fee for rent and services. Each practitioner maintained his or her own fee schedule. The difference between the highest charging and lowest charging clinician was $75 per session.

If you decide to become a preferred provider for an insurance company or for a managed care company, your fees will be set for you by contractual arrangement. Next are some key concepts and definitions.

PREFERRED PROVIDERS

A preferred provider is an individual who wants to be listed with an insurance company as providing mental health services. These companies are known as preferred provider organizations (PPOs). Providers agree to a set fee schedule and the client will be charged only a standard copay set by the company and any deductible that may be due. If potential clients consult their insurance plan and choose one of the preferred providers, they will be assured that their financial responsibility will be limited and the bulk of the fee for services will be covered by their health insurance plan. In theory the advantage for MHPs is that they will be able to see more clients because subscribers would likely prefer a situation in which their financial obligation is limited. People may be especially likely to choose a preferred provider when they have limited financial resources or they have no particular preference for which particular MHP they see. However, this does not mean they cannot see a clinician who has not signed up to be a preferred provider. Many plans allow for an out-of-network benefit (discussed further in chap. 9). However, in these cases there is usually a higher or separate deductible and a larger copay is due. In other words, the client bears a greater part of the cost of treatment.

MANAGED CARE PANEL

Some insurance companies have "carved out" or contracted with a separate company to manage the mental health benefits of the plan. These companies are called managed care organizations (MCOs). When subscribers want to access their mental health coverage, they call a telephone number on their insurance card and are given the name of an individual who is a member of their managed care panel. Once again, providers agree to a set fee schedule and the client will be charged only a standard copay set by the company and any deductible that may be due. All care must be authorized by the MCO or the sessions will not be paid. Furthermore, if these sessions are not paid by the insurance company, the clinician has contractually agreed that the client is not obligated to pay the fee.

CPT CODE

CPT is an acronym for Current Procedural Terminology. A CPT code is a uniform five-digit number that all insurance companies recognize as representing a particular type of service. For example, the CPT code 90806 represents 45 to 50 minutes of psychotherapy. The most common CPT codes used by MHPs are presented in Exhibit 6.1.

In addition to these CPT codes, behavioral assessment codes have been developed (see Exhibit 6.2). These codes specifically address assessment activities in behavioral medicine.

FEE SCHEDULES

When providers join a PPO or managed care panel, they agree to a set fee schedule for their services. The reimbursement schedule for doctoral-level psychologists is higher than it is for master's-level clinicians. It is also of interest to note there are no differences in amount reimbursed based on the experience level of the clinician. A licensed marriage and family therapist (LMFT) with 20 years of experience has the same fee schedule as does an LMFT with 2 years of experience.

USUAL AND CUSTOMARY CHARGES

Not all insurance companies have PPOs or have carved out their mental health services to an MCO. However, each insurance company has

EXHIBIT 6.1

The Most Common CPT Codes Used by Mental Health Professionals

CPT Code	Description
90801	Initial diagnostic exam
90804	Psychotherapy, 20–30 minutes
90806	Psychotherapy, 45–50 minutes
90808	Psychotherapy, 75–80 minutes
90846	Family therapy without client present
90847	Family therapy with client present
90880	Hypnotherapy
90885	Evaluation of records for medical diagnosis
90889	Preparation of report
96101	Psychological testing with written report
96117	Neuropsychological testing

EXHIBIT 6.2

Behavioral Assessment Codes

96150—the initial assessment of the patient to determine the biological, psychological, and social factors affecting the patient's physical health and any treatment problems.

96151—a reassessment of the patient to evaluate the patient's condition and determine the need for further treatment. A reassessment may be performed by a clinician other than the one who conducted the patient's initial assessment.

96152—the intervention service provided to an individual to modify the psychological, behavioral, cognitive, and social factors affecting the patient's physical health and well-being. Examples include increasing the patient's awareness about his or her disease and using cognitive and behavioral approaches to initiate physician-prescribed diet and exercise regimens.

96153—the intervention service provided to a group. An example is a smoking cessation program that includes educational information, cognitive–behavioral treatment, and social support. Group sessions typically last for 90 minutes and involve 8 to 10 patients.

96154—the intervention service provided to a family with the patient present. For example, a psychologist could use relaxation techniques with both a diabetic child and his or her parents to reduce the child's fear of receiving injections and the parents' tension when administering the injections.

96155—the intervention service provided to a family without the patient present. An example would be working with parents and siblings to shape the behavior of a child with diabetes, such as praising successful diabetes management behaviors and ignoring disruptive tactics.

made its own determination as to what it believes is a "reasonable and customary" charge for each CPT code. There does not appear to be any rhyme or reason as to how this is determined; two insurance companies can have different reasonable and customary charges for a specific CPT code for services provided in the same geographic area.

BALANCE BILLING

As noted earlier, when one becomes a provider for a PPO or MCO, one agrees to a set fee schedule. Providers are not allowed to charge the client the difference between their usual fees and those contractually agreed to with the PPO or MCO. For example, let us imagine Jane Doe, a licensed clinical social worker (LCSW), normally charges $100 for CPT code 90806 (50 minutes of psychotherapy). She receives a new client, Mr. Public, who was referred by his MCO, for which Ms. Doe is a provider. The contract Ms. Doe has signed indicates her fee for all clients of this MCO will be $60. On completion of the session Mr. Public pays his $10 copay. Ms. Doe then submits the claim to the MCO for the session and 2 to 4 weeks later receives a check for $50. Her fee for this session would then be considered paid in full at the contract rate of $60. She may not then subsequently bill Mr. Public an additional $40 to make up the difference between her usual fee of $100 and the contracted rate of $60. When she signed the contract with the insurance carrier, she agreed to accept its fee allowed as full payment regardless of what she typically charges.

However, let us imagine that Mr. Public's insurance carrier did not have a PPO or carve out its mental health benefits to an MCO. In such a plan, called *indemnity insurance,* Mr. Public is free to choose whatever licensed MHP he wants to see for psychotherapy. The carrier will then reimburse for psychotherapy services at 60% of its usual and customary fee. In the case of the psychotherapy session with Ms. Doe, Ms. Doe would submit a claim to the insurance company. Two to 4 weeks later she would then receive a check from the insurance carrier for 60% of what it believes is the usual and customary charge for this service. For example, if it believes $80 is the usual and customary fee then the check would be made out to Ms. Doe in the amount of $64. She may then bill Mr. Public $36 for the balance of her $100 fee. Even though the insurance carrier believes the usual and customary fee is only $80, Ms. Doe does not have a contractual agreement to abide by that fee schedule. Therefore, Mr. Public is financially responsible for the balance of her set fee.

Your values about money and your comfort level in asking for money for your services will likely play a significant role in fees that you charge and the percentage of what is billed that is actually collected. In chapter 1 we outlined many of the economic conflicts inherent in being an MHP working in the for-profit business called private practice. It is important that before setting a fee schedule the clinician in private practice resolve the issues presented by Rodino (2005) and Grodzki (2004). Without doing so, it will become impossible to ever comfortably say over the telephone, "My fee is $120 per session," or during a treatment session, "Ms. X, your bill is now up to $300 and it is important that we bring this balance down to zero." Martin-Causey (2005) described her journey:

> After many years of working hard in the mental health field and not seeing much financial return, I one day realized that I should be able to do what I enjoy doing and make lots of money doing it. That became my new mission. I've built a fee for service practice that I love. I have noticed that when I made the shift from "helping people" to "making money," my business goals changed but I did not give up doing what I enjoy or helping people. I am much more focused and the quality of my services has improved. (p. 64)

If it is difficult for clinicians to reconcile conflicts about the financial aspects of practice, we suggest that they seek out supervision or mentoring from a senior clinician to help them with this issue.

Through informal inquiries or by consulting salary surveys the clinician arrives at dollar amounts that the average clinician in the local area charges for services. However, this is group data and the question still remains, "What should I charge for *my* services?" Our answer is "as much as you can and still maintain a business." In many ways the fees that you set are educated guesses. You can set them and always evaluate whether they are optimal for you. For example, you could set your fees at $25 per session and likely garner a lot of business quickly. However, would this be enough to pay all of your overhead and still leave you enough of a profit? The answer is, likely not. However, you can set your fee at $300 per session. Because few people could afford this amount, you would likely not attract many clients. Unfortunately, there is no sage advice as to what fee you should set. Martin-Causey (2005) described the process that she went through:

> I started to get an idea of the range of fees people were charging. It appeared that the established psychologists who had a good reputation in the community charged more per session than some others. I decided that I would set my rates near the upper end. I told myself that I was very good and should charge as if I was one of the best. However, I didn't go as high as a few in the community that I really respected. I didn't see myself as that good. (p. 61)

In general, psychologists charge a higher rate than do providers at the master's level. There is no rhyme or reason to this except that lore has it that those with more education should be expected to charge at a higher rate. However, there is no reason that an LCSW in private practice should charge more, less, or the same as a PhD or PsyD in private practice for delivering the same service. Some of the most talented clinicians we have known have been LCSWs.

Private Practice Principle Number 12: Clinicians should charge fees that the market will bear. To charge less does not make good business sense. To charge more does not make good business sense.

Think of it this way. If you charge $75 per session, do you really think people would not come to see you if you charged $80 per session? The additional $5 is not likely to make or break whether or not a particular client sees you. There is a 6.25% difference between these two figures, and over the course of a year this amount can add up to a significant amount of money. Imagine that you see 20 clients per week for 48 weeks each year. At $75 per session the gross monies collected would be $72,000. At $80 per session the gross monies collected would be $76,800—a $4,800 difference. If this figure were $90, the amount collected would jump to $86,400—$14,400 more than if the fee charged were $75. As noted earlier, there is likely an upper limit to what you could charge (or, in business terms, what the market will bear), but why would you want to sell yourself short and not earn an optimal amount of money?

SLIDING FEE SCALE

An often asked question on Internet discussion lists is "Should I have a sliding fee scale?" For a variety of reasons clients may not have the ability to pay for psychotherapy on a regular basis. A true sliding fee scale that is used in public mental health agencies bases fees on ability to pay. The fee determination takes into account income and family size. To apply such a sliding fee scale to a psychotherapy practice would result in nothing short of chaos as you try to compute fees for each of your clients. Rather, we believe that on a case-by-case basis private practitioners would do well to accept a certain number of low-fee clients into their practice. Martin-Causey (2005) devoted 10% to 20% of her available psychotherapy sessions to low-fee clients. She capped it so as not to place the financial viability of her practice at risk. Both of us have always had the policy of seeing someone who called our office for services regardless of ability to pay. In these cases we have negotiated a fee that both we and the client felt was reasonable and affordable. In more than 25 years of practice we can count on less than two hands the number of times that we could not negotiate a fee that we and our clients could live with in the situation. On one of these occasions Steve Walfish wanted a schoolteacher who made $25,000 per year to pay a fee of $25 per session, but she felt she could not afford this amount. He then suggested she contact a university training clinic to pursue therapy services in that setting. Both of us have at times feared that such a policy would result in being inundated with low-fee clients. However, this feared situation has never materialized.

FEES FOR PSYCHOLOGICAL TESTING

As noted earlier, Norcross, Karpiak, and Santoro (2005) found that 72% of psychologists in private practice engage in activities related to diagnosis and assessment. There are two models of billing for psychological testing. We do not advocate one over the other. The first is to charge by the hour. The psychologist must add up all the time involved in administering and scoring tests, interviewing the client (and parents and teachers in the case of child assessment), writing the report, and having a feedback session. Then, to determine the fee, the psychologist would multiply his or her standard hourly fee by the number of hours spent on the case. The second method is to charge a flat fee for the completion of the evaluation. The fee would be the same whether it takes 5 hours or 10 hours to complete the evaluation.

Another issue to consider in deciding what to charge for psychological testing is the concept of time versus expertise. Having administered more than 4,000 Minnesota Multiphasic Personality Inventories, Steve Walfish usually takes less than 5 minutes to interpret and dictate an interpretation. Let us imagine that Steve charges $150 per hour for his services. If the time formula is used, he would be reimbursed $12.50 for this component of the evaluation. This compensation hardly seems appropriate (at least to him it doesn't!) for having the ability to competently interpret a psychological test. Consider a parallel situation in medicine: when a radiologist reads and interprets an X-ray. Radiologists are compensated for their ability to do so and not for how long it takes them to do so. In addition, the radiologists take responsibility for the correctness of the interpretation. This responsibility should be accompanied by compensation for the time and energy it took to become expert in this specialty. The same is true for psychologists when interpreting psychological tests. An old story regarding a similar issue with attorneys goes something like the following:

> A man has a problem with the criminal justice system because of a law that he may have inadvertently broken. He goes to an attorney and asks for her help. She listens to his story, goes over to her bookshelf, and pulls out one of her case law books and reviews it for a minute. She smiles and says, "There is good news. According to statutes you will not be responsible for this and you are not in any trouble." The man smiles until she says, "That will be $500 for my services." The man is shocked and he says, "We talk for five minutes, you look in a book for 30 seconds, and I owe you $500?" She replies, "Yes, because I knew which book to look in."

The same is true for psychologists. They know how to interpret personality tests, detect patterns on the Wechsler Intelligence Scale for Children— Fourth Edition and Woodcock-Johnson Tests of Achievement that may be indicative of a learning disability, and determine whether someone likely is malingering in a criminal or civil case. This skill set deserves compensation if someone is willing to purchase this expertise. It is up to each psychologist to determine what the compensation should be for providing these services.

FORENSIC SERVICES

Court-related services by definition are not reimbursable by a health insurance policy. Health insurance is used to pay for treatment of medical disorders and not court-related services. For those being referred forensic cases, Hess (2005) offered excellent advice related to ethics and the setting and collection of fees. Clinicians typically have a separate fee schedule for court-related work. This fee is subjectively set by each individual clinician. Forensic work can require a specialty skill, can be disruptive to a clinical practice if depositions or court appearances are required, and is subject to a scrutiny that is not typically associated with conducting psychotherapy in the confines of one's office. We have heard the higher fees for forensic work referred to as "combat pay" or a bonus for working under stressful conditions. One forensic specialty area in which psychologists are more often sued for malpractice is child custody work. It is almost inevitable that clinicians working in this area will be sued for malpractice because typically one parent is unhappy with the results of the case. In addition, in court and during deposition, MHPs occasionally have to tolerate rude behavior on the part of attorneys trying to cross-examine and discredit them.

Mart (2006) wrote an excellent book on starting a forensic mental health practice that we highly recommend for those MHPs considering forensic work. For court work most professionals bill for all of their time, including direct service time with the client, reviewing of records, relevant research, phone consultations with attorneys, report writing, and travel to and from the office to court or a deposition. Attorneys charge for such services. They should expect MHPs to do the same. Clinicians should prepare a letter of understanding with an attorney regarding the fees being charged. One excellent form titled "Terms of Engagement Contract" may be found in Blau and Alberts (2004). Many cases get settled at the last minute or are postponed. However, the MHP will have cleared his or her calendar (at the attorney's request), so this agreement should also include a cancellation policy.

CHARGING FOR OTHER SERVICES

Psychotherapists become involved in professional activities other than providing psychotherapy or assessment. Examples of such activities might include teaching a class in the community, consulting to a community agency, writing a chapter for a book, or supervising new clinicians for licensure. These are also examples of income-generating activities for private practitioners for which there is no set fee schedule. It is up to clinicians to determine for themselves what to charge for sharing their expertise in these ways. These activities provide an alternative to doing direct service work and we have found them to be invigorating, intellectually stimulating, and useful in preventing burnout. That they provide additional income and enhance your credibility in the community and profession is a bonus.

Both of us have contributed chapters to edited books and have been typically paid a few hundred dollars as an honorarium for doing so. This is not very much money for the amount of work involved but we do it because we find it enjoyable and believe it enhances our professional reputations. On a recent Internet discussion list Steve Walfish learned of a psychologist who contributed a module to a workbook to be used by a for-profit company. She asked for and was paid $2,500 for doing so, and Steve could only admire her ability to be paid so handsomely for her work.

Jeff Barnett engages in a wide range of compensated activities in addition to his psychotherapy and assessment practice. First, he teaches 1 day each week in the graduate programs of a local college. This position provides a salary as well as full health and retirement benefits. He also regularly provides continuing education workshops, an online licensure review course in his state, and online continuing education courses that require little additional work after the content is placed online. He provides clinical supervision and consultation to colleagues, ethics tutorials for MHPs referred by their licensure boards, and expert witness testimony in administrative law and licensure board hearings for MHPs. He also is an associate editor for an American Psychological Association journal. Each position and activity provides him with income beyond the revenues he generates in his practice.

When psychotherapists are asked to speak to for-profit groups, conduct workshops or seminars in their area of expertise, or consult to a business about a particular problem, the organizations may have a set fee in mind and then it is up to the clinician to decide whether the fee offered is acceptable. If it is not acceptable, then the clinician can attempt to negotiate (e.g., "my usual fee for consulting is . . .") and the organization can decide whether it wants to pay that amount.

> **Private Practice Principle Number 13:** Private practitioners need to become comfortable negotiating from a position of strength. If you are desperate for the job or income, you will negotiate from a position of weakness. Strength is found in the ability to say "No, thank you" and walk away.

A colleague was asked to travel from his home in Florida to conduct a workshop for a school system in New York. He didn't really want to do it, but he wanted to maintain an open relationship with the organization. So he asked for double his usual consulting fee, thinking he would be told, "Thanks, but that amount is not in the budget." Much to his surprise the organization said yes to what he thought was an outrageous fee. He was then happy to go to New York to do the workshop. This is an example of negotiating from strength. Early career professionals who are just building their practice may feel desperate to fill their hours. Some of this attitude is reasonable because $50 per hour is much better than $0 per hour if there is not another concurrent income source. However, as one's practice solidifies we recommend replacing negotiating from a position of weakness with negotiating from a position of strength.

RAISING FEES

Of course, you need to raise your fees periodically because expenses increase over time. You may also raise fees when you develop new areas of expertise. Although it is easy to raise fees periodically with new clients, for ongoing clients it may feel uncomfortable to tell them that their fee will increase by X amount next month. It may be better to just include in your informed consent agreement that on January 1 of each year your fee will increase by 10% (or some other amount). Letting clients know of this increase in advance is consistent with the requirements of Standard 6.04, Fees and Financial Arrangements, of the American Psychological Association's "Ethical Principles of Psychologists and Code of Conduct" (2002). This standard requires psychologists to "reach an agreement specifying compensation and billing arrangements . . . as early as is feasible in a professional or scientific relationship" (p. 1,068). Furthermore, clinicians need to be sensitive to each client's financial situation and consider it in all decisions regarding increasing fees. These standards are consistent with standards from the ethics codes of other mental health professions including social workers and counselors. All MHPs have the ethical obligation to appropriately attend to these issues.

Collecting Fees

There are two models for the collection of fees. The first model is "pay as you go." The second is to accept a client's insurance and to bill the insurance company on behalf of the client. In the pay-as-you-go model clients meet their total financial responsibility at the time of the session or are billed monthly for the full fees charged. Thus, if the fee for psychotherapy is $100, they pay this amount by cash, check, or credit card or debit card before leaving the office. If the clinician is not a member of their PPO or MCO, clients may be interested in submitting a claim to their insurer to be reimbursed for all or part of the fee paid for the ser-vices. In these cases clinicians may present clients with a super bill that they in turn may submit to their carrier. A sample super bill is presented in Exhibit 6.3. The basic information includes the client's name, diagnosis, date of service, service activity (CPT code), amount billed for the service, name of the clinician, and the clinician's tax identification number. Many practices have these super bills preprinted with all possible CPT service codes and then simply check off the appropriate codes and fill in the amount charged. Computerized billing programs can generate a super bill for a client once the data for the session have been entered into the system. An alternative is to develop a general template of a super bill on a word processing program. The clinician may then simply change the name, date, and diagnosis for the individual client for whom the bill is being generated.

In the second model the clinician accepts the client's insurance and at the time of service collects only appropriate deductibles and copays. After the session is completed the clinician completes a standard health insurance claim form titled CMS-1500. These forms may be purchased at any large office supply store or through companies online (a search on the term *CMS-1500* yields multiple purchase options). After these are submitted the clinician will then receive a check from the insurance carrier, typically 2 to 6 weeks later. In theory, if (a) the client has paid the deductible and appropriate copay and (b) the insurance has paid the appropriate portion, then the balance due for the service provided should

EXHIBIT 6.3

Sample Super Bill

Jane Q. Public, PhD
Licensed Psychologist No. 1234
2040 84th Street
Brooklyn, NY 11214
(212) 373-2437

March 12, 2007

Name of Patient:	James Smith
Diagnosis:	300.02 (Generalized Anxiety Disorder)

Date of Service	CPT Code	Units	Fee
3-12-07	90806 (Psychotherapy)	1	$100.00

Total Amount Billed:	$100.00

Consulting Psychologist:	Jane Q. Public, PhD
Tax ID Number:	012344567

---

be zero. If this is not the case, the clinician then has to bill the client for the remaining balance due. The clinician may do this by sending out a statement or by prearranging with the client that any balances not paid will be charged to his or her credit card.

> **Private Practice Principle Number 14:** Clients often misunderstand their insurance benefits. As part of the informed consent process clinicians should have procedures in place to clarify this issue.

One frequent misconception that clients have is their belief that their insurance company is responsible for paying for all their health care services. This is not the case. The client is responsible for payment of his or her health care services. A third party (e.g., an insurance company) may pay for these services on the client's behalf. The contract for payment of services, however, is between the client and clinician. We recommend that clients be presented with a written description of the billing and collection process as part of the informed consent process. In addition, this description should be reviewed with the client and any misunderstandings clarified at the outset. Clients should then sign this written agreement and be provided with a copy for their records.

CLIENTS WHO FEEL ENTITLED

The number one reason for bankruptcy in the United States is unpaid medical bills. As an MHP you may think of medical bills as being only for hospital services, medication costs, expensive imaging tests, or physician visits. However, to clients your services are lumped into the general category of health care costs, and a small percentage of the population does not feel obligated to pay for their health care. This is reflected in the attitude expressed by the following statement: "They're rich doctors. They drive fancy cars and live in big houses. It's a hardship for me to pay them the $300 that I owe them and they're so rich they won't miss it." MHPs are not immune from being the victims of such attitudes, and the result will be nonpayment of fees by these individuals. Policies and procedures can be put into place to minimize the extent of losses resulting from this nonpayment of fees earned. However, private practitioners have to be aware that when they are delivering a service there is a chance they will never see payment from these "entitled clients."

Getting Paid by Insurance Carriers

Clients purchase or are provided health insurance benefits through a third party. However, simply having an insurance card does not guarantee the private practitioner will be paid for providing services to his or her clients. Health insurance has a language all its own, as well as policies and procedures that must be followed for reimbursement to take place.

> **Private Practice Principle Number 15:** Although not to the point of having a disorder, it is helpful to have some obsessive–compulsive tendencies when dealing with insurance companies and collecting payments from clients.

Although we have no documented proof, it is our hypothesis that insurance companies factor in clinician error when calculating their profit margins. We can think of no other reason to justify denial of claims for not following certain procedures within a certain time frame. For example, some companies have a policy that claims must be submitted within 60 days of the date of service. If submitted on day 61, the claim will be denied. Even if the service is medically necessary, if preauthorization is required and not obtained, the claim will be denied. It is important to remember that if clinicians choose to accept their client's insurance in their practice, they do not make the rules about policies and procedures. All provider agreement contracts with PPOs or MCOs are written to be corporation-friendly, not clinician-friendly. In this regard it is important to understand three important parts of the reimbursement process: verifying benefits, obtaining authorization, and submitting a claim for payment. Each has specific steps that must be followed. If any are missed, payment may be delayed or denied.

VERIFYING BENEFITS

This step in the process can be approached by the clinician in various ways. Some take it on themselves (possibly through office staff or an outside billing agency) to verify that clients' overall benefits are in effect, whether they have mental benefits to begin with, and the nature and extent of these benefits. Many insurance carriers now provide benefits information on the Internet for clinicians who have contracted to be providers for their company. Other clinicians leave this responsibility to the client. However, if clinicians delegate this task to the client they should be aware that clients sometimes make mistakes. However, it will be the clinicians who will not get paid for the service provided. For example, some benefit plans indicate that authorization for services must be obtained from a managed care company before any services are delivered. If the client misses this piece of information when the claim form is submitted, the explanation of benefits (EOB) will indicate payment is denied because of lack of authorization. The EOB will further indicate that the client balance due for this session is $0.00 because care was not preauthorized. If weekly sessions are taking place, because of the submission–payment time frame, sometime between the fourth and sixth session the clinician will learn that he or she has just provided four to six sessions free. By contract, the clinician cannot ask the client to pay for services that have not been authorized.

When calling an insurance company to verify benefits, clinicians need to know a few pieces of information about each client. Without them, benefits information will not be provided to the clinician. Most (although not all) of this information is provided on the client's health insurance card and includes (a) name of client (with exact spelling); (b) name of the insured, if different; (c) relationship between insured and subscriber; (d) client's date of birth; (e) subscriber or member identification number; and (f) name of the employer and employer's group identification number.

The insurance company will likely also verify your name and tax identification number and address for your practice. When obtaining information from the client, be sure to obtain the following information: (a) name of the insurance company, (b) whether it is a health management organization or PPO, and (c) telephone number for customer service to verify benefits. Some insurance cards indicate only one central number (usually toll free) to call related to benefits or claims. Other cards have multiple numbers. In these cases it is not unusual for there to be a specific number to call for mental health or substance abuse services.

If so, call this number, which likely will connect you to the MCO the carrier has contracted with to provide services.

Many companies have developed an automated touch-tone telephone system to verify benefits. Such a system is able to confirm if coverage is in effect, when the benefits started, if the deductible has been met, and possibly the copay due per session (MHPs are paid under the category of "specialists" for copays). However, it may not provide information regarding mental health coverage. One then has to follow the prompts to speak to a customer service representative to obtain this specific information.

Related to mental health services the following information must be obtained: (a) whether preauthorization for services is required, (b) number of sessions allowed per calendar year, (c) how many sessions have been used thus far this calendar year, (d) whether there is a separate deductible for mental health services, (e) the percentage copay that is due for services, and (f) whether there is a lifetime maximum amount allowed for mental health services. There is a movement for parity laws to be passed at both the state and federal levels. Insurers traditionally could write benefits packages whereby the benefits provided for physical health treatment were treated differently than were the benefits for mental health treatment. Many policies include a separate deductible for mental health treatment, a higher copay, annual session limits, and lifetime benefits paid for a specific disorder. The passage of parity legislation across the board would eliminate such discrimination.

Insurance companies offer benefits packages to employers and business owners, and it is up to them to decide which benefits they want to offer to their employees. Therefore, it is important to know that just because one client has a certain insurance carrier does not mean another client with the same carrier has the same benefits package. That is, a BlueCross plan at Company X may have no mental health benefits, a BlueCross plan at Company Y may have limited mental health benefits, and a BlueCross plan at Company Z may have full mental health benefits with no limitations. Within large companies employees often have a choice of insurance packages. Therefore, the benefits for employees within the same company may be different.

It should be pointed out that a "verification of benefits" is not actually a verification of benefits. Customer service representatives will tell you the best information available as to whether or not a subscriber is enrolled and the benefits of the plan. However, the representative always provides a disclaimer. It differs by insurance company but essentially the message goes something like the following: "The benefits that we quote you are not a final determination of benefits. A final determination will be made when a claim is submitted for review." A written authorization of benefits from an unnamed managed care company reads as follows: "Payment for services described in this letter is subject to the member's eligibility at the time services are provided, benefit plan limitations, and availability of remaining coverage."

So you may be told (verbally or in writing, or both) that a client has benefits and that 80% of usual and customary charges will be paid. However, this may not be the case. It is rare, but it does happen (thus the caveat) that the customer service representative makes a mistake in quoting benefits or the employee is not actually enrolled in the plan. The employee may have lost benefits or switched plans and the insurance carrier was not immediately made aware of the change. Often the employee will remain on the list of insured for a while after his or her coverage has expired.

COMPLETING A HEALTH INSURANCE CLAIM FORM CMS-1500

Correctly filling out a health insurance form is not rocket science. However, it does require an understanding of the information being requested (especially the codes) and the ability to pay attention to detail. Figure 6.1 presents a correctly completed claim form to be submitted to an insurance carrier for reimbursement. What follows in the subsequent paragraphs are the steps necessary to complete the 33 boxes on this form.

Box 1—Insurer

This box identifies the name of the insurance carrier. Check the appropriate box. Unless one has a large Medicare or Medicaid practice, most times the box that will be checked is "Other."

Box 1a—Insured's ID Number

Each person has a unique ID number. It may be a Social Security Number or, because many companies are now trying to enhance privacy protection, a different number. It appears on most insurance cards as either a member number or a subscriber number. It may be totally numeric or it may be alphanumeric.

Box 2—Patient's Name

Last name, then first name, and then middle initial.

Box 3—Patient's Birth Date and Sex

Enter the date of birth of the client and not the subscriber. Indicate whether the client is male or female.

FIGURE 6.1

1500

HEALTH INSURANCE CLAIM FORM

APPROVED BY NATIONAL UNIFORM CLAIM COMMITTEE 08/05

PICA

| | | | | | | | PICA |

1. MEDICARE (Medicare #) — MEDICAID (Medicaid #) — TRICARE CHAMPUS (Sponsor's SSN) — CHAMPVA (Member ID#) — GROUP HEALTH PLAN (SSN or ID) — FECA BLK LUNG (SSN) — OTHER (ID)

1a. INSURED'S I.D. NUMBER (For Program in Item 1): **24683579**

2. PATIENT'S NAME (Last Name, First Name, Middle Initial): **Public, John Q.**

3. PATIENT'S BIRTH DATE: **11 14 68** — SEX: M **X** F

4. INSURED'S NAME (Last Name, First Name, Middle Initial): **Public, John Q.**

5. PATIENT'S ADDRESS (No., Street): **888 Eighth Street**

CITY: **Atlanta** — STATE: **GA**

6. PATIENT RELATIONSHIP TO INSURED: Self **X** Spouse Child Other

7. INSURED'S ADDRESS (No., Street): **888 Eighth Street**

CITY: **Atlanta** — STATE: **GA**

ZIP CODE: **30306** — TELEPHONE (Include Area Code): ( )

8. PATIENT STATUS: Single Married **X** Other / Employed Full-Time Student **X** Part-Time Student

ZIP CODE: **30306** — TELEPHONE (Include Area Code): ( )

9. OTHER INSURED'S NAME (Last Name, First Name, Middle Initial):

10. IS PATIENT'S CONDITION RELATED TO:

11. INSURED'S POLICY GROUP OR FECA NUMBER: **4396A**

a. OTHER INSURED'S POLICY OR GROUP NUMBER:

a. EMPLOYMENT? (Current or Previous): YES NO **X**

a. INSURED'S DATE OF BIRTH: **11 14 68** — SEX: M **X** F

b. OTHER INSURED'S DATE OF BIRTH: MM DD YY — SEX: M F

b. AUTO ACCIDENT? YES NO **X** — PLACE (State)

b. EMPLOYER'S NAME OR SCHOOL NAME: **Georgia State University**

c. EMPLOYER'S NAME OR SCHOOL NAME:

c. OTHER ACCIDENT? YES NO **X**

c. INSURANCE PLAN NAME OR PROGRAM NAME: **Blue Cross PPO**

d. INSURANCE PLAN NAME OR PROGRAM NAME:

10d. RESERVED FOR LOCAL USE:

d. IS THERE ANOTHER HEALTH BENEFIT PLAN? YES NO **X** — If yes, return to and complete item 9 a-d.

READ BACK OF FORM BEFORE COMPLETING & SIGNING THIS FORM.

12. PATIENT'S OR AUTHORIZED PERSON'S SIGNATURE I authorize the release of any medical or other information necessary to process this claim. I also request payment of government benefits either to myself or to the party who accepts assignment below.

SIGNED **Signature on File** — DATE **6/22/07**

13. INSURED'S OR AUTHORIZED PERSON'S SIGNATURE I authorize payment of medical benefits to the undersigned physician or supplier for services described below.

SIGNED **Signature on File**

14. DATE OF CURRENT: ILLNESS (First symptom) OR INJURY (Accident) OR PREGNANCY (LMP): **06 22 07**

15. IF PATIENT HAS HAD SAME OR SIMILAR ILLNESS. GIVE FIRST DATE MM DD YY

16. DATES PATIENT UNABLE TO WORK IN CURRENT OCCUPATION: FROM TO

17. NAME OF REFERRING PROVIDER OR OTHER SOURCE: **Jane Doe, MD**

17a. / 17b. NPI

18. HOSPITALIZATION DATES RELATED TO CURRENT SERVICES: FROM TO

19. RESERVED FOR LOCAL USE

20. OUTSIDE LAB? YES NO **X** — $ CHARGES

21. DIAGNOSIS OR NATURE OF ILLNESS OR INJURY (Relate Items 1, 2, 3 or 4 to Item 24E by Line)

1. **300.02** — 3.

2. — 4.

22. MEDICAID RESUBMISSION CODE — ORIGINAL REF. NO.

23. PRIOR AUTHORIZATION NUMBER

24.
A. DATE(S) OF SERVICE From / To	B. PLACE OF SERVICE	C. EMG	D. PROCEDURES, SERVICES, OR SUPPLIES (Explain Unusual Circumstances) CPT/HCPCS / MODIFIER	E. DIAGNOSIS POINTER	F. $ CHARGES	G. DAYS OR UNITS	H. EPSDT Family Plan	I. ID. QUAL.	J. RENDERING PROVIDER ID. #
1	07 13 07 07 13 07	11		90806	1	140 00	1		NPI	1111122222
2	07 20 07 07 20 07	11		90806	1	140 00	1		NPI	1111122222
3									NPI	
4									NPI	
5									NPI	
6									NPI	

25. FEDERAL TAX I.D. NUMBER: **000000001** — SSN EIN **X**

26. PATIENT'S ACCOUNT NO.

27. ACCEPT ASSIGNMENT? (For govt. claims, see back) YES **X** NO

28. TOTAL CHARGE: $ **280 00**

29. AMOUNT PAID: $ **0 00**

30. BALANCE DUE: $ **280.00**

31. SIGNATURE OF PHYSICIAN OR SUPPLIER INCLUDING DEGREES OR CREDENTIALS (I certify that the statements on the reverse apply to this bill and are made a part thereof.) **STEVEN WALFISH, PHD** — SIGNED — DATE **7/20/07**

32. SERVICE FACILITY LOCATION INFORMATION — a. NPI b.

33. BILLING PROVIDER INFO & PH # **(404) 728-0728** — **Steven Walfish, Ph.D.** **2004 Cliff Valley Way, Suite 101** **Atlanta, GA 30329** — a. NPI b.

NUCC Instruction Manual available at: www.nucc.org

APPROVED OMB-0938-0999 FORM CMS-1500 (08/05)

Sample form CMS-1500

Box 4—Insured's Name

Enter the name of the person whose name appears on the insurance card. It may be the client or it may be a spouse or other family member (e.g., parent) or a domestic partner.

Box 5—Patient's Address

Enter the client's address that is on file with the insurance carrier.

Box 6—Patient's Relationship to Insured

Check the appropriate box.

Box 7—Insured's Address

Complete this box if the insured's address is different from the address of the client.

Box 8—Patient Status

Check the appropriate boxes for both marital status and employment or student status.

Box 9—Other Insured's Name

Some people are covered by two insurance policies. Leave this blank if there is no secondary insurance plan. If there is a secondary insurance plan, fill in this box as well as the corresponding information in Boxes 9–9d.

Box 10—Is Patient's Condition Related To:

Check the appropriate box. If the condition is related to an employment injury, the client's workers' compensation insurance may be the appropriate payor for the service. If work stress is the reason for the treatment, do not check the Employment box. This box is only for treatment related to a workers' compensation claim. If the condition is related to a motor vehicle accident, the client's or the other driver's personal injury protection policy purchased with automobile insurance may be the appropriate payor for the service.

Box 11—Insured's Policy Group or FECA Number

Each employer has a unique identifier and once again this appears on most insurance cards. If there is no number, leave this blank.

Box 11a—Insured's Date of Birth

This is typically left blank.

Box 11b—Employer's Name or School Name

Enter the name of the employer or school. If there is no employer, as may be the case in individual plan, leave this blank.

Box 11c—Insurance Plan Name or Program Name

List the name of the insurance plan as found on the insurance card. Examples are BlueCross BlueShield of Washington PPO or CIGNA HMO.

Box 11d—Is There Another Health Benefit Plan?

Check the appropriate box. If the answer is yes, Boxes 9–9d must also be completed.

Box 12—Patient's or Authorized Person's Signature

This signature allows the insurance carrier to obtain any information from the mental health professional that may be necessary to process the claim, including the client's personal health information. In our experience this information is rarely requested. However, the insurance company wants to retain the right to obtain this information to ensure that services are being delivered and are medically necessary. Most private practitioners as part of their disclosure papers have clients agree to release this information. Without such an agreement by the client the insurance carrier may refuse to pay on claims. Rather than the client signing this box, usually "Signature on File" and the date this agreement was signed by the client are entered here.

Box 13—Insured's or Authorized Person's Signature

This signature allows the insurance company to pay the provider directly. This agreement is also usually included in the clinician's disclosure materials. If this box is not signed the insurance carrier will send a check to the client rather than to the clinician. This box is also usually filled in with "Signature on File."

Box 14—Date of Current Illness

Enter the first date of service provided by the clinician to the client.

Box 15—If Patient Has Had Same or Similar Illness, Give Date

This box inquires about previous episodes of the same condition the client may have experienced. This box is typically left blank.

Box 16—Dates Patient Unable to Work in Current Occupation

This box is typically left blank. This information may be relevant in workers' compensation or disability cases.

Box 17—Name of Referring Provider or Other Source

If a physician referred the client for services, the physician's name is written here. In most cases this information does not matter. In some cases in which a health maintenance organization is involved or a specific referral was made by a physician related to a client's medical condition, the insurance company may need to match up your name with the referral.

Box 18—Hospitalization Dates Related to Current Services

This box is completed if the services were completed in a hospital setting.

Box 19—Reserved for Local Use

Leave blank.

Box 20—Outside Lab?

Leave blank.

Box 21—Diagnosis or Nature of Illness or Injury

Enter the four- or five-digit *Diagnostic and Statistical Manual of Mental Disorders, Fourth Edition* (*DSM–IV*; American Psychiatric Association, 1994) diagnosis. When coding, be sure to include all digits possible in the diagnosis. For example, many insurance companies will return the claim if the diagnosis is presented as 296.3 (Major Depression, Recurrent) as they will consider this number incomplete. This particular diagnosis must have a fifth digit as a descriptor. The diagnosis code number 296.32 (Major Depression, Recurrent, Moderate Severity) would be processed correctly. Only one Axis I diagnosis is typically listed in this box, though there is room to list as many as four diagnoses. There is really no reason to list more than one diagnosis in the box.

All claims need a diagnosis to be processed through the client's medical insurance. If there is no medical illness then the plan will not see the need to reimburse for the service provided. As such, for clients entering psychotherapy for personal growth reasons, who have no accompanying diagnosis such as a mood disorder or anxiety disorder, their insurance is not likely to contribute to the costs of therapy. Also, listed in the *DSM–IV* are V codes, which are not typically considered covered under most insurance plans. For example, Partner Relational Problem (V61.1) and Parent–Child Relational Problem (V61.20) are frequent reasons why clients seek out the services of a mental health professional. However, if there is no accompanying Axis I diagnosis then the insurance carrier is likely to deem these diagnoses as not covered. The same is often true for school and educational diagnoses (e.g., learning disabilities). It is important for clients to verify ahead of time whether these services are covered diagnoses on their plans. Most insurance companies will not have marital therapy as a covered service when the diagnosis is partner relational problem. They may allow conjoint therapy when one partner has an Axis I diagnosis (e.g., major depression) and the best way to treat this problem is with the client's partner present. Before doing so either the clinician or client should obtain permission from the insurer or managed care organization (MCO) for doing so (and document the permission). However, the clinician has to be very careful here for two reasons. First, if the clinician uses a different diagnosis than the one that actually suits the situation just so insurance will cover the service, this action is likely to be viewed as insurance fraud. Take the example of a clinician who is doing couples therapy to improve an otherwise healthy couple's communication and problem-solving ability or enhance their sexual enjoyment together. Instead of submitting a diagnosis of partner relational problem the clinician may submit a diagnosis of major depression or adjustment disorder with anxious mood as these are Axis I diagnoses for one partner. Of course one would ask why a clinician would do such a thing. Motivators could include pressure from the clients to have their insurance cover the couple's treatment so they do not have to pay out-of-pocket or a clinician wanting to help out the client because he or she believes that insurance should cover couples therapy. Research completed by Kielbasa, Pomerantz, Krohn, and Sullivan (2004) and by Pomerantz and Segrist (2006) found that the diagnostic label a client receives can be related to the source of funding of psychotherapy (self-pay vs. managed care). In an early study Sharfstein, Towery, and Milowe (1980) found insurance claim forms to often contain inaccurate diagnoses, primarily because of concerns about client confidentiality. Second, in couples psychotherapy the general philosophy is that there is no particular identified patient. Rather, the couple is the unit for treatment. To then label one person as having major depression or an adjustment disorder goes against this philosophy. In addition, the person who receives this "misdiagnosis" then has a mental health diagnosis that will follow him or her on his or her record. In some cases this diagnosis may preclude this person from some types of insurance coverage (e.g., life insurance) or a security clearance at some point in the future.

Box 22—Medicaid Resubmission

This box is generally left blank unless there is a special situation with a Medicaid claim.

Box 23—Prior Authorization Number

With some insurers and MCOs, authorization for treatment is obtained before the first session. Each authorization is signified with a code number and may be entered here. However, we have always left this box blank and it has never resulted in a reimbursement problem.

Box 24A—Date(s) of Service

There are two dates to be listed and most often they are the same date for each line. For example, if the date of service was July 13, 2007, then the "From" date should be listed as 07/13/07 and the "To" date should also be listed as 07/13/07.

Box 24B—Place of Service

Enter where the service took place: in your office, a hospital setting, a skilled nursing facility, or a host of other places (the computer billing program Therapist Helper has 36 possible places where services may be rendered including the catch-all "other locations"). Each location carries a code (either numbers or letters) that is to be placed in this box. The most common codes for private practitioners are 11 (office), 51 (inpatient psychiatric facility), 55 (nursing home), and NH (residential substance abuse treatment facility).

Box 24C—EMG

Leave blank.

Box 24D—Procedures, Services, or Supplies: CPT/HCPCS and Modifier

The CPT code describes the type of service delivered to the client. The most common codes used by mental health professionals are 90801 (initial interview), 90806 (45–50 minutes of psychotherapy), 90847 (family psychotherapy), and 96101 (psychological testing with report). The complete list of CPT codes is presented in Exhibit 6.1 (p. 116). Leave the "Modifier" box blank.

Box 24E—Diagnosis Pointer

This information allows the insurance company to know for which diagnosis you are providing the service on that date. If there is only one diagnosis (usually the case), place the number 1 in this box. If more than one diagnosis is listed, then the number in this box should reflect the number of diagnoses listed in Box 21.

Box 24F—S Charges

S charges refers to your usual and customary charge for the service delivered. It does not reflect any discounted charges you may have contractually agreed to with a preferred provider organization or MCO. For example, if your usual and customary charge for one unit of 90806 (45–50 minutes of psychotherapy) is $100 and you know the MCO this client belongs to has a contracted rate of $80 per session, enter $100 in this box. When processing the claim, the insurer will make the appropriate adjustment.

Box 24G—Days or Units

Enter the number of hours the service took to provide. One hour equals one unit in this box; 1 is the most frequent number placed in this box. Some exceptions may be for psychological testing with report, which may involve more than one unit. Some behavioral assessment codes are reimbursed in 15-minute intervals. Thus 1 hour of time may need to be coded as four units. We suggest that you check with the company that you are billing for clarification on this issue.

24H, 24I, and 24J—EPSDT Family Plan, ID Qual, Rendering Provider ID

Leave blank.

Box 25—Federal Tax ID Number

This number identifies your business to the Internal Revenue Service (IRS). This is either your Social Security Number or your Employer Identification Number (EIN). Use the one that the insurance company holds on file associated with your name. Most solo practitioners who are not incorporated use their Social Security Number as their tax ID number. If you are a sole practitioner and prefer not to use your Social Security Number as your tax ID number, you will have to obtain an EIN. This number is used by the IRS to identify a business entity. You have to obtain an EIN if you are a corporate entity and cannot use your Social Security Number as a tax ID number. Instructions for obtaining an EIN may be found on the IRS Web site (http://www.irs.gov/businesses/small/article/0,,id=97860,00.html). An EIN is easy to obtain and may be applied for by telephone, fax, or mail or online. There is no fee to obtain an EIN.

Box 26—Patient's Account Number

If you do computerized billing, each client will be assigned a unique account number. It will automatically be added to the form when it is printed or electronically mailed. This number is not essential to include.

Box 27—Accept Assignment?

This box is related only to government-managed insurance plans. If you have agreed to be a provider for these entities (e.g., Medicare, Medicaid) then you have to check the box marked "Yes." This means that you agree to their fee schedule and you will be mailed a check. If you have not agreed to be a provider for these entities you can check the "No" box. However, if you do not accept assignment the insurance company may mail the check to the client instead of you and it will then be up to the client to pay you.

Box 28—Total Charge

Add up the charges entered in Box 24F. Each time an insurance claim is submitted for reimbursement, it may reflect one date of service or multiple dates of service (up to six per claim). Some clinicians submit claims weekly so likely only one session will be placed on the claim form. Some clinicians submit claims only once per month, preferring to receive a check for a larger amount reflecting payment for three or four sessions rather than receiving three or four checks for smaller amounts.

Box 29—Amount Paid

Enter the amount received from the client at the time services are delivered. This amount will be for the client's copay or any amount that is due toward his or her deductible.

Box 30—Balance Due

This is the difference between Box 28 and Box 29. For example, if the amount charged in Box 28 was $100 and the copay received in Box 29 was $20, the amount to be placed in Box 30 is $80.

Box 31—Signature of Physician or Supplier Including Degrees or Credentials

Sign and date this form.

Box 32—Service Facility Location Information

Fill this in if the place of service in Box 24B is other than the clinician's office. For example, if the service was delivered at the inpatient psychiatric unit of Northside Hospital, then this hospital would be listed along with its address.

Box 33—Billing Provider Information and Phone Number

List your contact information here. Use the information on file with the insurance carrier. Please note that if the tax ID number the insurer has for the clinician does not match up with the address on file, then the insurer may return the claim unpaid. Computerized billing systems such as Therapist Helper also place the National Provider Identifier (NPI) below the address in this box.

At the bottom of the form there is room for the clinician to enter his or her NPI. Each private practitioner has to obtain an NPI. Health care plans use this number in processing all of their financial transactions with providers. Practitioners will not be able to be reimbursed without this number. There is no fee to obtain an NPI and it may be applied for online (http://www.nppes.cms.hhs.gov/NPPES/Welcome.do).

SUBMITTING THE CLAIM

Claims may be submitted in one of two ways: on paper through the U.S. Postal Service or electronically through the Internet. Either way will get the claim paid. However, claims submitted electronically will generally get paid faster.

Computerized billing programs have the ability to bill electronically. Each company has its own unique payor address so the claim may be directed to it for processing. In addition, several insurance companies and MCOs allow electronic billing through their Web site. Because this feature reduces costs, companies provide this service free of charge and encourage clinicians to use it.

When submitting paper claims, pay close attention to whether the claim is sent to the insurance carrier or, if applicable, to a separate MCO. This information may be on the client's health insurance card or it may be listed on an authorization letter sent by the MCO. It is also important to understand that the same insurance carrier may have multiple claims processing centers. Therefore, not all Aetna, CIGNA, or United-Healthcare claims go to one centralized address. In his billing program Steve Walfish sends Aetna claims to three different addresses, CIGNA claims to five, and UnitedHealthcare claims to three.

Claims need to be submitted in a timely manner following the date of service. As noted earlier, some have a relatively brief (60-day) requirement, whereas some may allow for as long as 1 year. For this reason it is important that clinicians review their calendar once per month to ensure that all bills for services provided in the previous month have been submitted for reimbursement.

How often one submits claims depends on the individual's cash flow needs. In private practice there is no such thing as receiving a paycheck on the 1st and 15th of the month (unless this has been prearranged in a clinician's corporate structure). An analysis of one's personal and professional bills will help determine the frequency of claim submission. Claims are generally paid 2 to 6 weeks after submission. Many people have a disproportionate number of bills that are due at the beginning of the month (e.g., personal rent or mortgage, practice rent) so there is a need to have a disproportionate amount of cash available at that time to meet those obligations. With a computerized billing system it is not difficult to bill daily. Most people bill weekly. Those with a large cash reserve may be able to submit claims on a monthly basis.

W-9 FORMS

Insurance companies are required to maintain a running total of payments they make to health care providers. If this amount is over $500 in the calendar year, they are required to report these payments to the IRS. As such, the carrier will ask providers to complete a W-9 form that lists their name and address, corporate identity if different from their name, and Social Security Number or EIN. If you are a provider for an insurance company, the company will typically include such a form in the application packet. If you are not a provider for the insurance company, it will usually write to you and either provide you with a blank form or request that you mail one in. These forms are easy to complete and may be downloaded from the Internet (search on *W-9 form*).

Once You Are Paid by the Insurance Carrier

After you submit a proper claim to an insurance carrier, 2 to 6 weeks later payment for these services will arrive in the form of a check through the mail (although note some insurance companies are moving toward electronic payment of their claims directly into a bank account of your choice).

The check is accompanied by an EOB. Most often a copy is mailed to the client at the same time. This way the client will know the claim was paid and the breakdown of the payment of the claim as well as be able to notice whether any insurance fraud is taking place. For example, a client may notice that charges were paid for three sessions when he or she was out of the country on vacation. This would be a case of either the clinician making an honest billing error or an attempt to defraud the insurance company for services not provided. Lest one think that MHPs, because of strong ethical training and prosocial values, are above such behavior, an Internet search on the terms *psychologist* and *insurance fraud* should serve as an eye-opening, myth-dispelling exercise.

Each insurance carrier has a different format for its EOB. However, it typically contains information regarding the name of the client, the name of the provider of services, the date the service was provided, the amount the clinician charged for the service, the amount allowed by the carrier (either by contractual arrangement or by their algorithm for the charge it considers reasonable and customary), the copay or deductible due from the client, the percentage at which the charges are paid, the amount paid by the plan (which should correspond to the amount of the check that was received), and the remaining patient responsibility. A sample EOB is presented in Exhibit 6.4. As can be seen, after all of the discounts, the client is ultimately responsible for only $13.60 of the initial $140 charge for the session.

Insurance Company Mistakes

Insurance companies occasionally make mistakes. Some of these are mistakes of omission and some of commission. Some are a result of system difficulties on their part. On occasion a clinician will call an insurance company to inquire why a claim submitted 6 weeks prior has not been paid. The customer service representative will look in the system to track the claim and may discover that it had never been received or entered into the system. This may happen despite the clinician mailing it to the correct address or receiving verification of an electronic bill. At

EXHIBIT 6.4

A Sample Explanation of Benefits

Insurance R Us
1225 Christmas Lane
Juneau, AK 99802

Jane Doe, LMFT
1111 Main Street
Elmsville, IN 46381

Claim Number:	54321
Check #:	987601234567
Insured:	Santa Claus
Date:	6-7-07
Group:	Toy Factory USA
Provider ID #:	555555555
Provider:	Jane Doe, LMFT
Service:	Office Visit
Date of Service:	5/8/07–5/8/07
Total Charges:	$ 140.00
Excluded Charges:	$ 72.00
Copay/Deductible:	$ 0.00
Covered Expense:	$ 68.00
Paid at:	80%
Paid by Plan:	$ 54.40
Patient Responsibility:	$ 13.60

that point the clinician has no option but to resubmit the claim. On some occasions the carrier may allow the bill to be faxed to expedite its processing. For this reason it is important for clinicians to review the status of claims no later than 6 weeks after submission. Another error is a rejection for lacking preauthorization on record. This might occur despite the clinician having received a letter of authorization from the insurer or MCO. We have had conversations with customer service representatives (CSRs) that have gone something like the following:

> *CSR:* The claim was rejected because the services were not preauthorized.

> *Steve:* I am holding the authorization in my hand as we speak.

> *CSR:* I'm not sure how that happened because we have no record of it. Please resubmit the claim with a copy of the authorization and we will reprocess the claim for payment.

One frequent insurance error we have noted is related to billing for psychological testing, specifically CPT code 96101. In the "Days or Units" box of the CMS-1500 Claim Form (24G), most procedures are billed at one unit (e.g., an hour of individual or couples therapy). However, the number of units for psychological testing will most often be for multiple units (e.g., 3–4) for the same day of service. When the insurer codes the information in this box into the system, he or she may reflexively enter one unit instead of the three or four units sent in by the psychologist. This error has to be noticed by the psychologist (it is not difficult to miss because the check accompanying the EOB would be for much less than was anticipated because the insurance company paid for only one unit instead of four) and a correction has to be requested.

As noted earlier, we believe insurance companies may count on clinician error or lack of follow-through to increase their profit margin. Recall Private Practice Principles Numbers 2 and 15. You are responsible for your financial success. Collections have to be closely monitored, otherwise the amount billed and collected will fall below the 90% threshold we consider minimally acceptable. When a mistake is discovered, the clinician has two options. One is to call the insurer, point out the mistake, and ask the insurer to correct it. In most cases this will be successful if the carrier agrees that a mistake has been made. The second, and one we advocate, is not to spend time calling but rather to correspond in writing, providing a description of the mistake and appropriate documentation to support your case. This method leaves a paper trail related to the mistake that may need to be referred back to if the issue is not resolved in a satisfactory manner. Such a sample letter is presented in Exhibit 6.5.

EXHIBIT 6.5

Sample Follow-Up Letter to Insurance Carrier

Jeffrey E. Barnett, PsyD, ABPP
1511 Ritchie Highway, Suite 201
Arnold, MD 21012
(410) 757-1511

June 30, 2007

To: BC/BS Appeals
From: Jeffrey E. Barnett, PsyD, ABPP (123456789)
Re: Claim Rejection

I would appreciate it if you would review the enclosed rejection of services provided to Ms. Jane Smith.

In the enclosed explanation of benefits I have noted a denial for payment of a claim for services delivered to Ms. Smith. The stated reason for the denial is that there was no record of the patient in your files.

Please note that I have enclosed a copy of her insurance card. I would appreciate it if you would correct this denial and pay on the claim that was submitted.

Thank you for your attention to this matter and if you have any further questions please do not hesitate to contact me.

In completing retrospective reviews, an insurance company may discover it made a mistake and paid you, the clinician, when benefits were not actually in effect. The company will then write to you and ask for a refund. You may then ask the client for the funds, but the carrier is due the refund. If you do not refund the money, the insurance company will simply deduct it from a future payment it is making on behalf of another client. For example, suppose it paid you $100 for services delivered to Mr. Jones (who in retrospect was found not to be an enrollee) and you have not refunded the money. When you submit a claim for services delivered to Mr. Smith, the company will simply not pay you the first $100 and apply that to the refund due on the Mr. Jones account. Its obligation to pay on the claim for Mr. Smith will have been met.

There will be times when you disagree with a decision made by an insurance company or a MCO to either deny payment or refuse to authorize future services. Each has developed a protocol for handling disputes that should be followed to the letter. If you have signed a contract to be a provider for the insurer or MCO, then you have likely contractually agreed to abide by this protocol. If you are not a provider and have not been able to successfully negotiate an agreement regarding the dispute with the insurer or MCO, then you may have recourse to the office of the insurance commissioner in your state. In such disputes you should consult with this state agency to find out its policies and procedures for resolving such disputes.

COLLECTING THE CLIENT'S PORTION OF THE FEE

We strongly advise that clinicians ensure that clients understand they will be responsible for the copay portion of the fee on the day services are provided. Such a procedure accomplishes several things. First, it helps the clinician with cash flow. Although payments of $10 to $20 per session do not seem lofty, they can easily add up to several hundred dollars per week. Second, when monies due are paid in full at the time of session the clinician does not have to send out follow-up bills attempting to collect these funds. This saves staff (or personal) time and postage costs. Third, it prevents a large balance from accumulating.

It is impossible to correctly predict 100% of the time how much money the client will owe when insurance is involved. There are too many variations within insurance policies and reimbursements. When clinicians or clients attempt to verify benefits, some companies will not inform them what they consider to be their reasonable and customary charges. This information may only be learned later when the EOB is received with payment. Some insurers may not have information available as to whether the client's deductible has been met for the year. Because of this, clinicians have to then later collect the remaining balance due from the client. Computerized billing programs will generate financial account statements to be mailed to the client indicating they have a balance due and request that it be paid by a certain date. If a billing program is not used, the clinician may use his or her word processing program to send out financial statements. An example of such a statement is presented in Exhibit 6.6. We recommend that these statements be sent out monthly and designate a specific due date for payment.

WAIVING COPAYS

Because they are generally nice human beings, clinicians who know clients are not in a financial position to be responsible for their copay can be tempted to waive this fee. This is allowable on an occasional basis. Another option is to set up a payment plan for the client with a generous payback schedule.

However, copays cannot be waived on a consistent or systematic basis lest this be considered insurance fraud. Suppose the clinician's fee is $100 per session and clients with this same policy have a 20% (e.g., $20) copay. The insurance company will pay 80% of the fee (e.g., $80). If the clinician routinely waives this $20 copay, the insur-

---

EXHIBIT 6.6

A Sample Client Financial Statement

John Q. Public, LCSW
350 Fifth Avenue
New York, NY 10118
(212) 246-8000

June 2, 2007

Ms. Jill Smith
13579 Broadway
New York, NY 10120

Bill for Services

Name of Client:	Bobby Smith
Type of Services:	Psychotherapy (90806)
Date of Services:	5-25-07
Total Charges:	$ 120.00
Insurance Discount:	$ 20.00
Insurance Payments Received:	$ 80.00
Direct Payments Received:	$ 10.00 (5-25-07)
Total Balance Due:	$ 10.00

Please Pay This Amount by June 30, 2007

---

ance company will interpret the fee for psychotherapy as being not $100 but rather $80. If this is the actual fee, then it believes it should be paying 80% of this figure, or $64. Please be forewarned: Health care providers have been prosecuted for consistently and systematically waiving copays.

CREDIT CARD PAYMENTS

If clients are made aware the copay is due on the date of their session, they will usually bring cash or a check to make this payment. On occasion people really do forget their checkbook. They will then usually simply make a double payment at their next scheduled session. Clients may also prefer to pay all their monies due by credit card, and we think it important to provide this as a payment option. As noted at the beginning of the chapter, each time a client walks out of a MHP's office without paying the entire fee there is a chance this fee will never be paid. Because of this we also suggest that as part of the clinician's intake paperwork clients sign a "credit card guarantee of payment." A sample agreement is presented in Exhibit 6.7. This particular form allows clients to pay any unpaid balance that is due by check or credit card. This form also allows clinicians to collect any unpaid portions of their clients' balance by billing their credit card.

Clinicians may obtain a merchant account through their bank that will allow them to process credit card payments. Doing so requires a one-time purchase of equipment necessary to complete the transaction. Some of the national billing services provide a mechanism for credit card transactions, as do some of the computer billing programs. In addition, some companies focus solely on providing a portal for credit card transactions. Some clinicians accept payments through PayPal accounts. Although this is not an endorsement, two psychologists are the owners of http://www.professionalcharges.com, a Web site that allows credit card payments for MHPs.

Clinicians pay a percentage of the amount collected to the credit card company. This fee is usually a few percentage points and varies by company. Some companies also levy a transaction fee each time a charge is made. Clinicians are encouraged to shop around for the service that offers them the best price and convenience.

The term *credit card guarantee* is actually only a guarantee in name only. When clients do not pay the balance due as per the written agreement, we then process their credit card for payment. However, there have been cases in which the transaction was rejected by the credit card company. We then attempted to once again collect the money from the client, but to no avail. Although these cases are rare, they are once again examples of not being able to collect 100% of the amount billed for services.

EXHIBIT 6.7

Sample Credit Card Agreement

Credit Card Guaranty of Payment

I understand that Dr. Walfish will be billing my insurance company for therapy or evaluation services. I further understand that I am responsible for all reasonable and customary fees that my insurance company does not pay such as deductibles or copays.

I also understand that Dr. Walfish is billing my insurance company as a courtesy to me rather than my paying for services up front and waiting to be reimbursed by my insurance company.

I understand that Dr. Walfish will work with me and my insurance company to receive payment from them. For my convenience he will wait a reasonable amount of time to be reimbursed by my insurance carrier for services delivered. However, sometimes insurance companies do not pay in a timely manner and sometimes they do not reimburse at the rate that was initially expected. Because of this I am giving Dr. Walfish permission to charge my credit card for any services that have not been paid by me or my insurance carrier within 90 days of billing. If services have not been paid within 60 days Dr. Walfish will notify me in writing that he has not been paid by my insurance carrier and that he encourages me to contact the carrier to get it to pay for the services in a timely manner.

I understand that Dr. Walfish uses the credit card company professionalservices.com. On my credit card statement the charge will appear as if coming from that company and not from Dr. Walfish. I understand that this form is valid for 3 years unless I cancel the authorization in writing.

Patient Name

Cardholder Name (if different from the patient)

Cardholder Billing Address

Type of Credit Card (Visa, Mastercard, or Discover; American Express is not accepted)

Credit Card Number

Expiration Date

Signature and Date

COLLECTION AGENCIES

If they inform clients as part of the informed consent process, clinicians have a right to turn unpaid client accounts over to a collection agency. In doing so, clinicians can share only the basic information an agency would need to attempt to collect on the debt, not any clinical information.

However, we suggest that clinicians not take this route and simply take the loss. R. Woody (1988) has suggested that when a clinician attempts to collect from a client unwilling to pay his or her debt, frequently "that client suddenly seems to remember the practitioner's shortcomings" (p. 108). The client may then turn around and make a complaint about a clinician, bogus or not, to a state or national professional association or a state licensing board. At that point in time the headaches and the costs for attempting to collect this unpaid debt increase exponentially. We believe it is a better practice to implement procedures to minimize the amount of unpaid accounts and view the few hundred dollars as uncollected funds. An example of a preventive strategy is to include in the informed consent agreement that outstanding balances may not exceed the charges for three sessions. Addressing the issue at that time will be much less costly than if the balance owed is allowed to continue growing beyond that.

Other Fee-Related Issues

Every clinician should have a clearly stated no-show and late cancellation policy. Clients should know that time is scheduled exclusively for them and cannot be filled by someone else at the last minute. Most clinicians have a 24-hour cancellation policy. This means that clients will be billed for the session if they cancel the scheduled appointment less than 24 hours before the scheduled appointment. If they are a no-show for the appointment, they will be billed as well. It should also be explained to clients they are responsible for paying the entire fee that would be due for the session, not just their usual copay if they have insurance. An insurance company will not pay for a service that has not been delivered, which clients commonly do not realize. For example, consider a situation in which the contracted rate for psychotherapy is $100 and the client has a 20% copay. For a session that takes place the insurance company will pay the clinician $80 and the client will pay the clinician $20, and the entire obligation for the fee will have been met. However, if a session does not take place because of a late cancellation or no-show, the insurance carrier will pay $0 toward the $100 fee obligation. Therefore, the entire $100 fee becomes the responsibility of the client.

It is important that clients respect your time and therefore be responsible for no-show or late-cancellation fees. However, sometimes life events make missing a session unavoidable, and if a client runs late or misses an appointment on an occasional basis, you may use your discretion and waive these fees. For example, people wake up in the morning ill, and there is no way for them to know this 24 hours in advance. Sometimes cars break down on the way to the appointment. Children become ill or have accidents and have to be taken to a medical clinic. In major metropolitan areas on occasions interstates are backed up for several hours because of major accidents, and the client simply cannot get to the appointment on time. We attempt to be compassionate about this and will not charge when it appears that circumstances are out of the client's control. An exception is when a client has to work late. We do not consider this an emergency and will bill for this time.

Many psychotherapists also use credit cards to ensure payment for appointments cancelled with less than 24 hours notice and for missed appointments. Information on this policy must be included in the informed consent agreement. But with that done, the clinician can directly charge the client's credit card for these fees when they arise. This practice helps reduce the likelihood of not being paid for one's time.

Embezzlement

There is no shortage of stories in the popular press regarding embezzlement of funds by trusted advisors of entertainers. It is common to hear stories in which accountants and stockbrokers have escaped to a foreign country courtesy of the funds they have embezzled from their clients.

Of course, such a thing could not happen to MHPs in private practice because they are generally a group of prosocial caring human beings. Wrong! Although we have no reason to believe it happens with great frequency, any small business is at risk of employee theft.

We have heard stories of many clinicians who were the victims of embezzlement in their practice. Exhibit 6.8 presents an interview with Jennifer Kelly, a psychologist who generously agreed to share her experiences in hopes they can help to prevent similar occurrences.

MHPs often have partners in their practice. MHPs are human beings, too, and are not immune from the problems that many of their clients face: alcoholism, drug addiction, gambling addiction, abuse of credit cards, making faulty investments, and other problems that may be associated with financial distress. When people become desperate they do desperate things, and on rare occasions this may mean stealing from their partners. Support staff may be envious of the "big bucks" earned by MHPs in private practice, especially if they are involved in the fee collection process and see how much money is flowing into the practice (they may not see how much money is flowing out). If they are financially stressed or have financial envy, on a rare occasion they may be tempted to siphon off a small percentage for themselves, thinking that "these small amounts won't be missed by these rich doctors."

EXHIBIT 6.8

A Story of Embezzlement From Jennifer Kelly, PhD

I know many people who have been victims of embezzlement, including psychologists, psychiatrists, and other physicians. Many of the victims whom I have talked to about it indicated they were too embarrassed to mention it, as if they had done something wrong. The physicians find out about it, terminate the person, and just move on without taking further action.

I thought I had insulated myself from embezzlement by the precautions I had set in place. No one else has access to my checkbook or corporate credit card.

In the past I used an internationally based office staffing company to hire my office manager. After she abruptly left the job, I found out from several of my clients that she had borrowed money from them. I had no idea this was taking place but after she left clients revealed this information to me. I checked with my attorney and was informed that I would have to pay the clients back because the office manager was an extension of me. The attorney indicated that I had to ask all of my clients if she had borrowed money from them and if so to tell them I would be responsible for the debt.

I also informed the staffing agency about this, and the agency indicated that I would not have to pay the person the last paycheck. At that time I asked if it had conducted a background search on the employee and the agency assured me that it did.

When I began the process of looking for a replacement office manager, the staffing agency asked for a second chance, saying that my experience was an anomaly and that a background search on the person would be conducted. The agency recommended someone and I hired her on the basis of their recommendations. As time progressed I became increasingly concerned with the income. I was busy seeing patients, but was not seeing the accompanying increase in my deposits. I started to review my books because it seemed that something was not right but I could not put my finger on it. I was expecting a check in the range of $800 for work I had done with a client. I went through the client's chart and saw an explanation of benefits (EOB) indicating the fee was paid for services rendered. The deposit was listed as paid on my billing system. However, this check was not on my deposit slip. When I questioned her about this the following day she corrected the deposit slip to reflect the deposit. Still not feeling confident in her response, I went through the system and compared the postings in the system to the actual deposits made. That's when I knew there was some form of embezzlement.

I then called my bank. I had been with this bank for 10 years and did all of my personal and business banking there. I spoke with someone in the Fraud Unit of the bank. He said that he could not help without the checks. I then had contact with an account representative of the bank. He noted that my history indicated something was wrong and that I needed to get the image on the back of the checks. I spent time gathering the EOBs and copies of the checks and faxed them to this person. He said he would get on it right away. Despite repeated calls, he never responded. Once I was able to get in touch with him, he told me that he was busy as it was the holiday season and that he would get back to me. He never did. I was eventually told that he was no longer employed there.

I then went to my certified public accountant (CPA), who is also a tax attorney, and he referred me to the City of Atlanta Fraud Department, which opened a case. The detective made numerous attempts to contact the bank manager about the matter, but she never responded to his calls and was never available. My accountant eventually went to the bank to find out what happened to the checks. She discovered that my employee had used the signature stamp that I use for insurance claim forms to endorse the checks and cash them. When I attempted to discuss this with the bank manager, she indicated that the tellers told her that I gave them permission to cash the checks, and that the bank would not talk with me. I was flabbergasted because I never gave such permission. I was further told that I needed to have

(Continued)

EXHIBIT 6.8 (Continued)

my attorney contact the bank. The manager said I couldn't have access to my own records! Furthermore, the bank continued to allow my office manager to cash checks even after I notified the bank that I never gave her permission to do so. For example, on January 5, 2005, at 10:00 a.m., my attorney made it clear to the bank that she had cashed checks without authorization and at 1:00 p.m. she cashed an additional set of checks.

The investigator did not want me to fire the office manager because a criminal investigation was under way. He wanted to be able to catch her in the act. Because I had to continue working with her, I obtained a Post Office box and had my mail forwarded there. The office manager, sensing something was not right, called the post office and asked why the mail was being forwarded.

Shortly thereafter I received a call from my CPA/tax attorney and was told the police were getting ready to arrest her. I told the police I had a client scheduled and the detective told me to cancel the appointment. He said the City of Atlanta did an inmate search and found out that she was a convicted felon on parole while working for me. She had three prior convictions for forgery and fraud. I asked how someone on parole for these charges could get a job in a doctor's office and I was informed, "There are good parole officers and bad parole officers." I had previously asked the staffing company if it did background checks on the employees it was recommending. At first the agency told me that it did. Two years later the agency told me it did not conduct background checks. I thought I had all the checks and balances in place. This was unbelievable to me.

My office manager was arrested and given a high bond. However, because of overcrowded jails the bond was lowered. It has been 2 years and the case has still not gone to trial. However, my CPA sent her a 1099 form for the money that she took so she will likely have trouble with the Internal Revenue Service. She admitted cashing the checks but said that I had given her permission to do so.

I found out later from clients that she said extremely negative things about me to my clients. No one said anything until after she was gone.

Since this has happened no one touches my mail except me. I have a finger on the pulse of my practice. Opening the mail takes me 2 hours each week but now I feel that it is well worth it. I will let my office staff post charges but no one but me makes deposits. I had let my previous office staff do this but never again. Since I diagnosed the problem I have noticed a significant rise in the amount of money in my account. I believe that if you are not looking at the finances very closely, somebody can take money in small amounts and you would never know it. I think if you are making a lot of money you will not miss a little bit here and there.

I have also learned never to trust a bank. The bank said it had a great fraud unit but the bank put the burden on me to prove that the embezzlement was not my fault. I had to hire someone to review my records. The bank had everything and would not cooperate. The bank said it was my fault because I had an "out-of-control employee." It turned out that she had stolen $128,000 from me. I have a lawsuit filed against the bank, which is trying to break me financially as it is making it my responsibility to produce a tremendous amount of records. It takes time, energy, and people to do this work, along with attorney fees. Everyone has told me to go to the media and let them know about the bank and the international staffing company.

I also have learned that I can't trust an employment agency. I'd advise everyone to do his or her own background check. It's not an expensive thing to do through the sheriff's department. I would also advise doing a credit check. It is important to know that the people working in your office are trustworthy, especially because they are dealing with clients (remember that the previous office manager was borrowing money from my clients) and finances.

I have talked with numerous physicians and psychologists, and a number of them told me that embezzlement has happened to them. I have come to the conclusion that as hard as we work to make money, there are people out there working as hard to take it away from us.

Broskowski (1984) indicated that organizations, because of their internal complexity, must develop mechanisms for monitoring internal self-regulation and balance. He viewed internal control mechanisms as a process of feedback. Many years ago we had a colleague whose husband was an ophthalmologist. He asked that Steve Walfish and two of his friends come to his office for an examination and that they pay cash (that he had given to them) for the services rendered. The ophthalmologist then tracked the flow of this cash to ensure that it had been properly dealt with in his practice. This is one example of internal monitoring of the financial aspects of a practice. As Epstein (2006) elaborated,

> Many people start their operation by carefully hiring people they think they can trust thinking, "We're family. They'll never steal from me." Unfortunately, those who have learned the truth are the ones that have put too much faith in just one employee. Too often a business finds out too late that even the most loyal employee may steal from the company, if the opportunity arises and the temptation becomes too great—or if the employee is caught up in a serious financial dilemma and needs fast cash. (p. 109)

Epstein presented guidelines for reducing the likelihood of theft. These include not letting any one person handle more than one of these four functions: bookkeeping, authorization of expenditures, money handling, and financial report preparation. He also viewed it as essential to review bank statements on a monthly basis, review the checkbook to ensure that checks are not missing, and observe how cash is handled in the office. Most certified public accountants will also have suggestions as to how a practice can develop controls to increase the likelihood that embezzlement does not take place, and we strongly advocate putting such systems into place. Not doing so places one's hard-earned funds at risk (albeit a low one) of theft.

Conclusion

Fee setting and fee collection are influenced by both pragmatic and emotional issues. Private practitioners have to know how to set fees, submit claims to insurance companies, and have mechanisms to collect unpaid monies. It is also important for clients to understand the fees involved in professional services. Herron (1995) advocated that this process be as visible as possible. In addition, private practitioners have to give themselves permission to ask for reasonable fees, have an expectation that these fees be paid, and have an internal strategy for how to respond if these expectations are not met. Ignoring either the pragmatic or the emotional aspects of billing and collecting will have a negative impact on the bottom line of the profitability of the private practice.

Understanding Basic Accounting and Taxes   7

A s operators of small businesses, mental health professionals (MHPs) have to learn how to "keep the books." In this chapter we detail what all practitioners need to know, what they can do for themselves, and when they will need the help of an accounting professional. We highlight the types of information to track to determine the profit and loss of the business. This record keeping may be accomplished the old-fashioned way through keeping a written ledger, but is easily handled through the use of simple (or more complex if desired) computer software programs. This information is vital in preparing income tax forms and determining amount owed or due back from the government. Tax issues discussed include payment of estimated quarterly taxes and self-employment taxes, what may be deducted as a professional expense, and options for reducing tax liability. In addition, the tax implications of having employees versus independent contractors are presented.

Before we explore any of these issues, we must emphasize that you should not take any of the following as financial or tax advice. Please consult with the appropriate professionals regarding the accuracy of the information and how particular situations may apply to your own particular circumstances. In addition, because tax forms are always changing and individual situations may call for specific forms it is imperative that clinicians consistently consult with their tax advisors to ensure they are in compliance with state and federal laws.

What Is Bookkeeping?

According to http://www.dictionary.com (Bookkeeping, n.d.), the word *bookkeeping* is (a) the work or skill of keeping account books or systematic records of money transactions and (b) the practice or profession of recording the accounts and transactions of a business. As can be seen from these definitions, keeping the books is as simple as documenting each financial transaction within a private practice. Although this task may not sound fun, it is essential for understanding the financial health of a practice. Epstein (2006) noted that bookkeepers must be detail-oriented, enjoy working with numbers, and be meticulous. A bookkeeping system will allow you to understand how much money is coming into the practice and where money is flowing out toward practice expenses.

Private practitioners have only two ways to increase their incomes. The first is to bring in higher revenues. The other is to reduce overhead expenses. A good bookkeeping system will enable the small-business owner to make data-based decisions to accomplish these goals. Without such information it is difficult to know whether efforts need to focus on revenue enhancement or cutbacks on expenses. This knowledge is essential for making data-based, as opposed to seat-of-your-pants, decisions in managing your small business.

A Bookkeeping System

Both authors of this volume started working in private practice in the early 1980s before computers were routinely integrated into office operations. Bookkeeping was simple. We kept a written ledger listing monies collected from clients or consulting activities and another listing monies spent on the business by category. This process has not changed since we started practicing but has become easier to do with the development of computer software specifically geared toward bookkeeping and money management.

KEEPING TRACK OF INCOME

Computer billing systems allow you to know how much money is coming into the practice and the sources of these revenues. You can look up this information either for the practice as a whole or for each client.

When a client account is first entered into the computer, basic information on who referred the client, insurance carrier (if any), and where the client lives is logged. Then the dates of service and the amount billed are entered after the date of service. When payments are made by either the client or his or her insurer, these are entered into the system and matched with the date of service. With this information alone many reports may be generated allowing clinicians to understand the income flow regarding their practice. Although this is not an endorsement of this product in particular, the following reports, among others, can be generated by the billing system Therapist Helper.

- *Overall summary:* Allows you to see how much money has been generated into the practice.
- *Market analysis:* Examines how money is coming into the practice. Includes geographic distribution of the clients, which providers have billed the most sessions, and who is referring clients to the practice.
- *Transaction summary:* Produces a summary of procedures (Current Procedural Terminology codes), payments, and adjustments or write-offs.
- *Insurance payments:* Allows you to see which insurance companies you work with the most and what the reimbursement patterns are for each company.

These reports can be generated for an individual client or for all of the clients ever seen in the entire practice. Reports can also be generated for individual clinicians or for the practice as a whole. Reports can be generated for the entire history of the practice or for specific time frames of interest.

All computerized billing systems have capabilities of generating multiple reports about practice income. Used in this way, the computerized billing system not only keeps track of collections but also may act as a management information system. Key decisions can be made regarding marketing efforts if this information is available. For example, a clinician may see a pattern in which more and more referrals are of clients with a particular insurance that pays less than others. Targeted marketing efforts may be used to increase the number of referrals of clients with insurance that has a much higher usual customary fee. The bookkeeping system allows clinicians to view data indicating where their money (e.g., customers) is coming from in their practice. As the dictionary indicates, bookkeeping is simply a recording of transactions. Entrepreneurial private practitioners will then interpret and act on the data provided by this system to enhance their business.

Clinicians may contract out their billing services. Most companies who provide such a service would be able to generate any reports needed by the private practice.

If a computerized billing system is not used to track income that comes into the practice, clinicians must develop an alternative method. A simple way is to use a spreadsheet that has columns for date of payment, source of payment, and the amount collected. An example of such a system is presented in Table 7.1. However, unlike with computerized billing systems the payments received are not linked with the amount billed, the amount discounted, or the balance due from the client. A subsequent step of generating a separate invoice must take place if a balance is due (see the example in Exhibit 6.6, p. 144). Furthermore, unlike bookkeeping software programs, the spreadsheet method does not generate reports.

KEEPING TRACK OF EXPENSES

Epstein (2006) suggested that the business ledger serves as "the figurative eyes and ears of bookkeepers and accountants who want to know what financial transactions have taken place historically in the business" (p. 49). It is important that the private practitioner maintain accurate records of business expenses for two reasons. First, it is the only way to determine if too much money is being paid for overhead or for specific subcategories of overhead. Second, practice expenses are used in profit-and-loss statements when filing income taxes.

TABLE 7.1

Sample for Tracking Collections With a Spreadsheet

Date	Name of client	Payment type	Amount paid
6-1	Mr. A	Insurance	$ 60.00
	Ms. B	Direct Pay	$ 120.00
	Mr. C	Direct Pay	$ 25.00
	Ms. D	Insurance	$ 80.00
6-4	Mr. E	Direct Pay	$ 15.00
	Ms. F	Direct Pay	$ 10.00
	Mr. G	Insurance	$ 40.00
6-7	Mr. H	Direct Pay	$ 120.00
	Ms. I	Direct Pay	$ 100.00
	Mr. J	Insurance	$ 62.75
6-10	Ms. K	Direct Pay	$ 60.00
	Mr. L	Insurance	$ 80.00
	Ms. M	Insurance	$ 60.00
	Mr. N	Insurance	$ 103.96
	Ms. O	Direct Pay	$ 27.25
	Mr. P	Insurance	$ 40.00

On its Web site the Internal Revenue Service (IRS; 2006) defines "business expense" as follows:

> Business expenses are the costs of carrying on a trade or business and they are usually deductible if the business is operated to make a profit.

There are two key concepts in this simple sentence. First, the expense must be related to you conducting your private practice. This requirement is fairly broad and can be subject to interpretation. However, the primary motivation must be to enhance profitability of the business and not for personal use or gain. Second, the business must be profitable lest it be considered a hobby—expenses related to a hobby are not deductible. For example, consider private practitioners who see only two clients per week. They do this because they enjoy it and see it as sideline to the primary way they earn their living. After the clinician purchases malpractice insurance, consults with attorneys as needed, and pays office rent it is possible to speculate that more often than not this sideline will be a losing venture. IRS rules indicate that a profit must be made in a certain percentage of years to deduct expenses incurred; otherwise the IRS categorizes the activity as a hobby.

Expenses may simply be kept on a spreadsheet. The columns will list the different practice expense categories and the rows will contain the date and the amount for each entry. However, we advocate that expenses be tracked in a basic computerized checkbook program, such as Quicken by Intuit or Money by Microsoft. These are easy to learn and take little time to input if done on a regular basis. In addition, important reports may be generated to better understand how the practice is spending its money. For example, Quicken can readily generate these reports: (a) income and expense summary by category, (b) income and expenses by category for two time periods, and (c) itemized category spending. These data can help private practitioners decide whether they are spending their money wisely. For example, they may discover they are paying $1,200 in office supplies in a given year. They may then consider whether they can reduce this amount by purchasing supplies in an alternative way (e.g., from a chain bulk discount store or the Internet). Or they may see they are paying $18,000 per year for support personnel and they may then explore whether switching to a model of hiring independent contractors to perform the work would save money. However, it is only by inspecting and analyzing the data that practitioners may make meaningful data-based decisions related to their expenses.

GENERAL EXPENSE CATEGORIES

Most practices have similar expense categories. Some may have special circumstances that are unique to them or an expense category that may be applicable in certain years and not others (e.g., purchase of capital equipment or furniture).

These are the expense categories used in our practices:

- bank charges
- books and journals
- capital equipment
- continuing education
- dues for professional associations
- insurance
- marketing
- office supplies
- parking
- photocopying and printing
- postage
- professional services
- psychological tests
- rent
- telephone
- office personnel

Accounting

In describing the interaction between bookkeeping and accounting, Tracy (2005) elaborated,

> Bookkeeping refers to the record keeping aspects of accounting. It is essentially the process of recording all transactions and financial activities. Accountants design the bookkeeping system and establish controls to make sure the systems are working well. (p. 44)

Tracy further explained that accountants (a) design documents, (b) establish rules and methods of financial transactions, (c) establish classification schemes, (d) perform oversight and reviews, (e) prepare internal reports for managers, and (f) prepare tax returns to be submitted to government agencies.

Bookkeepers provide the essential data for the management of the practice. It is up to practice owners to use these data to their advantage. As Barry Melancon, certified public accountant (CPA), described in his interview (see Exhibit 5.2, p. 87), accountants can be invaluable in helping a practice owner understand financial data related to his or her practice. However, an accountant likely cannot do this without understanding the mental health business. Therefore, a collaborative relationship must be developed between clinician and accountant. For example, an accountant may simply say, "Well, in order to earn significantly more money you must now start seeing 45 clients a week." There is no reason why the CPA would understand this would lead to burnout in the clinician and likely weaken their therapeutic effectiveness with clients. However, such a statement may lead to brainstorming regarding other ways to earn money such as seeing clients in groups rather than individually, taking on an associate, or developing other new sources of revenue.

Tracy (2005) described several ways in which *"savvy* business managers" use accounting data. These include

- *Making smarter profit decisions:* He suggested that one must have a "profit model" in mind; that is, one must understand how the business earns money. In this way one can diagnose profit and analyze what happened to profit when there is a change in one of the key factors that drive it.
- *Not confusing cash flow with profit:* One may be able to generate large amounts of income, but if expenses are not controlled in a reasonable way the profit potential of the business will be significantly compromised.
- *Governing cash flow:* Even if a practice is profitable, if usable cash flow is not available, problems or lost opportunity may develop. Usable cash flow is necessary to contribute to the operation and growth of the business, to distribute profits and salaries to the personnel involved in the business, and to meet debt obligations.

Tracy (2005) suggested it is important to analyze profit and loss and the effects they have on the business. Along these lines, as small-business owners it is important for private practitioners to be able to explain what causes their profit or loss. If you cannot do so, then your business's success or lack of success would appear to be caused by random factors. As clinicians, MHPs are aware of the importance of clients analyzing their attitudes and behavior and which ones produce positive outcomes and which produce negative outcomes. In this way MHPs can reinforce attitudes and behaviors yielding positive outcomes and modify those producing unhappiness. The same holds true for profits or losses in a practice. Aside from significant environmental or sociopolitical factors, clinicians are the makers or breakers of the financial success of their practices.

In our experience we have found cash flow to be a particularly difficult area to manage, especially when developing a practice, because not much cash is flowing in at first. Under ideal circumstances, practices will have a few months' reserve sitting in a bank account accruing interest and being there for "a rainy day." The number of clients seen may ebb and flow depending on the nature of the practice. For example, it is not unusual for August to be a slow month because many families go on vacation or people wait for the summer to be over before beginning to work on personal growth issues. For those who work with children and adolescents, the telephone usually rings off the hook after the first report card comes out and it is discovered that students are experiencing academic difficulties. Clinicians working in the area of weight loss often find that February brings a flood of new referrals because of the inability of most people to maintain their New Year's resolution of losing weight. After clinicians have had a few years of data to analyze they may be able to make reasonably reliable predictions regarding income that will be coming to the practice and thus plan expenses accordingly (i.e., not plan significant purchases during low cash-flow times).

Taxes

The only way to avoid paying taxes is to not earn any money. However, there are ways to reduce tax liability and to legitimately claim expenses as tax deductions. It is important that private practitioners consult with accountants and tax attorneys to learn how to reduce their tax liability. This should be done at the beginning of the calendar year, not the end, so that proactive planning may be implemented. Tracy (2005) suggested that accountants can help small-business owners think through income tax factors in choosing an optimal corporate structure (see chap. 4).

TAX FORMS

In computing tax liability for the federal government one is required to complete a Form 1040. To this form individuals who are employed by an institution attach a copy of a W-2 form that reflects the income received from their employer. Because private practitioners do not have an employer, they have to complete a separate form titled "Schedule C: Profit or Loss From Business," which is for sole proprietors (this is the case for most private practitioners; those who are incorporated have separate reporting requirements). Part I of the Schedule C form focuses on income. This figure is the cumulative amount of gross monies that have come into the practice from all sources that are not part of a paid position in which a W-2 form would be issued. For example, if you teach one course at a local university, a W-2 form will likely be issued in January of the following year indicating what was paid to you and taxes withheld. However, this information would not go on the Schedule C but rather on another part of the 1040.

Part II of the Schedule C form summarizes expenses for the business. These expenses are all the business-related costs of your attempts to make your practice profitable. These expenses are deductible. For an explanation of what a legitimate business deduction is, visit the IRS Web site (http://www.irs.gov/pub/irs-pdf/p535.pdf) and consult your accountant. Practices that are incorporated may have more items that could be considered deductible (depending on the rules of the corporation that are adopted) than would a sole proprietor. Therefore, it is best to understand your own particular business tax structure when deciding whether an expense is a legitimate deduction. Furthermore, costs at one point in a career may not be deductible, but they could be at a later point. For example, fees paid toward initial licensure may not be deductible, but fees toward obtaining a license in another state once already licensed may be deductible. Educational fees for earning a degree may not be deductible, but continuing education postlicensure is deductible.

Some business expenses we took as deductions last year include office supplies, telephone (company charges, answering service, long-distance calls related to the practice), legal and professional services (e.g., consultation with attorneys, accountant fees, payments for transcription services), office rent, postage, automobile (e.g., parking for practice-related activities, mileage allowance for consultation or volunteer services), bank charges, books, subscriptions to journals, psychological tests, photocopying, continuing education (e.g., registration fees, all costs of attending professional meetings including hotels and meals), professional dues, licensure fees, marketing (e.g., development of promotional materials, taking to lunch potential referral sources), furniture, malpractice insurance, office overhead insurance, computer hardware and software, cell phone and pager, staff salaries, and benefits. Note the similarity of these categories with those previously listed as bookkeeping categories. Keeping the categories closely aligned with business expense deductions facilitates the computation of tax liability at the end of the year.

It is important to consult your tax professional regarding how to best compute some of these deductions. A few categories allow multiple methods to determine the deduction. For example, automobile expenses may be calculated using a mileage allowance (in 2008, 50.5 cents per mile) or an actual expense method. The full cost of capital equipment, such as furniture or computer equipment, may or may not be able to be deducted in one calendar year. These deductions may need to be depreciated or spread out over the expected lifetime of the capital purchase. Basic descriptions of the IRS guidelines regarding depreciation may be found at http://www.irs.gov/newsroom/article/0,,id=164589,00.html.

ESTIMATED TAXES

Individuals who work for an organization and receive a paycheck from that organization have taxes taken out of each check to meet tax obligations. This process is referred to as withholding taxes, and the amount is based on income earned and number of dependents claimed. Monies are also deducted for Social Security and Medicare, and the employer makes these payments to the federal government.

In private practice as a sole proprietor there are no paychecks and therefore no structure or format to pay these deductions every 2 or

4 weeks (this may not be the case if the clinician is part of a corporate structure). As such, private practitioners meet this obligation by making estimated tax payments on a quarterly basis. Estimated payments can be made for federal taxes and state taxes (as applicable). IRS regulations regarding making these estimated payments are described at http://www.irs.gov/businesses/small/article/0,,id=110413,00.html and http://www.irs.gov/publications/p505/ch02.html#d0e4537. Although the exact due dates may vary (if they fall on a weekend, they are moved to the following Monday), these quarterly payments are generally paid on April 15, June 15, September 15, and January 15. If these payments are a significant underestimate of the actual tax liability due (e.g., if they total less than 90% of the tax due that year), the IRS also assesses a penalty (see http://www.irs.gov/taxtopics/tc306.html).

There are different methods for computing the estimated taxes due. First, one may simply pay one fourth of the tax liability that was due from the previous year. For example, if you paid $12,000 in taxes the previous year, you may make four payments of $3,000 each as estimated taxes to avoid penalties. However, if you made significantly more money, you will still owe taxes come April 15. Second, using your bookkeeping system each quarter, you may total your income and your practice expenses. Then, knowing your income tax bracket, you may send in the amount due.

> **Private Practice Principle Number 16:** Be sure to make accurate estimated tax payments. We have known too many clinicians who have had an "oh my goodness, what am I going to do now" experience on April 14 when they learned of their tax liability.

SELF-EMPLOYMENT TAXES

Paying self-employment taxes is one of the downsides of not being employed by an institution. Epstein (2006) explained that employers and employees pay equal shares of the monies owed for Social Security and Medicare taxes. However, sole proprietor private practitioners do not have anyone to split the bill with, so they are responsible for paying the full 15.2% themselves. Self-employment taxes are described at http://www.irs.gov/businesses/small/article/0,,id=98846,00.html. In 2006 only the first $94,200 of income was subject to these taxes. Epstein (2006) indicated that the federal government adjusts this figure annually.

1099 FORMS

In January insurance companies send out forms summarizing the amounts they have paid to the MHP over the course of the calendar year. Copies of these forms are simultaneously sent to the clinician and the IRS. These forms resemble traditional W-2 forms that employers provide to employees. However, whereas W-2 forms are attached to tax returns, the 1099 forms are not. They are simply kept for your records. This form allows the IRS to determine whether the monies you are claiming as income are reasonably compatible with the amounts the insurance carriers indicate paying out to you. Take the example of claiming that you have collected $60,000 in fees from clients during the previous year on your tax return. At the same time the 1099 forms received from insurance carriers indicate they have paid you $70,000 in fees. The IRS may want to have a discussion with you about such a discrepancy.

You will also receive a 1099 form from any organization or corporation that has paid you more than $500 during the year. For example, if a company has paid you $750 to conduct a stress management seminar or an attorney has paid you $900 to complete a psychological evaluation, each will be sending you a 1099 form. The same holds true in reverse. If you have paid a nonemployee more than $500 during the course of the year, you are required to send them a 1099 and a copy to the IRS (for employees, the end-of-the-year W-2 form will reflect all you have paid them in salary). For example, if someone (other than an office employee) provides transcription services for you and you paid them $1,200 during the course of the year, or someone has provided computer consulting services and you paid them $850, you will send each of them a 1099 (with a copy to the IRS) with the respective amounts paid to them indicated on the form. These forms are available through the IRS, although many CPAs provide them as a courtesy to their clients.

TAX PREPARATION

We are aware of four ways to prepare tax forms to be submitted to the IRS. The first is obtaining copies of all of the relevant forms, computing the appropriate numbers, and completing the forms on your own. This process is tedious and not one we particularly recommend. The second is to go to an outside tax preparation service. These are commercially available in national chains (e.g., H&R Block) or local businesses may provide such a service. The third is to use a commercially sold tax preparation software program, such as TurboTax by Intuit or TaxCut by H&R Block. These relatively inexpensive programs will walk you through the completion of the tax return step by step and do all computations. However, no tax planning advice is provided in this format and the private practitioner has to be familiar with all deductions available. The fourth way is to establish a relationship with a CPA. CPAs can prepare your forms and also offer advice. However, this level of personal attention is also accompanied by the greatest cost of all of these methods. We especially advise new private practitioners to consult with a CPA rather than using the commercially sold tax software programs. Too many aspects of owning a small business have tax implications for a private practitioner to consider. Perhaps after several years of such consultations it may be possible to switch to the software method. However, tax situations (e.g., retirement planning, estate planning) change throughout one's career. Thus, it still may be wise to spend the extra money to ensure that your individual circumstances are receiving optimal attention.

Conclusion

Knowledge of basic bookkeeping and accounting practices is valuable for all psychologist small-business owners. Although being an expert in accounting principles is not necessary, having enough expertise to apply the basic practices described in this chapter is a must. Even if you choose to use the professional services of a CPA, it is still important to know bookkeeping and accounting basics so you will know what records to keep and how to keep them to make your CPA's job that much easier when it is time to do payroll, itemize deductions, and prepare your tax returns.

Understanding the Insurance Needs and Options of the Independent Practitioner

8

When mental health professionals (MHPs) are employed by a corporation, university, or government agency, their insurance needs are typically met by that institution. In other words, benefits of many employed positions include health insurance, life insurance, disability insurance, and malpractice insurance. In this chapter we describe each type of insurance and discuss the rationale for it, the pros and cons, where to get it, how to get it, options available, and how to get the best coverage for the money. The implications of going without purchasing these products at all or purchasing a suboptimal amount of coverage are discussed. Liability issues in independent practice are also detailed, along with ways to decrease exposure to malpractice claims.

What Is Insurance?

We know of no one who enjoys purchasing insurance and paying the premiums. We have marveled at how much we have paid in premiums over the past 25 years for health insurance, life insurance, disability insurance, auto insurance, homeowners insurance, and malpractice insurance. Pity the poor person who has to make claims against every one of these policies! However, when a claim does have to be made, and there is no difficulty in the execution of payment on this claim, everyone is glad to be covered.

An Internet search yields interesting definitions for the word *insurance*. These include

- the act, system, or business of insuring property, life, one's person, etc., against loss or harm arising in specified contingencies in consideration of a payment proportionate to the risk involved (http://www.dictionary.com; unabridged);
- coverage by contract in which one party agrees to indemnify or reimburse another for loss that occurs under the terms of the contract (http://www.dictionary.com; unabridged);
- any means of guaranteeing against loss or harm (http://www.dictionary.com; unabridged);
- a protective measure (http://www.AmericanHeritageDictionary.com);
- protection against future loss (http://www.WordNet.com); and
- a contract (policy) in which an individual or entity receives financial protection, or reimbursement, against losses from an insurance company, which pools clients' risks to make payments more affordable, in exchange for a premium (http://www.Investopedia.com).

As these definitions suggest, purchasing insurance is a way to attempt to mitigate or buffer against losses or potential costs. If your car is totaled in an accident, automobile insurance will rebate you the current value of the car. If you become ill and need expensive medical tests, health insurance will likely pay a portion (if not all) of the costs of your care. If a client successfully sues you for malpractice, your carrier will pay the amount of the judgment on your behalf up to the limits of the policy you have purchased.

Rarely do people really believe they are going to need insurance. Levine, Perkins, and Perkins (2004) indicated, however, that stressful life events are not the exception but the rule. From their perspective, "life is a soap opera" and there is no reason to believe MHPs are immune from life's negative events. Norris (1992) reviewed epidemiological data on the incidence and prevalence of nine traumatic events. In a community sample, lifetime frequencies for the total sample ranged from 4.4% for sexual assault to 30.2% for tragic death (i.e., loss of a loved one by homicide, suicide, or accident). Of those deaths, 3% involved spouses, 6% involved children, 9% involved parents, and 82% involved someone else. Robbery and injury-causing motor vehicle crashes were also quite common, each occurring to about one fourth of these respondents at some point during their lives. We highly recommend reading the special section of the December 2007 issue of *Professional Psychology: Research and Practice,* which contains eight articles on the life of the psychotherapist. Private practitioners have no special shield of protection against being involved in a significant motor vehicle accident or contracting a serious and debilitating illness, and their spouses and children are not inoculated against experiencing a significant or fatal illness. It is for these reasons that it is important to purchase insurance. As Tyson (2006) stated, "Buying insurance based on your perception of the likelihood of needing the coverage is foolish" (p. 310). Rarely do people believe they will become involved in a significant motor vehicle accident in the next year, but the data from Norris (1992) suggest that 2.6% of a community sample did experience such an accident in the previous year. Lest you believe that you do not need malpractice insurance, know that psychologists, social workers, professional counselors, and marriage and family therapists all have suits filed against them. Bennett et al. (2006) reported that approximately 1% of psychologists are subject to either a licensing board complaint or malpractice action each year. Any one of your clients is capable of filing such a suit at any time, whether it be for just cause or not.

Some Concepts Regarding Insurance

Zevnik (2004) indicated that laws regulating the business of insurance may differ from state to state. The insurance laws that apply in Oregon may not apply in Washington. Therefore, it is important to understand the insurance laws in the state in which the insurance is purchased. What you choose to insure, and how much you choose to insure it for, is most often a matter of values and risk tolerance. Some aspects of life require insurance. For example, owning an automobile requires insurance coverage in most states, owning a home with a mortgage requires homeowners insurance, and if you want to be a provider for a preferred provider organization (PPO) or a managed care organization you are required to carry malpractice insurance. However, in general there is no requirement that private practitioners purchase health insurance, life insurance, disability insurance, or malpractice insurance. Tyson (2006) advocated buying insurance for "the big stuff" and not to "sweat the small stuff." He noted that "the point of insurance is to protect against losses that would be financially catastrophic to you, not to smooth out the bumps of everyday life" (p. 308).

Private Practice Principle Number 17: Whether you see one client per year or 1,000 clients per year, it is imperative that you purchase malpractice insurance. It takes just one lawsuit to create havoc in your financial life.

As Tyson indicated, one malpractice suit, even if unsuccessful, will likely be catastrophic, and we recommend buffering against this possibility.

Insurance is sold through a number of outlets. It may be purchased directly from the company or through an agent affiliated with the company, an independent agent, or many organizations. In addition, insurance may now also be purchased over the Internet. Tyson (2006) suggested buying insurance directly from the company. He elaborated that "most insurance is sold through agents and brokers who earn commissions based on what they sell. The commission can bias what they recommend" (p. 310).

Tyson (2006) went on to say that the higher the number of policies an agent or broker writes for a certain company, the higher his or her commission rates become. Therefore, it is important to be an informed consumer and ensure the rates and coverage you are being quoted are competitive. Tyson also noted the following:

> Insurance salespeople aggressively push cash value policies because of the high commissions that insurance companies pay them. Commissions on cash value life insurance range from 50 to 100 percent of your first year's premium. An insurance salesperson can make *eight to ten times more money* selling you a cash value policy than selling you term insurance. (p. 331)

Once again, we suggest becoming an informed consumer and making sure that you are purchasing a product that is in your best interest.

There are many insurance companies. As Tyson (2006) suggested, make sure that you are buying coverage from a financially stable insurer. He urged obtaining ratings of the companies from two or three insurance rating services. The major rating companies are A.M. Best, Fitch, Moody's, Standard and Poor's, and Weiss.

Tyson (2006) noted that when possible it is advantageous to purchase insurance as part of a larger group, as doing so generally results in lower premiums. Many organizations or professional associations have contracted with insurance carriers to offer policies to their members. For example, the American Psychological Association Insurance Trust (APA Insurance Trust; http://www.apait.org) offers insurance in the areas of professional liability, life insurance (term), income protection (e.g., disability), office overhead, and long-term care. They also offer automobile and homeowners insurance options. Other professional groups such as the National Association of Social Workers, American Counseling Association, and American Association for Marriage and Family Therapy also offer some of these group-buying opportunities to their members. Major discount retailers such as Costco and Sam's Club also offer a variety of insurance packages to their customers.

Other factors contribute to the costs of insurance coverage. These may have a large effect or no effect, depending on the type of insurance being purchased. These factors are (a) age of the insured, (b) whether the insured is a smoker, (c) whether significant health problems are present when applying for insurance, (d) the duration of the term of coverage applied for, and (e) the limits or benefits of the policy.

The reason for cost differences should be obvious. Life insurance will cost more if you are applying at age 55 than if you are applying at age 35. Smokers are actuarially considered a higher risk related to the use of health insurance or life insurance. The longer the term of insurance (20 years vs. 10 years), generally the less expensive the monthly premiums will be. A million dollars' worth of life insurance will cost more than a policy that would pay one half of that amount in the event of death.

Within most types of insurance coverage the consumer can choose from multiple options. For example, Zevnik (2004) stated, "There are undoubtedly dozens, if not hundreds, of permutations of life insurance contracts" (p. 209). Within health insurance are traditional indemnity plans, catastrophic coverage plans, long-term-care plans, health maintenance organizations (HMOs), PPOs, and health savings accounts. Zevnik (2004) suggested a careful review of all available options before choosing the policy that is best for your particular situation. The insurance needs may be similar but not identical for Private Practitioner A, who is 28 years old and single, and Private Practitioner B, who is 46 years old, married, and has three children.

Most insurance policies offer options regarding size of deductible and level of benefit. In general, the larger the deductible, the less expensive the policy. The more sizable the benefit, the more expensive the policy. Tyson (2006) suggested opting for the highest deductible that you can possibly afford. This saves on premium dollars spent and eliminates the hassle of filing for claims that are only a small amount of money.

Each policy has its own language and terms to be understood. For example, within health insurance terms such as *reasonable and customary, network provider, maximum out-of-pocket costs,* and *lifetime maximum* are common. Within disability insurance terms such as *waiting period, partial versus total disability,* and even *disability* have to be clearly defined. A glossary of insurance terms can be found on the APA Insurance Trust Web site (http://www.apait.org/apait/resources/definitions). Without totally understanding this language, private practitioners will be purchasing a product that may or may not meet their needs should the situation arise in which they have to use their insurance. Therefore, if you are using an agent be sure to have him or her explain any terms that are not clearly understood. If you do not educate yourself about insurance before signing a contract to purchase a specific policy, you are counting on chance that the policy will pay exactly as you hope or even that it will pay at all.

Malpractice Insurance

As noted earlier, malpractice insurance for MHPs is optional. It is not a condition of licensure to practice in a state. However, PPOs and managed care organizations require clinicians to carry malpractice insurance (and they will specify the minimum amounts acceptable), and hospitals require it as well for those MHPs who seek privileges on their staff.

Barnett and Henshaw (2003) described the two types of malpractice insurance: claims-made and occurrence. Claims-made insurance covers the insured only while the policy is in effect. If coverage is discontinued for any reason (e.g., if you switch carriers or retire, or the company stops writing policies), then the coverage ceases. Occurrence insurance remains in effect over the course of your career and the coverage never ceases. For this reason occurrence insurance is more expensive than claims-made insurance.

Let's look at a hypothetical example. Mary Smith, a licensed marriage and family therapist who maintains claims-made insurance, decides to retire on December 31, 2008. She has had this coverage with Insurance Company X for the past 10 years and no malpractice suits have been filed against her. Because she is retiring she does not renew her policy for the coming year. On January 5, 2009, a client files a malpractice claim against her related to services provided a year earlier. Because the statute of limitations to file a suit in their state had not expired, the client was within her rights to do so. However, in this scenario Ms. Smith is not covered by her carrier even though she had insurance in effect while the alleged malpractice took place. If Ms. Smith had purchased occurrence insurance instead she would have been covered for this claim (or any other claim made against her in the future) and likely have breathed a sigh of relief.

Steve Walfish initially had his malpractice coverage with the St. Paul Companies. For many years they were the largest writers of malpractice policies for health care professionals. However, one day the company decided that this insurance product was no longer profitable. As such, it gave proper notice that it would no longer be renewing policies, and Steve then had to purchase this coverage from another company. He had claims-made insurance at that time. Therefore, he would not have been covered if a suit had been filed against him by a client whom he had seen in all those years he was covered by this carrier. Insurance companies allow for such a case by selling a product called a *tail*. This tail then covers private practitioners for any suits brought against them for services during the period they were covered by the previous insurance carrier. It is essential that a tail be purchased once the private practitioner ceases to practice. Imagine retiring at age 70 and then at 72 a former client files a malpractice suit against you and you have opted not to have coverage in effect. Recall one of the definitions of the word *insurance* presented at the beginning of the chapter: "a protection against future loss." Tails are expensive to purchase. The decision between occurrence insurance and claims-made insurance is a matter of "Pay me now or pay me later" as the savings from buying the latter instead of the former may be erased when you purchase the tail. Bennett et al. (2006) advocated continuing to purchase malpractice insurance during retirement years. They suggested that any activities that the retired MHPs may do following retirement (e.g., summarizing records of former clients, testifying in deposition or court regarding a previous case, making referrals to specific professionals) may be considered professional activity and subject to a malpractice action. If coverage is not in effect, then the private practitioner is 100% liable for any judgment against him or her.

When it comes to the amount of malpractice to purchase, we advocate, "The more, the better." There are two figures to consider when choosing the extent of your coverage: amount made per claim and amount made in 1 year. For example, malpractice insurance in the amounts of $1,000,000/$3,000,000 means a policy limit of $1,000,000 per claim and $3,000,000 for the year in total. So if you are successfully sued by one client for $1,000,001, your insurer will pay the first million dollars and you will be left paying the client the remaining $1. However, if you are successfully sued for $1,100,000, you are responsible for the remaining $100,000. If three people successfully sue you in 1 year for no more than $1,000,000 each, your financial obligation would be covered. However, if a fourth stepped forward and did the same, you would owe $1,000,000.

Table 8.1 presents amounts charged by an unnamed insurance carrier for claims-made malpractice insurance for different policy limits. The numbers presented are based on the 5th year of coverage being in effect (The costs are less expensive across all disciplines for the years leading

TABLE 8.1

Malpractice Rates From an Unnamed Insurer

Each wrongful act/Aggregate	PhD/PsyD	MSW	LPC	LMFT
$1,000,000/$1,000,000	$700	$364	$314	$242
$1,000,000/$3,000,000	$798	$358	$358	$276
$1,000,000/$4,000,000	$868	$370	$389	$300
$1,000,000/$5,000,000	$896	$381	$402	$310
$2,000,000/$2,000,000	$945	$366	$424	$327
$2,000,000/$4,000,000	$1001	$379	$449	$346

Note. PhD/PsyD = psychologist; MSW = master's in social work; LPC = licensed professional counselor; LMFT = licensed marriage and family therapist.

up to this time frame). The cost difference between a minimum amount of insurance and a maximum amount of insurance for a MHP is minimal. For example, for a person with a master's in social work, the annual cost difference between coverage of $1,000,000/$3,000,000 and $2,000,000/4,000,000 is only $39. We believe the better policy is well worth the extra money. For psychologists this difference is greater ($203), but we still think it is well worth the extra cost. You would be kicking yourself if by saving a couple of hundred dollars a year you were responsible for paying out $1,000,000 (or even $100,000). Most insurance companies also offer a discount on these rates if you participate in one of their risk management continuing education programs. We suggest that you take advantage of such a program not only because of the financial incentive but also to keep current in the latest risk management issues and procedures.

Most insurance companies also offer the opportunity to purchase additional coverage for legal defense for a licensing board complaint. We strongly urge all clinicians to purchase this extra coverage. For example, the unnamed insurance company from Table 8.1 offers $25,000 of such coverage at an annual cost of $75. If you ever do need it you will be extraordinarily grateful that you purchased this much coverage for such a small amount of money. Even if a frivolous complaint is filed against you with a licensure board, it can easily cost $10,000 to $20,000 to pay for your legal representation to include preparation of your defense and representation at hearings.

Most companies also provide a consultation service through which you may speak with an attorney or another MHP well-versed in ethics and legal issues should you have dilemmas or questions arise in your practice. The insurance company's goal is to be helpful and an advocate for you to conduct your practice in the most risk-averse manner possible. The more they can do to help prevent a client from filing a suit or board complaint against you, the more money they will be able to earn as an insurance company. Therefore, they are motivated to help.

It may be noted in Table 8.1 that psychologists have the highest rates for the same amount of coverage when compared with the other three disciplines. Indeed, psychologists pay nearly three times the amount that a marriage and family therapist does. It is unclear why this is the case, although it is possible to speculate that actuarially insurance companies have determined that psychologists are at a higher risk to be sued than are those in the other professions.

The rates presented in Table 8.1 relate to clinicians in full-time private practice. Each company also has rates (that are proportionally less expensive) for those individuals who are in part-time practice.

One can never eliminate the possibility of (a) committing an act of malpractice or (b) a client filing suit against you for an alleged event of malpractice. No one is perfect, and events out of one's control may happen despite one's best efforts. MHPs make mistakes by acts of either commission or omission. MHPs also have clients, some with Axis II diagnoses, who may feel entitled or enjoy the drama of a lawsuit. However, the private practitioner can engage in risk management behaviors that decrease the likelihood that these events will take place.

Bennett et al. (2006) pointed to the difficulty in knowing exactly what behaviors result in malpractice suits being filed against psychologists. However, after reviewing several data sets, they noted that common themes do arise. They concluded that in order of frequency (most common to least common reason) the highest areas of risk are sexual relationships, nonsexual multiple relationships, insurance and fee problems, participation in child custody cases, breaches of confidentiality, practicing outside of one's area of competence, test misuse, inadequate supervision, inappropriate follow-up or termination, inappropriate response to crises, and inadequate record keeping (p. 22). Strom-Gottfried (1999) examined 894 ethics complaints filed against clinical social workers. Her study revealed that 56.1% of the cases were violations involving some form of boundary infraction (sexual activities, multiple relationships). Reamer (1995) found that the most frequent malpractice suits brought against social workers involved sexual misconduct or incorrect treatment.

Bennett et al. (2006) identified three key elements of risk management—informed consent, documentation, and consultation—and then applied them to a variety of clinical applications. We highly recommend following the model presented in their book as a method of reducing risk of being involved in a malpractice case.

On the basis of years of service on a state psychological association's ethics committee, Barnett (1996) formulated principles to minimize the risk of malpractice. These included (a) placing primary emphasis on serving and being helpful to the consumers of your services; (b) having a full and complete informed consent process; (c) being aware of and informing clients of the limits of confidentiality; (d) practicing within the standard of care of the profession; (e) maintaining boundaries and avoiding exploitative multiple relationships; (f) maintaining sound business practices and making clear all fee and financial arrangements; (g) seeking consultation and supervision; (h) not abandoning clients and making appropriate referrals; and (i) maintaining timely, relevant, and thorough documentation.

Along these lines we recommend that clinicians regularly attend continuing education programs on ethical issues and also be current with the major texts on ethics for their profession. Excellent books on the topic include those by Barnett and Johnson (2008), Knapp and VandeCreek (2006), Nagy (2005), Pope and Vasquez (2007), Reamer (2006), and J. Woody and Woody (2001). Clinical practice is complex, and often unique clinical situations and application of professional skills call for an examination of ethics issues as they relate to these areas of practice. For example, special attention has been paid to ethical and legal issues in forensic practice (Bush, Connell, & Denny, 2006; Hess, 1998, 2005), HIV psychotherapy cases (J. Anderson & Barrett, 2001), practicing in organizations (Lowman, 2006), health care settings (Hanson, Kerkhoff, & Bush, 2004), rural practice (Barnett & Henshaw, 2002; Schank & Skovholt, 2005), dealing with suicidal clients (Barnett & Porter, 1998), termination and abandonment (Barnett, MacGlashan, & Clarke, 2000), informed consent (Snyder & Barnett, 2006), online counseling (Mallen, Vogel, & Rochlen, 2005), practicing in the context of managed care (Barnett, 1998), and even closing a practice (Barnett, 1997a). As private practitioners expand the scope of their practice to areas beyond traditional individual psychotherapy, ethics and legal issues must be considered as part of a risk management process.

It is important to make a final point related to malpractice and sexual activity with a client. As noted earlier, this is the area with highest risk for a malpractice suit to be initiated. Most malpractice policies contain a sexual activity exclusion in their policy. If a suit is filed related to inappropriate sexual activity by an MHP, this misbehavior will not be covered by his or her malpractice insurance policy.

Disability Insurance

Disability insurance is also known as income-replacement insurance. Tyson (2006) asked the question, "If you were disabled and unable to work, what would you live on?" (p. 309). He pointed out that the purpose of disability insurance is to protect your income for yourself and dependents. If you are employed by an organization, most likely one of the benefits includes paid sick leave. Some organizations allow employees to donate sick leave hours to their coworkers in need. Paid sick leave is a way for income to continue despite an inability to work. In private practice, unless it is structured in a corporation, there is no such thing as paid sick leave. MHPs are in a service business. If no service is provided, no reimbursement is received.

Disability insurance is different from paid sick leave in that it is not designed to cover periods of short-term inability to work. If you are unable to practice for a few weeks, no method or product is available to cover that short-term loss of income. For example, we have a colleague who had a heart attack and was unable to practice for 2 weeks following the incident. He then gradually returned to work, as he was physically unable to return to his previous full-time schedule right away. This time off, and the gradual return to work, was a lost income opportunity. Disability insurance is designed for the times when one is unable to return to work in fewer than 30 days. It is especially valuable when one is unable to work for several months or years because of illness. No one likes to think about this as a possibility, but "life happens." As Tyson (2006) pointed out, the majority of disabilities are caused by medical problems typically associated with advancing age. However, he further indicated that more than one third of all disabilities are experienced by individuals under the age of 45 and that the medical problems associated with disability cannot be predicted in advance, especially those caused by accidents.

KEY ISSUES IN DISABILITY POLICIES

Zevnik (2004) indicated that disability policies contain many variables that merit close attention. Furthermore, within each are several variations that are crucial to understand.

The first variable is the waiting period. This is the length of time one has to be disabled before benefits begin. One is not eligible for payments from the first day the disability occurs; payments begin only after this waiting period has expired. The length of the waiting period is chosen by the person purchasing the coverage. The choices are typically offered at 30, 60, 90, or 180 days following the onset of inability to work. For example, imagine you are disabled for 45 days and have purchased a 30-day waiting period. A total of 15 days of benefits would be paid because there would be no payment for the first 30 days.

The shorter the waiting period, the more expensive the insurance premium will be. Therefore, it is important to examine your own financial situation to determine the waiting period that would best suit your needs. For example, if you believe that you have enough assets to cover 3 months of lost income, then choose a 90-day waiting period because it will be less expensive than a policy with a 30-day waiting period.

The second variable is the time period for which benefits are payable. Most policies are not in effect from the onset of disability until the time of death. When disability benefits are provided in organizations, short-term disability payments are usually (depending on the organization) payable for 6 months and long-term disability benefits for 2 years. In private practice there is more flexibility in this choice. The period may be as short as 2 years or may last until the claimant is 65 years of age (Zevnik, 2004). However, the longer the period of coverage, the higher the premium costs will be.

The third variable is amount of coverage. When disability benefits are provided in organizations, the amount is usually based on a percentage of the employee's salary. Zevnik (2004) reported that this figure is usually either 60% or 80% of an employee's gross salary. Zevnik also indicated that these benefits are not taxable and not subject to Social Security or Medicare taxes. However, in private practice the benefits are not based on an annual salary level, but rather individual practitioners choose the amount of coverage they want to purchase. The coverage, which is for X number of dollars per month, depends on the extent of the clinician's practice and how much the clinician would be willing to receive in income if he or she were disabled. For example, a clinician might want to purchase $3,000 per month of coverage or $10,000 per month of coverage (2 years of tax returns are required to document general level of income to avoid someone earning $3,000 per month purchasing $10,000 per month of coverage; the maximum amount of coverage purchased needs to be similar to the amount historically earned). The higher the monthly benefit, the higher the premium costs will be for that coverage. We also recommend a periodic review of the amount of coverage that is needed. For example, Jeff Barnett recently increased the amount of his disability coverage. In reviewing his insurance needs he realized that the monthly payable amount was the same as when he initially purchased his policy 20 years prior. Because his income had increased significantly since then, it was time to update the benefit to reflect his current needs.

The fourth variable is definition of disability. This issue is important to consider when purchasing a policy. Private disability policies provide options of purchasing either *usual occupation* or *any occupation* benefits. Take, for example, a licensed professional counselor in private practice who has a stroke and has speech aphasia. It would be difficult, if not impossible, for her to continue in her private practice. Indeed, there may be no other aspect of mental health counseling in which she could be gainfully employed. If she has usual-occupation benefits, she would receive full benefits. If she had any-occupation benefits and if it were determined that she could not do professional counseling but could be employable (at a relatively comparable salary level) in another occupation, then benefits would not be available to her. The other issue within the definition realm is whether someone is partially or totally disabled. Take the example of the counselor who has a stroke; suppose that through rehabilitation efforts she is able to return to work half time. If her policy contains a clause indicating partial disability benefits are available, she could earn her income from the practice and the insurance carrier would then make up the difference between her half-time and full-time pay (within the limits of her policy).

Zevnik (2004) also suggested paying attention to other aspects of a disability policy, including a cost-of-living adjustment provision, noncancelable and guaranteed renewal clauses, and a future insurability feature. If you are disabled for 10 years and do not have a cost-of-living adjustment benefit, then inflation will whittle away the value of the disability benefits. Zevnik (2004) indicated that certain policies may require periodic medical exams. He suggested that if a claimant falls into ill health without the noncancelable and guaranteed renewal clauses, coverage may be canceled. Disability benefits are purchased at a certain level (monthly dollar amount payable) and are in effect for a certain number of years (e.g., 5, 10, 20 years) with a fixed monthly premium cost. Suppose a psychologist purchases a policy at age 28 and it is in effect for 20 years. He then becomes fully disabled at age 38 and collects benefits for the 10 years remaining on his policy. However, at age 48 this coverage will end. If a future insurability option was not purchased, it will be near impossible to obtain further coverage. In addition, some policies also include clauses regarding retraining. If the professional counselor in the earlier example had such a clause, she might be eligible for training for another comparable-level occupation in which speech aphasia is not an impediment to being employed.

When describing the need for income protection insurance, the APA Insurance Trust (n.d.) indicated that the chances of disability are much greater than the chances of death for individuals in the 25- to 65-year-old age range. Indeed, it cited data to suggest a 50% chance that a 30-year-old individual will be disabled for more than 3 months before reaching the age of 65. We believe these important data should not be overlooked by private practitioners trying to protect their financial future.

OFFICE OVERHEAD INSURANCE

Office overhead insurance is separate from disability insurance. Let us take the example of a psychologist in private practice being unable to work because of an injury in a motor vehicle accident and need for rehabilitation. However, during this time he still maintains his obligations to pay his office rent (or mortgage if he owns) and salary obligations for any employees. He may have to pay for telephone services related to his practice and to maintain memberships in professional associations. If he has office overhead insurance, all of these bills will be covered. Insurance premiums related to practice may also be paid with these funds. Overhead insurance is typically time limited (e.g., 2 years) and generally not very expensive.

A description of benefits, limits, and exclusions of a sample plan for psychologists may be found on the APA Insurance Trust's Web site (http://www.apait.org/apait/products/officeoverhead/detail.aspx). To find other private insurance companies that write policies for this type of coverage, perform an Internet search on the term *overhead insurance.*

PREMISES INSURANCE

Imagine the unfortunate circumstance that a client is injured in your waiting room when a piece of the ceiling breaks off and falls on his shoulder. Who is financially responsible for his injury? Is it the building's owner or the private practitioner who leases space in the building? Take another scenario in which a client slips and falls because children's toys in the waiting room were not put away. Who is financially responsible for this injury?

To cover these unlikely scenarios, purchase premises insurance. It is generally inexpensive and provides financial protection for the private practitioner.

BUSINESS INTERRUPTION INSURANCE

Imagine that your practice premises are subject to the wrath of a natural disaster, such as a hurricane, flood, tornado, or earthquake. Or perhaps because of a fire your office building is condemned or cannot be occupied for 4 months because of reconstruction. All of these events are unlikely to happen. However, if they do, in addition to the emotional distress of the event, you now have no income (remember—private practice is a service business; no service equals no income).

Business interruption insurance will allow income to continue at the same rate as it was before the disaster took place. We know of no clinician who has actually purchased this type of insurance for his or her practice. However, this does not mean it should not be considered in an overall protection plan.

Other Insurance

The insurance needs of private practitioners as described earlier relate to the business of their practice. However, as previously stated, when one is employed by an organization, several types of insurance are often provided as a fringe benefit. These usually include health insurance and life insurance.

Purchasing these types of insurance is totally optional. The decision to purchase health or life insurance on the part of the private practitioner may depend on available monies, life circumstances, and personal values. In terms of available monies there is no such thing as inexpensive health insurance. Some policies are just less expensive than others. Private practitioners who are not married or do not have children may decide to forgo the purchase of life insurance. Some people who are young and healthy may decide to take the chance of forgoing health insurance. This is not a position we advocate (because "life happens"), but some people are willing to take such risks.

HEALTH INSURANCE

We do not go into a detailed discussion of health insurance options for the private practitioner because they are quite numerous. As discussed earlier, if a group plan is available for purchase through a national organization or retail membership club, we encourage the private practitioner to take advantage of such an opportunity. The purchasing power of the group may allow purchase of health insurance at a more reasonable price than on an individual basis. Health insurance options may be explored through Internet searches or by contacting large insurers (e.g., your local BlueCross BlueShield, Kaiser Permanente) directly.

A variety of plans are usually offered, including traditional indemnity plans, PPOs, and HMOs. Varying levels of deductible are usually offered as well. As noted earlier, a plan with more coverage and a lower deductible will cost more. The less the coverage and the higher the deductible, the less will be the cost of the insurance. Variables entering into your choice may depend on your health and life circumstances. For example, if you are healthy and have no dependents you may opt for a high deductible (e.g., $5,000 per year) and coverage only for hospitalization. This type of coverage is typically referred to as catastrophic. Recall the advice of Tyson (2006) who suggested purchasing insurance not for everyday costs but only for large costs. With such catastrophic coverage there may be no coverage for office visits or medications. However, if you know that you or a family member will have a consistent need for medical attention and medications, then a plan with more coverage and a lower deductible may be a better fit.

Many private practitioners are opting to purchase health savings accounts for their health insurance needs. As Tyson (2006) explained, these accounts are meant to accompany a high-deductible (at least $1,000 for an individual and $3,000 for a family) health insurance policy. Monies can be set aside for medical expenses into an investment account. These health expenses are then paid with pretax monies. Information about health savings accounts may be found on the U.S. Department of Treasury Web site (http://www.treas.gov/offices/public-affairs/hsa).

LIFE INSURANCE

The main reason to purchase life insurance is to provide a source of income protection for your dependents. Choosing the right policy takes education and a significant amount of study.

There are two primary categories of life insurance: term and whole life. As Zevnik (2004) explained, term insurance is "pure" insurance, whereas whole life is a combination of insurance and investment. Term insurance is limited to the specified dollar amount of the policy for the term the policy is purchased. There is no cash value, dividend, or investment component for term insurance. Policies may be purchased that remain in effect for a varying amount of years. When the policy term expires, you must apply for a brand-new policy. There is no automatic renewal. If a short-term policy is purchased (e.g., 5–10 years) then the premiums will be higher when a new policy is sought because it is being purchased at a higher age. If the insured develops a serious health problem, he or she may not be able to obtain a replacement policy because a physical examination and reporting of medical conditions are requirements of the application. As such, it may be safest to purchase a policy for the greatest number of years possible (Zevnik, 2004).

In whole life policies, a portion of the premium goes toward the purchase of a death benefit and another portion is channeled into building a cash value that pays a dividend. There are two advantages to this approach as opposed to term insurance: (a) one can borrow against the cash value if money is needed for any reason and (b) if the policy is surrendered, the built-up cash value is paid to the policy holder (Zevnik, 2004).

Zevnik (2004) reported that the rate of return on whole life policies is generally lower than on other investments. However, the forced savings involved in whole life policies may make it attractive to investors. Whole life policies cost more than term policies. There is an adage in the insurance industry that it is financially better to buy a term insurance policy and invest the difference in a better returning account than to buy a more expensive whole life policy. However, Zevnik (2004) noted that not everyone is disciplined enough to make this extra investment.

As noted earlier, there are many combinations and permutations of life insurance and it is best to choose the one that best fits your needs. In terms of finding a reputable insurance agent, we suggest asking professional colleagues who they use as their agent if you are not going to purchase directly from a company.

Conclusion

If we may borrow from a Donna Summer song, private practitioners "work hard for the money." We know of no successful practitioner who does not. The purchase of insurance is a way to protect what you have earned, what you will earn in the future, and what you may want to leave to others when you have passed on. As we noted at the beginning of this chapter, no one enjoys paying insurance premiums. However, not to do so places your financial security at risk.

BUILDING YOUR PRACTICE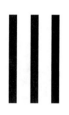

To Managed Care or Not to Managed Care

That Is the Question

9

S ay the phrase *managed care* to a private practitioner and you'll generally hear all sorts of visceral negative reactions and corrective phrases such as *mismanaged care* or *mangled care*. Paradoxical to this response is the fact that one of the more common questions asked by early career professionals is, "How can I get on managed care panels (MCPs)?"

Many authors have discussed the deleterious impact of managed care on the provision of psychotherapy (e.g., Alleman, 2001; Fox, 1995; Karon, 1995). In a survey by Phelps, Eisman, and Kohout (1998), four out of five psychologists reported that managed care was having a negative impact on their practices. A survey in one state found that higher involvement in managed care by independent practitioners resulted in a reported adverse effect on morale, professional identity, and approach to psychotherapy compared with lower involvement levels by practitioners (Rothbaum, Bernstein, Haller, Phelps, & Kohout, 1998). Cohen, Maracek, and Gillham (2007) similarly found that psychotherapists believed that contracting with managed care organizations (MCOs) demanded several practices that violated the psychotherapists' standard of care and professional ethics. Kremer and Gesten (1998) found that clients, and potential clients, showed less willingness to self-disclose under managed care conditions than in other circumstances.

It is clear that insurance companies save money when they (a) reduce fees paid to mental health professionals and (b) limit the number of psychotherapy sessions or psychological testing hours they will authorize for payment. However, managed care did not arise from a vacuum just to fix a system that was functioning effectively and efficiently. Barnett (1997b) pointed out that regardless of how individual practitioners may feel about managed care, out-of-control health care costs created a need for changes in the health care system. Our colleague Tony Broskowski used to refer to 30-day treatment programs for alcohol and drug addiction as *cashectomies*. Treatment protocols were designed to be 30 days in length because most insurance carriers provided 30 days of coverage. Individualized planning for length of stay was not a part of the determination unless an extension of more than the 30 days was going to be requested. Psychological services were not always being delivered because of medical necessity. When Steve Walfish first moved to Washington state, during an initial session his client informed him, "I've been in counseling for years. I intend to be in counseling for years. I have this good Boeing insurance that will pay it for me." Steve, who generally practices short-term cognitive–behavioral psychotherapy, replied, "Well, not with me." They met for 10 sessions to work on issues related to anxiety and depression and episodically over the next 4 years she went in for "booster sessions" or to deal with a specific crisis that emerged in her life. So in some ways managed care came about because there were no internal controls within the profession. Broskowski (1991) contended that managed care in the mental health industry emerged as a marketplace response to concerns for service cost, quality, and accessibility on the part of employers and insurers. Strom-Gottfried (1998) similarly argued that participation on MCPs need not be equated with unethical practice and is no less ethical than the unregulated fee system that existed before the advent of managed care. Clinicians choosing to provide services within a MCO system can consult Barnett (1993) for helpful guidelines for working ethically within such a system.

Why Be on a MCP?

The answer to this question is simple. MCOs control the mental health insurance benefits of a massive number of clients. A large segment of Americans with health insurance have had their mental health care "carved out" to a MCO by their insurance carrier. By *carveout* we mean that insurance carriers have contracted with the MCO to be responsible for all of the mental health (and usually substance abuse) care for their subscribers. The largest MCOs are Magellan Health Services, United Behavioral Health, ValueOptions, and CIGNA Behavioral Health. Therefore, if this large segment of the American population wants to access their insurance benefits to pay for part or all of their mental health care, they may have to go through these MCOs. There are exceptions to this if the insurance plan has out-of-network benefits, which we discuss later in the chapter. Therefore, MCOs are a large player in the mental health care system.

It is unclear how many mental health professionals there are in this country. However, with psychology being the second most popular major on college campuses today (Princeton Review, n.d.), it is safe to assume that the number is still growing. Many of these graduates will want to earn an advanced degree in the mental health fields. With the number of mental health providers growing there is more competition for attracting clients (e.g., customers) to their practices. As MCOs may serve as gatekeepers for their subscribers, if psychotherapists want access to these clients they may have to become providers for the MCOs.

Being on a MCP may be an advantage to your practice. It may be a disadvantage to your practice. However, before we elaborate on these issues, we examine how one gets on panels in the first place and how mental health care is delivered in managed care systems.

Joining a MCP

MCPs are not open to everyone who wants to join them. Membership is controlled by the self-defined needs of the MCOs. Frager (2002) indicated that it is financially advantageous to MCOs to limit the size of their panel because of the administrative costs associated with maintaining them (e.g., credentialing and recredentialing, mailings). The best way to find out if panels are open is to contact the companies directly through the preferred contact method they list on their Web sites. They will let you know if there are any openings on the panels. The panels tend to be closed especially if the clinician (a) is located in an urban area or an area in which there is a large concentration of mental health professionals or (b) is a generalist and does not have a specialty that is currently lacking on the MCP. If the panels are closed, then we suggest recontacting them every 3 to 6 months as the MCO's needs may change, especially as more providers opt out of MCO participation. The monthly newsletter *Psychotherapy Finances* (http://www.psyfin.com) often lists the names of managed care companies (and employee assistance programs) that are looking for providers.

Consider the following example from the Magellan Health Services Web site:

> Magellan's provider networks are managed by our local service centers. Providers are invited to participate in our networks on the basis of their
>
> ■ credentials,
> ■ specialties,
> ■ Magellan's business needs, and
> ■ in accordance with applicable state laws. (Magellan Health Services, 2007)

From the United Behavioral Health Web site:

> Please note that United Behavioral Health/US Behavioral Health Plan, CA are accepting applications based on assessed network need, unless otherwise required by state law. In order to be considered for network inclusion, please complete the "Network Request Form and Specialty Attestation" and fax them to the Network manager of your state. If it is determined that a business need exists in your area, you will be sent a *Join Our Network* letter via fax or e-mail within 10 business days advising you to continue with the UBH application process. If we determine that there is not an immediate business/network need in your area, you will be notified and we will retain your name should future network needs arise. (United Behavioral Health, 2007)

As can be seen, no one has a right to be a provider for a MCP; rather, membership has to fit in with the MCO's needs and interests.

If the MCP is open and needs providers, you will be invited to complete an application. The application will request information regarding your educational history, professional experience, approaches to psychotherapy, populations served, availability of hours, hospitals at which you have staff privileges, arrangements made for after-hours emergencies, information regarding past problems you may have had with licensure, and if there is any reason that you cannot currently safely practice (e.g., substance abuse problem, mental health problem). The MCO will then review this application and determine whether you are a fit for the current needs in its panel. Clinicians who primarily conduct long-term insight-oriented psychotherapy with adults are likely not going to be a good fit for a MCP. Clinicians who primarily practice short-term psychotherapy (either cognitive behavior therapy or solution-focused therapy) are likely better fits for the philosophy of most MCOs. Clinicians who see children and adolescents (because there is a shortage of individuals skilled in seeing this population) are likely to be more attractive to a MCP than are clinicians who solely see adults. Some MCPs also require a minimum amount of experience postlicensure (2 years for some, 5 years for others) for membership in their network.

For anyone interested in working within the MCO system, Frager (2002) presented excellent advice as a former insider. Once employed as a case manager for a large MCO, she offered direction for both joining a MCP and optimally functioning within a system that has its own set of rules. She provided specific advice for initially approaching the MCO, how to proceed if the MCP is closed, and completing the application and credentialing process. After receiving your completed application, the MCO will then review your credentials, verifying the accuracy and credibility of what you have reported. The process from initial inquiry to being granted membership on a MCP usually takes several months. Therefore, to reduce frustration, understand from the beginning that the process can be long and is completed at the pace most advantageous to the MCO and not the clinician. After all, you are asking to join the MCO; the MCO is not courting you.

Once you have been credentialed, the MCO will send you a contract that outlines the policies and procedures to be followed by panel clinicians, an appeals process if there is disagreement, and a list of reimbursements for services provided. Please note that these contracts are written to be MCO-friendly and are not in the best interest of the clinician. Why would they be? The MCO is looking out for its own best interests. Frager (2002) described this step as "signing your life away" (p. 61); the contracts, at least initially, are rarely if ever open for negotiation. It is a take-it-or-leave-it situation. Reimbursement rates for services rendered are especially nonnegotiable in the beginning, unless the person is being courted by the MCO to fill a special need on its panels. We are aware of some cases in which the MCO did negotiate fees because it wanted a valued member to either join or remain on the panel. The April 2007 issue of the newsletter *Psychotherapy Finances* featured a story on Noreen Keenan, a licensed clinical social worker. She became aware of a MCO that was expanding in her area and seeking panel members. When she received the packet, she noted that the reimbursement rate was different for social workers than for psychologists. In completing her application she crossed out the social worker rate and inserted the higher rate offered to psychologists. The MCO indicated that it could not honor the request for the higher fee. Dr. Keenan then said, "No, thank you" to the offer and thought that was the end of the story. However, the company quickly called back and agreed to the higher fee. It is unclear why the company changed its mind. One can speculate that the company needed to demonstrate to its subscribers that there was an adequate number of clinicians on their panel. However, Dr. Keenan was willing to walk away. The result is that she was reimbursed at a rate 25% higher than she would have been had she been desperate and negotiating from a position of weakness.

Provision of Clinical Services Within Managed Care

If you are on the MCP, you are eligible to see clients covered by a MCO. You may also be able to see clients if they have out-of-network benefits. Clients may access you in a number of ways. First, they may call their MCO and be given your name as a potential provider. When clients call, they are usually given three to five names of panel members in their zip code for geographic convenience. Second, they may get your name from a provider list (often on the Internet). Third, they may be referred by a friend or former client and inquire whether you accept their insurance or are a participating provider.

Once the client has scheduled an initial appointment with you, he or she most often then has to call the MCO and request an authorization for care. The first X number of sessions are then authorized for provision and payment. This number varies from MCO to MCO and may range from 4 to 10 sessions. Time frames in which the services must be delivered are usually specified. Some MCOs have gone to an open-access system in which this initial authorization step is not necessary. If more sessions are needed beyond the authorized number of sessions, the clinician then has to complete an outpatient treatment form and submit it to the MCO for authorization. This form usually includes information regarding diagnosis, severity of symptoms, number and frequency of sessions being requested, and a treatment plan with estimated end of treatment. When managed care first came into existence, these forms were quite onerous but have since been streamlined. Some MCOs have made it possible to complete these forms online. These forms should be completed before the last of the authorized number of sessions. If you go over this allotment (or beyond the end date of the authorization), you may not be paid for unauthorized sessions even if they have been deemed medically necessary. You may not seek payment from clients for unauthorized services. It is important to be meticulous regarding the tracking of the number of sessions provided and the number of sessions authorized (as well as dates) when working in a managed care environment. Although we have no way to prove this, we believe that MCOs count on a certain percentage of clinician error to avoid paying for services and increase their profit margin. Otherwise there would be no reason for a service delivered 4 weeks beyond the authorization date not being reimbursed, even when deemed medically necessary.

If further sessions are authorized, care may continue. If additional sessions are needed beyond this authorization, the same outpatient treatment reports need to be completed once again. It is our experience that beyond the initial authorization the MCOs begin to examine client progress and need for further care with closer scrutiny. If clients are not progressing, they might like to know why they are not. They may ask for medication consultations with a psychiatrist. They may request to review chart notes. They have the right to do all of this on the basis of the contract you have signed to be a member of the MCP. They want to ensure that clients are moving toward measurable goals and not using psychotherapy for continued support, maintenance of gains, or personal growth reasons. These circumstances are usually not viewed as medically necessary services.

If at any time the MCO decides that care is not medically necessary but the clinician disagrees, treatment should continue and the adverse utilization review decision should be appealed. Barnett and Sanzone (1997) reviewed court decisions and ethics issues for the mental health professional in the situation in which the MCO has denied authorization. These authors pointed out that terminating a client's treatment solely because of an adverse utilization review decision would be inappropriate. The psychologist's responsibility for each client's welfare remains regardless of payment decisions by MCOs. Barnett and Sanzone concluded the following: "Regardless of utilization review decisions, patients in need must be provided with continued care, either by the health care provider personally, or by making alternative arrangements through an appropriate referral" (p. 13).

Psychological testing must be preauthorized by the MCO. The MCO will typically have a form that has to be completed by the psychologist requesting authorization for the testing. The current form for United Behavioral Health asks for information regarding referral source, background information (symptoms, setting in which the testing will take place), the purpose of the testing, provisional diagnoses and rule-out diagnoses, and a listing of the tests and the amount of time requested for authorization. The form for Magellan Health Services is similar but also asks whether the referral question for the testing could not be answered by a diagnostic interview, a review of records, or a second opinion. This form is then faxed to the MCO, who reviews the request and decides to authorize the service or not as requested. The MCO may reduce the number of hours it will authorize. The psychologist may not bill the client for time not authorized by the MCO. If the request is not authorized, the psychologist then has to decide whether he or she is going to complete the evaluation anyway and accept only the time allotted or decline to complete the evaluation. If the evaluation is completed, we suggest the psychologist not reduce the length of the testing battery just because the reimbursement for the evaluation is lower than he or she would like it to be. It is incumbent on the psychologist to complete the evaluation using the test instruments he or she deems necessary to answer the referral question regardless of how long it takes to do so or what the reimbursement rate may be from the MCO.

To do otherwise would be compromising the integrity of the assessment process.

> **Private Practice Principle Number 18:** Participation in a managed care plan is not a requirement for being in private practice. If you choose to participate, you must clearly understand and emotionally accept all of the financial and clinical ramifications and limitations beforehand. If you do not, you will set yourself up for a great deal of frustration during your participation.

Alleman (2001) pointed out that a percentage of clinicians have a personality that will not allow them to peacefully participate on MCPs. They simply cannot tolerate someone inspecting their credentials, having influence on their treatment decisions, deciding how long they may work with a client, and defining the appropriate goals of psychotherapy. We think it important that clinicians do a self-analysis to see whether they can practice under these stipulations. Recall the data of Walfish and O'Donnell (in press) in which "relationships with managed care companies" was found to be the most stressful variable when working in a private practice. To practice within a MCP and believe the circumstances should be different than they actually are will only result in an angry psychotherapist. We also believe there is a high likelihood that such resentment will trickle down to interfering with the client–psychotherapist relationship.

It is also important that all psychotherapists who participate on MCPs have practice patterns and areas of competence consistent with managed care's needs. These areas may include brief forms of treatment, group treatment approaches, and evidence-based treatment methods. In addition, one should have a willingness to monitor treatment outcomes and share these data with the MCOs.

Fee-for-Service Practice

A fee-for-service practice model is simple in concept. The private practitioner sets his or her fees, informs the client of these fees, and then the client pays that amount. Although this concept is simple, it has historically been difficult to put into action for some private practitioners.

Comas-Diaz (2006) suggested that to remain autonomous, many private practitioners have diversified their practices by going outside of managed care. Two pioneering books in the area of developing a fee-for-service practice—*Breaking Free of Managed Care* (Ackley, 1997) and *Saying Goodbye to Managed Care* (Rodino, Haber, & Lipner, 2001)—are "must-reads" for those considering this path for their practice. Rodino et al. (2001) indicated that all private practitioners have anxiety about developing a fee-for-service practice. The anxiety is related to the "uncertainty of private practice without (or limiting) the safety net of managed care" (p. 33). These authors suggested that anxiety can best be reduced by lowering overhead expenses and maximizing income potential. Ackley (1997) found that when he decided to move from an insurance-based practice to a fee-for-service practice, only 10% of his clients were private pay. However, within 14 months this number increased to 70% to 90%. He suggested that "clients are far more ready for this approach than you would believe" (p. 10). He added that a significant portion of people will forgo using their insurance to pay for treatment so as to have customized attention, real privacy, and no psychiatric diagnosis on record. Both Ackley (1997) and Rodino et al. (2001) presented strategies and frameworks to follow in developing a successful private pay practice. Rodino et al. (2001) also suggested that clinicians focus on developing a comfort level in dealing with money in terms of "how to ask for it and how to get it because people can pay for therapy" (p. 30). In fact, with the combination of deductibles and copays, the average psychotherapy client (not the insurance company) has been found to pay for a significant portion of his or her mental health treatment (Walfish & Jannsen, 1988). Rodino et al. (2001) stressed the importance of specialization in practice as well as identifying and marketing value-added services they can provide for other professionals. They mentioned the innovative example of networking with bridal salons and offering wedding stress packages. Anyone who has ever been involved with wedding planning knows how stressful it can be for all involved. This is a non-managed-care way of delivering a service that people will gladly pay for to optimize the joy they will experience from this happy occasion. In the following chapter we focus on other non-managed-care ways of earning a living.

As briefly mentioned in chapter 6, many insurance plans allow for out-of-network benefits. These benefits are often seen in preferred provider organization plans but rarely, if ever, in health maintenance organization plans. If out-of-network benefits are available, clients may see anyone they choose to for psychotherapy regardless of whether the clinician is a preferred provider for them. The insurance companies provide a disincentive for using out-of-network benefits by raising the amount of the deductible that has to be met and requiring the client to pay a higher percentage of the amount due. In other words, clients bear the cost of a larger part of their treatment. As a hypothetical example, a client may have in-network benefits that include a $100 deductible and then pay 80% of the designated usual and customary charges. With an out-of-network psychotherapist, this deductible is raised to $500 and the client pays 50% of the designated usual and customary charges. Clients who do not have a preference for who they see and whose primary concern is having their insurance cover most of the costs of psychotherapy or evaluation will not likely want to go out of the network.

Jeff Barnett does not participate on any MCPs and he is not a provider for any insurance companies. This position evolved for him over time. He believes that he stayed in managed care an extra 2 or 3 years after the fees paid to him stopped being reasonable. He feared that no one would pay for his services, and therefore he held on while his reimbursement rates dwindled by 52% from where they had originally started several years prior. However, as the reimbursement rates decreased, he noticed his irritation level going up, and he became especially annoyed at the paperwork, telephone utilization review, and the mismanagement of, and excessive delays in, the payment of his claims. He finally decided that it was not worth it to him to continue in this manner. He had been trying to build his out-of-network practice, but the MCO contracts that he signed required him to make appointments with new clients within a certain time frame. He found himself giving away prime-time psychotherapy hours (after school and in the evening) to these lower fee clients because of contractual obligations and was not happy about doing so. He was most concerned about disappointing his referral sources if he dropped off of panels. When he decided to drop off of all panels he did notice a brief drop in his volume, but then it quickly picked up in response to active marketing efforts. He has raised his fees several times in subsequent years, and the majority of clients have been fine with that and his referral sources did not vanish. When he receives a telephone call from prospective clients he is careful to explain his out-of-network status and how it affects them. Only a handful of clients have decided not to work with him and instead chose an in-network provider.

Jeff has been able to maintain a very busy out-of-network practice in which he feels very fairly compensated by actively marketing his practice, by providing clients and referral sources with timely and personalized service, and by providing high-quality treatment and assessment services. He felt unable to do any of this under the constraints of managed care.

As discussed in chapter 6, with out-of-network benefits clients are presented with a super bill that they then submit to their insurance carrier for direct reimbursement. If the insurance carrier or MCO requests a treatment plan, the clinician is responsible for completing these forms. The authorization request is not asking the payor to authorize payment on the clinician's part but rather so the client may potentially be reimbursed. The client is responsible for payment regardless of whether the insurer reimburses him or her for services delivered. However, the insurer or MCO may not reimburse the client without completion of such forms. Clinicians could ask for a fee to complete this paperwork, but we advise against doing so. The client is also likely paying a significant fee for psychotherapy, and we view this extra work as a courtesy to the client.

We recently discussed practice issues with a colleague who a few years earlier had moved to a completely fee-for-service practice. He indicated that he is now earning more money than when he practiced primarily under managed care. At the time he was seeing 35 clients per week. He is now able to charge his self-defined (rather than insurance-company-defined) usual and customary fee of $140 per session and sees 22 to 25 clients each week. Consider the math involved with these numbers: 35 clients per week at $75 per session on average equals $2,625 per week in billings; 22 clients per week at $140 per session equals $3,080 per week in billings. The conclusion is simple: more money earned in 63% of the time. In addition, his overhead for billing services became virtually zero. He provides each client with a super bill following the session, which they submit for reimbursement. Clients have the option of paying by check or credit card at the end of the session. Therefore, he does not have to hire support staff or contract out a percentage of his earnings to a billing service. In addition, his rate of collections is 100%, whereas when he practiced under managed care money was often lost because of missed filing deadlines, personnel mistakes in filing claims, clients not always honoring their portion of the bill, or benefits initially described when authorization was requested not actually being in place when the claim was submitted for final review and payment.

As Rodino et al. (2001) pointed out, "people can pay for therapy" (p. 30). However, it is a matter of taking the plunge and clinicians forcing themselves to (a) develop new revenue sources that do not fall under the purview of managed care and (b) emotionally allow themselves to ask for and earn money. In the next chapter we explore avenues that mental health professionals follow that allow them to earn a living outside of managed care. Often, clinicians indicate that they do not want to see only rich people in their practice. To begin with, this notion is a mistaken one because the average length of psychotherapy is less than 10 sessions and most people can afford this cost, even if they have to place the fees on a credit card (as they might for a big-screen TV or a family vacation). In addition, recall the example of Martin-Causey (2005), who devoted 10% to 20% of her time to seeing low-fee clients. Enough full-fee clients will allow one to choose to see lower fee clients without feeling that it is a financial hardship.

A Hybrid Model

Unlike Jeff Barnett, Steve Walfish is a provider for selected insurance companies and on selected MCPs (he avoids those with the lowest fees). He does see some fee-for-service clients for psychotherapy and psychological evaluation, but this portion of his practice is small. Steve's practice has always been one that he considers to be a hybrid model in terms of some of his income coming from insurance-based sources and the other part from non-insurance-based sources. In addition, as we describe later, some of his consultation agreements insist that he be a provider for insurance companies and a member of MCPs. He is aware that he does have to work longer and harder than if he developed a practice that is solely fee-for-service. However, he has always had a successful practice and found that this model has provided a fine income.

In his professional career Steve has built three private practices. The first was in Tampa, the second in Edmonds and Everett, Washington, and the current one in Atlanta. The nature of how he has practiced has changed because of evolutions in the health care delivery system and opportunities that have developed for him. In Tampa in the mid- to late 1980s, the bulk of his income came from completing psychological evaluations in residential alcohol and drug treatment centers. Reimbursement for this treatment was insurance-based, so if he was not willing to be a provider for insurance companies the treatment center would not have referred him the 2,500 evaluations that he completed during this time. He rounded out his schedule with consultation to community agencies (e.g., grant writing, supervision of paraprofessional counselors) and a moderate number of psychotherapy hours each week. When managed care affected reimbursement for these treatment centers, this evaluation-based consultation practice came to an end. However, he was then able to contract with an eating disorders hospital that paid him directly for each evaluation. The hospital in turn billed the insurance companies for his services.

When he moved to Washington state he practiced primarily in a small working-class city that was dominated by one employer. He felt that these circumstances were not conducive to leaving insurance companies and MCPs. However, the bulk of his income revolved around three non-managed-care activities. These were the completion of Social Security Disability evaluations, evaluation and treatment of workers' compensation clients (which was quasi-managed by a claims manager), and the completion of forensic psychological evaluations for civil court cases (e.g., posttraumatic stress disorder following accidents). He rounded out his schedule by seeing managed care psychotherapy clients. In Atlanta the bulk of his income has come from completing presurgical psychological evaluations for gastric bypass surgery. Although a portion of these clients are self-pay, the vast majority are insurance-based. To secure his role as a consultant with a busy surgery group he had to agree to accept clients' insurance because the surgeons wanted to keep the out-of-pocket costs to a minimum. The previous person did not, and his fees were high. This became a source of unhappiness for the patients, and the surgeons were unhappy that their patients were unhappy. The trade-off for this agreement is that this surgery group uses him exclusively and insists that each patient undergo a psychological evaluation. He has now completed more than 1,000 such evaluations. In addition, he also completes psychological evaluations at a substance abuse and psychiatric residential treatment center. A few of these evaluations are paid by the treatment center, some are paid by the clients themselves, and about 70% are insurance-based. Once again he has agreed to accept insurance and is usually the psychologist first called to complete these evaluations. If he did not accept insurance, the center would not be referring the self-pay and treatment center paid clients (it is all or none). He rounds out his practice hours with MCO psychotherapy clients.

It is possible to speculate that if Steve stopped being a provider for insurance companies and MCPs he would develop practice opportunities that would match, or surpass, his current income level and he would not have to work quite as hard. He has colleagues who have been able to do so. However, he is not willing to risk his good income at this point in time. Perhaps if market opportunities present themselves, he will seize them and move in another direction, but until then the hybrid model works for him.

Conclusion

Managed care in and of itself is not evil. It has its strengths (preventing abuses of the system by health care providers, the possibility of increased referrals) and its weaknesses (the profit motive by private companies may interfere with quality of care, reduced reimbursement rates, increased administrative demands). If one wants to practice long-term individual psychotherapy, it is likely best to not follow this path because such treatment models are inconsistent with the values of MCOs. If one is a hyperindependent thinker who does not like restrictions placed on one's professional practice patterns, then it is also best to avoid being on MCPs. There is an inducement to be a provider for an insurance company or a MCO because they are gatekeepers for a large percentage of clients. However, with a bit of courage and innovative thinking many individuals have opted to not participate in these systems and have found success. Others have opted for the safety of working within these systems and feel positive about the large client flow, although unhappy about the reimbursement rates. We encourage clinicians to examine their goals, values, and personalities and shape a practice life with or without managed care as best suits them.

How Independent Practitioners Earn Money | 10

E arning money was simply a topic that was not discussed in our graduate training programs. Either the professors thought it taboo or they knew little about how to do it effectively because they were employed primarily in an academic setting. They may have done practice "on the side" but our exposure to clinicians who earned their living as full-time private practitioners was quite limited. Therefore, what we learned about this topic has come from trial and error, reading, consulting with colleagues, and our own creativity.

Private practitioners are not restricted in how they can earn money. The only caveat is they are bound to adhere to their professional ethics code, including not practicing outside their areas of competence. Most mental health professionals earn their living by providing traditional individual and couples psychotherapy or assessment services in the confines of their office. Yet, there are many other options for earning a living beyond providing these traditional services. For independent practitioners with the spirit of a small-business entrepreneur, there is a whole range of ways to provide needed services for which they may receive compensation. The autonomy provided by owning such a business allows mental health professionals (MHPs) to use their creativity and skill set outside of the consultation office. MHPs conceptualize earning a living in private practice as composed not solely of the fees earned in their offices but rather of the cumulative revenues generated from their skill sets. MHPs' activities include not only assessment and psychotherapy in their offices but also teaching, supervision, consultation in the community, research, speaking, writing, and anything else where opportunity meets their skill set. In this chapter we discuss issues related to MHPs' skill sets, how private practitioners earn money outside of managed care, and how passive income can be earned.

The Clinician's Skill Set

It is a common belief that earning a living with a bachelor's degree in psychology is difficult to accomplish. In addressing this issue, Ware (2001) counseled,

> Employers hire people primarily because they need problems solved and tasks performed. You can infer that knowledge about your skills should help you find occupations in which you can be satisfied and successful. Skills developed in college can contribute to career success. Liberal arts programs that include a major in psychology emphasize generalized or transferable skills. Transferable skills are those a person can use in a variety of settings, including work environments. (p. 12)

He suggested that students conduct a self-analysis of their own education and experience level to determine what skill set might transfer into an opportunity in the marketplace.

The same philosophy can be used by private practitioners to create income opportunities for themselves. Through graduate training, MHPs have developed skills in completing literature reviews, synthesizing data from a number of sources, applying statistics to better understand a problem or evaluate a program, teaching, presenting before groups, facilitating groups, completing assessment in a wide variety of settings with a wide variety of populations, working in teams, leading teams, and so on. Plante (1996) presented advice to new graduates to expand the array of skills and their applications to window of opportunities beyond the traditional roles demonstrated during graduate training. Plante believed that new professionals often underestimate their job skills and how these can be applied in a wide variety of jobs in business and industry, schools, hospitals, the media, and other agencies. The diversity of skills can easily be reflected in the income-generating activities identified by private practitioners in this chapter for practicing outside of managed care.

Practicing Outside of Managed Care

For mental health professionals wanting to practice outside of managed care, earning a living takes innovative thinking on how to apply one's skill set as an assessor, clinician, teacher, and organizational consultant. Walfish (2001b) asked psychologists in private practice to identify strategies that they used in their practice to earn a living that fall out of the purview of managed care. In this study, 180 separate strategies were identified by these practitioners. These strategies were conceptually organized into 10 categories and fell under the general headings of (a) business psychology, (b) consultation to organizations, (c) fee-for-service activities, (d) forensic psychology, (e) group psychotherapy, (f) health psychology, (g) psychoeducational services, (h) services to government, (i) teaching and supervision, and (j) miscellaneous. A complete list of the 180 strategies is available from Steven Walfish at psychpubs@aol.com. However, for illustrative purposes, Exhibit 10.1 presents each category along with five of the items that fell into the category.

Psychology in the corporate world has become attractive because industry is in need of the skills clinicians have to offer and companies usually can afford to pay for these services. Perrott (1998) described business psychology as the "application of clinical psychology's traditional knowledge base to people working in business settings for the ultimate purpose of enhancing the business's performance" (p. 31). Clay (1998) described the experiences of three clinical psychologists moving into the realm of organizational consulting. One recent area that has developed as part of business psychology is executive coaching (Kilburg, 2000, 2006). To learn more about this aspect of practice, along with training and certification programs, perform an Internet search on the term *executive coaching*. For clinicians wanting to branch out into the world of business, it would be prudent to heed the warning of Lowman (1998) that the practice of psychology in industry and organizations occurs in a complex and at times litigious environment. As such, a mental health professional should review ethics standards as they apply to the business world before applying assessment and intervention skills in the corporate world.

Consulting to organizations requires that psychologists leave the comfort of their consulting office and venture into the community. Lorion and Hightower (2001) highlighted errors that individuals often make when attempting to initiate clinical or consulting efforts in the community. They pointed to the need for clinicians to not be interpersonally distant, to be well prepared for the tasks at hand, to be patient and willing to overcome obstacles, to be practical and not grandiose, and to be willing to earn the trust of their consultees. If the clinician does these things both the clinician and the individuals in the agency will find

EXHIBIT 10.1

Non-Managed-Care Activities of Psychologists in Independent Practice

Business Psychology
- Consulting to corporate executives on behavioral science and policy issues
- Disability evaluations for individuals attempting to return to work
- Executive coaching in corporations
- Fitness-for-duty evaluations related to dangerousness
- Psychological evaluations for executives for hiring and promotion decisions

Consultation to Organizations
- Case consultation to teachers and counselors in schools
- Conducting a support group for staff at the Humane Society
- Consultation at nonprofit agencies on clinical issues for staff
- In-service training for a medical center on psychological issues
- Team-building consultation for a rehabilitation unit

Fee-for-Service Activities
- Coaching group for adults with attention-deficit disorder
- Divorce consultation to couples who are separating or divorcing
- Hospital consultation by contract to provide psychological assessments
- Premarital counseling
- Psychotherapy for residents in a private girl's boarding school where parents pay out of pocket

Forensic Psychology
- Assessment of law enforcement officers
- Child custody evaluations
- Evaluations for competency to stand trial
- Psychotherapy for individual referred by probation or parole
- Sex offender evaluations

Group Psychotherapy
- Group psychotherapy for adult children of alcoholics
- Group psychotherapy for children with attention-deficit/hyperactivity disorder
- Group psychotherapy for anger management
- Group psychotherapy for individuals with chronic pain
- Group psychotherapy for men's issues

Health Psychology
- Diagnostic evaluations with nursing home residents
- Hypnotherapy consultation to teach self-hypnosis and relaxation
- Neuropsychological evaluations for individuals experiencing a traumatic brain injury
- Running a weight management and fitness program
- Stress management training as part of a work-hardening program

Psychoeducational Services
- Counseling for children who have learning disabilities
- Parenting guidance for children with attention-deficit/hyperactivity disorder
- Psychological evaluations for special education eligibility
- Psychotherapy on-site for special education students by contract with the school system
- Testing for placement in gifted programs

Services to Government
- Evaluations of applicants for Social Security Disability
- Psychological evaluation of adolescents in a county-run long-term facility
- Psychological evaluations with individuals through state vocational rehabilitation services
- Psychological evaluations with individuals who are on workers' compensation
- Psychotherapy for foster children paid through Medicaid

EXHIBIT 10.1 (*Continued*)

Teaching and Supervision
- Consultation groups for other mental health professionals
- Psychotherapy supervision of graduate students in training
- Teaching courses in a department of psychology
- Teaching adult education classes at a university
- Continuing education for mental health professionals

Miscellaneous
- Daily radio show educating the public on psychology issues
- Employee assistance program assessment and short-term psychotherapy
- Evaluations of individuals considering entering the priesthood
- On-call psychotherapist as part of an emergency response team
- Writing of self-help books

Note. From Walfish (2001b).

the experience to be mutually beneficial. As can be seen from the examples presented in Exhibit 10.1, many organizations or agencies need the skills of mental health professionals. However, they may not want to (or have the funds available to) hire someone on a full-time basis. Private practitioners may be able to fill a need for specific skills for specific projects for the organization.

Ackley (1997) and Rodino, Haber, and Lipner (2001) make the case that psychologists in independent practice can earn a living in a fee-for-service manner without having to take referrals from managed care companies. We discussed this topic in chapter 9 (this volume), primarily focusing on traditional assessment and psychotherapy activities. Kolt (1999) presented a list of 125 market niches for psychotherapists based on consumer needs, and Walfish (2001b) presented 20 direct fee-for-service activities for which insurance reimbursement is not applicable.

The practice of forensic psychology is an area of practice activity focused on by respondents to the survey by Walfish (2001b). Thirty-seven separate clinical activities were mentioned, slightly more than one fifth (21%) of the entire list. This area of practice is well paid and will most likely never fall under the purview of managed care. These may be the reasons why this area has become attractive for independent practitioners. Hess (1998, 2005) elaborated on issues for psychologists to consider when accepting forensic cases, with a special focus on ethics. Psychologists may have an advantage in this area over the other disciplines because of their ability to provide psychological testing. However, we do know of clinical social workers who complete child custody evaluations and serve as expert witnesses in court on a variety of clinical issues.

Group psychotherapy is a cost-effective way to deliver psychological services. Compared with individual psychotherapy, clients can receive services in a relatively inexpensive manner. Participants can gain by being involved with other people who are struggling to solve problems similar to those they are trying to solve themselves. Many of the group activities delineated by the survey respondents in Walfish (2001b) are general in nature (e.g., group psychotherapy for adolescents, men's groups), but many are very specific in nature (e.g., adult children of alcoholics, anger management). Those wanting to learn more about group psychotherapy may want to consult Fuhriman and Burlingame (1994) and the journals *Group Dynamics: Theory, Research and Practice, Social Work With Groups, Journal of Group Psychotherapy and Psychodrama,* and *The International Journal of Group Psychotherapy.*

The survey participants in Walfish (2001b) identified a variety of health psychology services. Hersch (1995) cited several examples of how psychologists can better incorporate themselves into the delivery of health care. Clinical and counseling psychology are becoming more integrated with medicine (Haley et al., 1998; Pruitt, Klapow, Epping-Jordan, & Dresselhaus, 1998) as is social work (Gelhert & Browne, 2006). Recently, Steve Walfish was consulting with an early career professional just starting her practice in an office of family medicine physicians. On one of his Internet discussion lists he noticed an article summarizing psychological interventions for arthritis pain management (Dixon, Keefe, Scipio, Perri, & Abernathy, 2007). He suggested that she photocopy the article and distribute it to the physicians in her practice as well as local rheumatologists. He also suggested that she consider starting a psychoeducational group for these types of patients based on the empirically based programs documented in the article. The need for health psychology interventions in the community is significant and can easily be met by appropriately trained private practitioners.

School systems often provide assessment and psychotherapy services for children who have special needs. The traditional focus is on developing individual educational plans for students who have problems with learning or behavior. However, school systems are often understaffed and therefore a long waiting list may exist. Parents may prefer to have an expert outside of the school system serve as a consultant and advocate for their child and be willing to pay out-of-pocket for such services. Private schools often need outside consultants to complete assessments of children experiencing difficulties because they may not have the resources to hire professionals for their staff. Jeff Barnett completes more than 50 comprehensive psychoeducational evaluations each year, with referrals coming from several private schools in his local area. These schools have been a steady referral source for him for a number of years.

One way to deliver important services and to be paid for clinical services is to do work for the federal or state government. Psychologists routinely complete evaluations for individuals who apply for Social

Security Disability benefits. In a similar way, mental health professionals are often seen as important parts of a vocational rehabilitation services team in terms of assessment and psychotherapy. There is no lack of individuals who have become injured on the job, and a significant percentage experience emotional difficulties as a consequence of their injuries. It should be pointed out that services that the government pays for do not traditionally fall under the general heading of personal growth and insight-oriented psychotherapy. Rather, the goal is to treat specific problems in a focused time-efficient manner to facilitate the likelihood that an individual may obtain and maintain a job.

Teaching courses at universities and through adult education has been viewed by a panel of experts as an important strategy for building and maintaining an independent practice (Walfish & Coovert, 1989). The respondents to Walfish's (2001b) survey agreed that independent practitioners could add to their overall income levels by becoming involved in these activities, as well as supervising psychotherapists in training. Korn (2001) pointed out that most individuals who care about teaching usually learn their skills through trial and error. Individuals interested in becoming better teachers should consult the work of Korn (2001); McKeachie (1999); and Perlman, McCann, and McFadden (1999), as well as the archives of the journal *Teaching of Psychology*. There are often opportunities to teach courses through adult education programs sponsored by agencies or colleges and universities. For example, we know of a psychologist who teaches a stress management course at a local hospital as part of its wellness program. The catalog of adult continuing education classes at Everett Community College in Washington State includes courses titled "Resolving Emotional Eating," "Take Control of Your Life Now," and "Taoist Psychology," all taught by mental health professionals. Although these courses may not pay a great deal, they add to a clinician's income and also are a way of becoming better known in the community. Teaching jobs may also be available at community colleges or in master's or doctoral training programs. Providing supervision to both psychotherapists in training and those seeking postgraduate licensure hours can also serve as an income source for private practitioners. Individuals wanting to become more familiar with issues related to the development of supervision skills may want to consult Falender and Shafranske (2004); Hess (1980); Hess, Hess, and Hess (2008); and Watkins (1997) as well as the journals *Counselor Education and Supervision* and *The Clinical Supervisor*.

FOLLOW-UP STUDIES

Steve Walfish and his colleagues (Le & Walfish, 2007; Walfish, Keenan, & Tecala, 2008b) have conducted follow-up studies to the original 2001 study on non-managed care activities that generate income for private practitioners. The study by Le and Walfish was conducted with a sample of private practice psychologists, albeit 6 years later. The study by Walfish et al. (2008b) extended this work to a sample of 248 clinical social workers in private practice. Exhibits 10.2 and 10.3 present 20 of the strategies identified by each group in these studies. The complete list is available from Steve Walfish at psychpubs@aol.com. As can be seen, mental health professionals have found some interesting and creative ways to earn a living without having to fall under the scrutiny and limitations of managed care organizations.

EXHIBIT 10.2

Non-Managed-Care Activities of Psychologists in Independent Practice

- Consultation provided to the Pals for Life Breast Cancer Support Group by attending their monthly meeting and being available for any members to talk with me privately at that time.
- Offering corporate seminars on such topics as stress management, assertive management, dealing with the troubled employee, and anger and violence in the workplace.
- Serving as a utilization reviewer for insurance companies.
- Performing psychological evaluations for the Compensation and Pension unit of the local Veteran's Affairs medical center.
- Doing small-group observations and feedback on psychological testing and behavioral observations for a leadership program.
- Presenting trainings and team building using the Myers-Briggs Type Indicator to various business and community groups.
- Writing books for children, parents, and mental health professionals on feelings and relationships (three published).
- Speaking at schools, libraries, hospitals, and community group meetings on topics related to my books or general mental health issues.
- Completing criminal forensic evaluations.
- Consulting with guidance counselors and administration in private high schools with regard to student and staff issues (on a monthly basis).
- Offering executive coaching; usually paid by companies but also some individuals buy it for themselves and their own plans for success.
- Consulting with clergy about pastoral counseling issues and how to know when to refer out into the psychology community.
- Serving as a court-appointed "special master" or "parenting coordinator" to resolve disputes between parents in a high-conflict divorce.
- Conducting workshops for parents whose children have obsessive–compulsive disorder.
- Conducting pre-employment interviews of public safety officers (e.g., police, firefighters, correctional officers).
- Consulting with nursing homes on medication and compliance issues.
- Teaching couples the art and science of effective communication and problem-solving skills.
- Conducting learning disability evaluations with welfare clients planning to return to the workplace or education.
- Conducting IQ testing for children to determine eligibility for the gifted program in the public school system.
- Evaluation and treatment for those caught driving while intoxicated.

Note. From Le and Walfish (2007).

EXHIBIT 10.3

Non-Managed-Care Activities of Clinical Social Workers in Independent Practice

- Play therapy with foster children through a contract with a private nonprofit child placement agency.
- Community presentations for laypersons, with a door fee.
- Ethics investigation for the social work licensing board.
- Staff and program consultant for a residential care facility that serves men and women with developmental impairments.
- Case consultation to certain parish pastors regarding marital, family, organizational, and mental health issues that present during the course of ministry.
- Parenting training for parents of children with oppositional defiant disorder.
- Grant writing for local school districts.
- Staff in-service training presentation for nonprofit organizations.
- Substance abuse evaluations and treatment to ensure an oversight of adherence to treatment goals involving withdrawal and addressing comorbid issues.
- Workshops for couples to enhance their relationship.
- Mitigation expert witness in death penalty cases.
- Teaching a class entitled "When Parents Divorce, What Happens to the Kids." Monthly participants pay to attend.
- Court testimony regarding primarily child custody (civil) issues.
- Training or workshops for other professionals as continuing education for them.
- Family (small) business consultation.
- Facilitation of a family support group for the Huntington's Disease Society of America.
- Consultation to agency administration about employee issues.
- Therapy with clients who are victims of crime and referred by the judicial system.
- Home studies (I was contracted by attorneys to conduct home studies with parenting evaluation for adoption and custody determination).
- Consultation for in vitro fertilization program (I screened egg donors and egg and sperm donation recipients for participation in a program).

Note. From Walfish et al. (2008b).

KEEPING AN EYE OUT FOR OPPORTUNITIES

In chapter 2 (this volume) we tried to make the point that the entrepreneurial process includes (a) generating an idea or the recognition of an opportunity, (b) gathering resources to help bring the idea or opportunity to fruition, and (c) launching the opportunity and helping it to grow (Baron & Shane, 2008). Consistent with this entrepreneurial spirit Pope and Vasquez (2005) suggested two strategies that are helpful in bringing to fruition opportunities that may not have previously existed. First, they suggested "asking the community" what it is that they need from a mental health professional that they are currently not receiving. This may be done through either formal or informal needs assessment. A colleague who owns a mental-health-related company once told us that he conducts focus groups with his current customers to find out how he can be of further help to them. In this way he can tailor products or services to meet these needs. For example, if the private practitioner can get the gatekeepers of mental health services (e.g., physicians, employee assistance program counselors) to let them know where there are voids or missing pieces related to mental health treatment, then the practitioner can develop programs or services. If business leaders (if you want to work in the corporate world) or human resource managers would do the same, then the private practitioner may be able to fill the void. Second, Pope and Vasquez (2005) suggested paying attention to problems that emerge in the community and seeing if mental health services may be of help. Take for example the school shootings at Columbine and others that have followed. Soon after these tragedies mental health professionals were asked to conduct threat assessment with adolescents considered to be at high risk for violent behavior. The astute mental health professional who is aware of how to conduct such evaluations could fill such a need.

Other Sources of Income

As can be seen from the discussion thus far and what we have attempted to stress in this volume, a vast array of opportunities exists for private practitioners to earn a living. There is nothing wrong with a clinician who solely wants to be in an office and provide traditional psychotherapy and assessment services. However, with an entrepreneurial spirit and a willingness to use skill sets in ways that may not be traditional, clinicians' options are exponentially expanded.

We strongly advocate developing alternative methods of earning money other than providing direct services of psychotherapy and assessment. This variety helps to prevent burnout, allows one to work more hours in activities that generate income, and helps to keep one fresh and learning. For example, although we know people who conduct 40 hours of psychotherapy each week (or more), we are also aware how straining this can be for the psychotherapist. It is the rare individual who can keep this pace up for very long without becoming physically or emotionally exhausted or making a significant clinical mistake. However, a combination of activities that might include X number of hours of psychotherapy, plus Y number of hours of assessment, plus Z number of hours of other activities such as speaking, writing, or supervising may make it possible to generate 40 hours per week of billing.

WORKSHOPS

Workshops can be presented either to laypeople in the community or to professionals seeking to stay current in the field, upgrade their skills, or fill in their continuing education hours for licensure. Of course, one must become an expert in something to be able to provide such a service.

We have a colleague who is a specialist in early childhood development and developmental disabilities. He is based in Florida and spends approximately 1 week each month on the road presenting workshops on these topics to mental health and early childhood education professionals. He has contracted with a national continuing education company to provide these workshops. He is by no means "a biggie" such as Aaron Beck, David Barlow, Marsha Linehan, John Gottman, or David Burns who by name recognition alone could achieve a sold-out registration. However, he is competent in his area of expertise and makes excellent presentations. He is paid a percentage of the registration fees plus his travel and hotel and meal expenses. The other 3 weeks of the month he sees clients in his psychotherapy and assessment practice. He enjoys the diversity of meeting new people and going to new places and occasionally has developed consulting arrangements following his talks.

Claire Hatch, who has a master's of social work, is a clinical social worker who practices in Kirkland, Washington (just outside of Seattle). As can be seen on her Web site (http://www.clairehatch.com), her specialty is in the area of couples counseling. In addition to providing psychotherapy for individuals and couples, she provides a structured 12-week program for getting marriages back on track as well as a four-session program for couples before they get married. On her Web site she indicates that she has completed a certificate program in dispute resolution and has also had advanced marital psychotherapy training at the Gottman Institute in Seattle. She has taken the time to develop her area of expertise and interest through education and further training and has placed herself in a position to offer a service that is needed in her community.

PUBLIC SPEAKING

A common phobia is public speaking. Mental health professionals are not immune from this fear and may also want to avoid this activity. However, if this is an area of interest, public speaking is a good way to become better known in the community and to also earn income from making the presentations.

Nonprofit groups in the community frequently have no budget to pay for outside speakers. Talks to these groups should be done as a pro bono community service and as a means of increasing visibility in the community. Rarely have we done one of these talks and in the next month not received a call from someone who attended the talk and asked to become a psychotherapy client. However some groups, mostly in the business community or professional organizations, do budget funds for outside speakers. Some communities have speakers' bureaus for professionals to align themselves with to do these types of talks. In general, if you have written a book or have become noted in the community for some reason, you will be seen as a more attractive speaker. An Internet search on the phrase *become a professional speaker* yields a significant number of hits. We do not endorse any particular organization, but it could be an interesting way for the private practitioner to generate income.

Those wanting to overcome their fear of public speaking can join a local chapter of Toastmasters. This group takes a successive approximation approach in helping people overcome anxiety and become more effective public speakers. An interesting and emerging approach being developed by Page Anderson (panderson@gsu.edu) and her colleagues (P. Anderson, Zimand, Hodges, & Rothbaum, 2005) uses virtual reality to treat public speaking anxiety.

DEVELOPING PRODUCTS

Product development would fall under the general category of expending a lot of time and energy with no guarantee of a financial payoff. Products can take a lot of advance preparation and possibly an investment of some capital. However, if effective they can provide a source of passive income for the private practitioner. By passive we mean generating income not by delivering a direct service but rather by reaping the rewards of a previous investment of time and energy. Private practitioners traditionally earn money only when they see a client for assessment or psychotherapy or provide consultation to another professional or organization. In other words, the practitioner has to be present when these services are being delivered. With passive income, the practitioner is not present when the product is being used. Let us examine some sources of passive income.

> **Private Practice Principle Number 19:** There are only so many hours in the week during which a private practitioner can earn income. Therefore, it is financially advantageous to develop revenue streams of passive income.

Jeff Barnett has written several online courses. One is a licensure review course for his state's exam on state law and ethics. This course is offered four times each year online. Once the course was written, he spent only a little time updating content. He has also written four online continuing education courses for the Zur Institute related to ethics (http://www.drzur.com/outofofficecourse.html). Once each course was written nothing else was required, but he can update the material to keep it timely and relevant. For these courses he receives a percentage of all fees collected. He also has developed two other online continuing education courses that similarly bring in revenues from each person who completes them.

A second example is writing books. We will be the first to attest that writing a book is no easy task. However, many people believe "they have a book in them," and we encourage you to take the time and energy to work on this if you believe that you have something to say. If you discipline yourself to writing just five pages each week, most manuscripts can be completed in 1 year. If there are aspects that you need help with, you can hire an editor or writing coach. You may attempt to publish the book through traditional publishers, but in recent years self-publishing has become a reasonably priced option for authors. An Internet search on the term *self-publishing* yields a myriad of options. Books can be a way to enhance your practice credibility and enhance your visibility in the community. Dr. Cherry Collier is an example of a social psychologist who has written books (http://www.thefruitsoflabor.com/products.html) that have enhanced her consulting firm which specializes in employment and personal development issues. The royalties received from sales of the book are considered passive income.

A third example is developing self-help tapes. Michael Broder, PhD, is a psychologist who has developed an audiotherapy tape series (http://www.mindperk.com/Broder.htm). Although we are not endorsing these products, he sells tapes that address issues of depression, anxiety, stress management, overcoming anger, developing self-confidence, and making better choices. The royalties received from sales of the tapes are considered passive income.

A fourth example is the development of psychological tests. Although many psychological tests are developed by academic psychologists, this does not mean that private-practice psychologists cannot (a) develop tests on their own or (b) collaborate with an academic psychologist. E. Michael Lillibridge, PhD, is a psychologist in private practice who has developed a psychological test and integrated it into training programs for use in industry (http://www.peoplemap.org). Barry Bricklin, PhD, is a psychologist in private practice who has developed the Bricklin Perceptual Scales (http://www.tjta.com/products/TST_005.htm). These scales are often used in child custody evaluations. Once the test has been developed, the royalties received from sales of the tests are considered passive income.

Conclusion

We have tried to convey the message that for creative private practitioners, the sky is the limit in the number of ways to earn money. Baron and Shane (2008) suggested that opportunity recognition is central to the process of creating business opportunities. The multidimensional skill sets that clinicians learn in graduate training and postgraduate training arm them with the ability to apply their craft in many ways to help people and improve their communities. To create ways in which to be well paid to do so is icing on the cake.

BUILDING A RETIREMENT | IV

Attending to Your Finances
"What Do You Mean I Don't Get a Pension?"

11

Discussing ownership of a small business in an editorial in *Money Magazine*, Schurenberg (2007) noted, "The average self-employed American's family has five times the net worth of the average wage earners. So the payoff can be high if you succeed. Only problem: Success comes hard" (p. 16).

Data from salary surveys of mental health professionals bear out Schurenberg's contention. For psychologists with 10 to 14 years of experience, the average salary of those employed in a community mental health center is $50,143, a public psychiatric hospital $59,500, and solo private practice $91,767 (Singleton, Tate, & Randall, 2003). For marriage and family therapists working in organizational or agency settings, the average salary is $46,850, whereas those working exclusively in private practice earn an average salary of $58,787 (American Association for Marriage and Family Therapy, n.d.). A 1999 survey of clinical social workers found the median salary to be $39,800 for those working in social service agencies, $51,110 in child welfare agencies, and $62,500 in solo private practice (National Association of Social Workers Practice Research Network, 2002).

These data confirm what we have previously discussed in this volume. Those willing to take the most risk usually reap the most benefit. Walfish, Keenan, and Tecala (2008a) found a strong positive correlation (.52) between satisfaction with income and degree of job satisfaction in a sample of clinical social workers in private practice. However, increased income is not necessarily accompanied by financial security. In addition to earning money it is up to the private practitioner to manage the money appropriately and help it grow if financial security is the chosen goal. It is the sole responsibility of small-business owners to provide for their retirement. Therefore, in this chapter we discuss issues related to money management. As with previous chapters we must play "The Lawyers' Chorus": The information that follows should not be construed as financial advice. Readers should consult with their investment professionals regarding the accuracy of the information presented and how these issues may relate to their own individual situation.

Attitudes About Money

Earlier we discussed the importance for psychotherapists in private practice to examine their attitudes regarding money to resolve any economic conflicts they may have about being in private practice. When such conflicts exist, Rodino (2005) recommends a self-examination regarding one's psychodynamics about this topic. This exploration covers the topics of family history regarding money, experience of financial role models, ambivalence about success and accomplishment, feelings of unworthiness that may emerge out of values about competition, and conflict with religious, ethical, and moral upbringing that stressed altruism over financial success.

Although not a psychoanalyst, financial guru Suze Orman (1998) wrote in a similar vein regarding becoming financially successful. She expounded,

> I'll go so far as to say that in my experience, most of my clients'
> biggest problems in life today—even those that appear on the
> surface not to be money-related—are directly connected with
> their early, formative experiences with money. (p. 7)

She elaborated in Orman (1999), "Harder to recognize, and harder to overcome, are the internal obstacles, the emotional obstacles, that keep us from having what we want and enjoying what we have" (p. 10).

Orman (1998) offered exercises related to early memories about money that may be connected to current attitudes and potential problems with money. It is important to examine fears about money and how these may relate to early childhood experiences. With this knowledge, she suggested, it is possible to replace old fears about money with "new truths."

Orman (1998) also discussed financial issues from this perspective. She proclaimed that "financial freedom begins not in a bank or even in a financial planner's office, but in your head. It begins with your thoughts" (p. 7). In other writings Orman (1999) concluded the following:

> I have come to believe that the way each of us thinks and feels about money is the key factor in determining how much we ultimately have. Our thoughts and feelings about money have become obstacles that prevent us from having or keeping what we want. (p. 10)

Orman (1999) further added, "You must listen to the language of money around you and the words you choose to express your thoughts" (p. 29).

Kiyosaki (1997) described the influence of role models on shaping attitudes related to money in his book, *Rich Dad, Poor Dad*. He also elaborated on internal struggles as to which model to follow in his own life. "One dad would say, 'The love of money is the root of all evil.' The other, 'The lack of money is the root of all evil'" (p. 13). These opposing views had implications for Kiyosaki in terms of views about debt and if and how money is spent, how much energy is or is not placed on creating wealth, attitudes about taxes, educational path to take, choice of working for oneself or someone else, and beliefs about investments.

Educating Yourself About Money

Walk into any large bookstore and it will be a toss-up as to which section, psychology and self-help or personal finance, is the largest. There is no shortage of books related to basic financial information, sophisticated financial information, or even how to get rich quick. The Internet also contains a great amount of information on the topic. The only reason that mental health professionals do not get a financial education is because they have not taken the time to do so. Kiyosaki (1997) saw power in a financial education: "Money comes and goes, but if you have education about how money works, you gain power over it and can begin building wealth" (p. 19). There is a cliché that says "Knowledge is power." This statement is clearly true with financial information. Without basic financial information, private practitioners shortchange themselves and place their financial future on tenuous grounds.

Howard and Meltzer (2001) suggested that most people believe they have little chance of becoming wealthy, short of winning the lottery. However, they stated the following:

> The secret to creating wealth is really no secret at all. You do it with good habits, not investment wizardry. Regardless of what you make, put some money aside every month—preferably

10 percent or more—and in time you will accumulate a significant amount.

This advice is borne out in the data presented in *The Millionaire Next Door* by Stanley and Danko (1996). Contrary to popular opinion Stanley and Danko indicated most millionaires in this country did not inherit their wealth or win the lottery. Rather, they have "followed a lifestyle conducive to accumulating money" (p. 3). These authors have identified seven common denominators among those who accumulate wealth: (a) living well below their means; (b) being efficient in allocating their time, energy, and money in ways conducive to building wealth; (c) placing a higher value on financial independence than on social status; (d) not receiving economic help from their parents; (e) not financially supporting their adult children; (f) being skillful in recognizing market opportunities when they arise; and (g) choosing the right occupation for themselves. The data presented by Stanley and Danko (1996) suggest that financial security can be accomplished by slow and steady accumulation of savings and living a modest (though not deprived) lifestyle.

As noted earlier, it is not difficult to achieve a financial education if one makes the time. There are resources, resources, and even more resources. In addition to sources one may find at a local bookstore are online resources and courses and seminars that are available in most communities. In terms of basic books one can simply start with books such as *Personal Finance for Dummies* (Tyson, 2006) or *The Complete Idiot's Guide to Investing* (DeSalvo, Koch, & Kennon, 2006) and then expand into more specialized ones on such topics as stocks and mutual funds, real estate, and retirement planning. One online resource for a basic financial education recommended by consumer activist Clark Howard on his radio show and Web site is the Money Library at the *Los Angeles Times* newspaper (http://www.latimes.com/business/la-moneylib,0,3098409.html story). An explanation of basic concepts for investing in stocks may be found at http://www.schaeffersresearch.com/schaeffersu. In addition, classes on personal finance issues are frequently offered as part of adult education programs in colleges and universities.

Setting Financial Goals

Once you are educated on these issues, the next step is to set financial goals. Mary Farrell (2000), an executive at a major brokerage company, discussed the importance of defining financial goals. She noted that "the only person who can define what financial success looks like to you is you" (p. 20). Tyson (2006) pointed out that "one of the biggest mistakes people make is rushing into financial decisions without considering what is really important to them" (p. 60). As such, before setting goals private practitioners need to examine their values, their wants and desires, and what role they want money to play in their lives.

However, once these goals are identified, the people who achieve their financial goals have five things in common. First, they clarify their goals. Second, they develop and implement an investment plan. Third, they make savings an integral part of their budget. Fourth, they regularly review and update their plan. Finally, they continue to learn about financial issues (Farrell, 2000). In terms of continuing education about money we are strong advocates of regularly reading publications concerning money management and investing. Periodicals such as *Money Magazine, Business Week, Forbes, Fortune, Kiplinger's Personal Finance,* and *SmartMoney Magazine* are among the most popular. Many of these are available in local libraries. Each magazine has an accompanying Web site that carries most, though not all, of the stories that appear in the print edition. In addition, there are daily newspapers such as *The Wall Street Journal* and *Investor's Business Daily.* Although we do not think it possible to keep up with each source, we think it prudent for money managers to regularly read at least a few, to ensure they are staying current.

The behaviors outlined by Farrell (2000) are similar in nature to the problem-solving framework of D'Zurilla and Goldfried (1971) and should be familiar to most mental health professionals (e.g., define the problem, develop alternative solutions, make a decision and execute, and evaluate the outcome). Financially successful individuals are able to apply this strategy to achieving their fiscal goals. For those who are ambivalent about money, conflicts in values or goals may be interfering with achieving stated outcomes. For individuals who want to reach certain goals but find themselves not reaching them, applying motivational interviewing (Miller & Rollnick, 2002) concepts to themselves may be of value. They can examine how their income generation, spending habits, and saving habits are consistent or inconsistent with reaching those self-defined goals. Behaviors consistent with those goals should be retained. Behaviors inconsistent with these goals should be examined as to why they are present and then considered for elimination.

Self-Directed Versus Professional-Directed Investing

At one point in time if you wanted to purchase stocks the only option available was to go to a full-service broker who would do so on your behalf. Self-directed investing emerged in the 1980s, and with the advent of the Internet numerous options are available to the investor.

Kennon (n.d.) noted the differences between full-service and discount brokers. He indicated that with full-service brokers you will likely have your own personal stockbroker. The stockbroker will offer investment ideas, track how well your investments are doing, and be available to make trades on your behalf. Full-service brokerage firms (e.g., A. G. Edwards, Morgan Stanley Dean Witter, Merrill Lynch) have large research departments that rate how well businesses are doing and make predictions regarding stock performance. Kennon indicated that purchasing stocks through a discount broker is for individuals who are not interested in investment advice, want to make their own decisions, and do not need any customer service related to investing.

The responsibility for purchase or sale of all stock lies with the investor and not the broker (unless you give the broker permission to trade on your behalf). However, as can be seen with the full-service model, most of the work is done on the investor's behalf; the investor just has to decide if he or she agrees with the recommendations. The cost for this professional advice comes in the form of paying commissions on stock transactions or a management fee (usually a small percentage of the total portfolio). As we discussed in chapter 5, at times you have to spend money to make money. With the discount broker, little or no investment advice is offered. It is up to the investor to conduct all necessary research. Transactions may be placed through touch-tone systems over the telephone or online. The trade-off for this approach is that the fees for buying and trading stocks are much lower than with a full-service broker. In addition, it is possible for individuals doing their own research to purchase research information. An Internet search on the term *investment newsletters* results in no shortage of possible sources to find information on individual stock or mutual fund recommendations.

We do not think self-directed investment strategies are better than professional-directed ones, or vice versa. If you choose the self-directed path we strongly urge you to become an educated investor. Doing so will require an allocation of time, energy, and study. If you choose the professional-directed strategy we suggest that you monitor the performance of the investments recommended to you and not simply abdicate responsibility to the individual. In either case the ultimate responsibility for the investments lies with the investor.

Finding a Financial Advisor

Farrell (2000) suggested two methods for locating a financial advisor. The first is to ask your certified public accountant (CPA) to recommend a money manager. The second is to ask for a recommendation from someone you trust.

Orman (1998) indicated that it is important to understand how your financial advisors earn their money. Some may be fee-based and are paid only for the service they provide for you. With these individuals there are no added incentives for good or poor performance. They want only to provide you with their best advice. Their incentive is that if their advice is sound you will come back for more advice at a later date or recommend them to others to provide a similar service. Some may receive a fee plus a commission. These individuals receive a basic fee for providing the service and a commission for products that are purchased on their recommendation. Some may receive their fees on the basis of commission only. As previously noted individuals selling insurance in this manner may have an incentive to recommend those products that pay the higher commissions or recommend purchasing from companies that pay them a higher commission rate for being a high-volume producer for that company.

Orman (1998) provided a list of expectations one should have when looking for a financial advisor. These expectations focus on a willingness to have open communication, a willingness to explain all transactions and costs, the need to have a paper trail for all transactions, controls being set in place for the flow of money into and out of the account, and a high level of customer service. She suggested that if these are not all present then it is time to find a new financial advisor.

If you are unable to get a recommendation, another way to find a financial advisor is through the Financial Planning Association (http://www.fpanet.org/plannersearch/search.cfm?WT.svl=0). The Certified Financial Planner Board of Standards also presents a helpful online checklist of questions to ask when interviewing prospective financial planners (http://www.cfp.net/Learn/knowledgebase.asp?id=8). This group also provides basic information about several aspects of financial planning (http://www.cfp.net/Learn/default.asp).

Short-Term Investing

Investors may focus on making money in the short term or the long term. Short-term investments tend to be riskier. Howard and Meltzer (2001) suggested that longer term investments (10 years or longer) generally smooth out the bumpy ride that most investments have over the course of time.

Conservative short-term investments may be found in bonds, money-market accounts, and certificates of deposit. These investments usually provide steady but relatively small returns compared with investments in a bull stock market. However, they don't lose money in a bear stock market. For the short term it may be possible to pick individual stocks or mutual funds that are on the way up. Many people have speculated in real estate as a way to earn large rates of return in the short run. However, it should be noted that many short-term investments of this nature can be volatile in nature. Financial advisors usually stress that if money is needed in the short run (next 3–5 years) to pay for certain milestones in life (e.g., college education, wedding), then it should be in conservative and not risky investments.

It is also possible for practitioners to diversify their investments; that is, part of their portfolio can be allocated for investment in the short run and part for retirement. The balance allocation will depend on the individual goals chosen by the clinician and his or her particular circumstances. In the blessed situation in which someone knows he or she is going to inherit family money at some point in the future, the emphasis may be more on short-term investing rather than on retirement planning. However, people may choose to focus on saving as much for retirement as possible so they can count on a certain lifestyle later in their life.

Retirement Planning

At one point in time the American dream included finding a job with a well-known company, working one's way up the corporate ladder, and then retiring 40 years later with a gold watch and a fine pension. Although this scenario still is a possibility for some in the current economic system, it is no longer the path of most Americans. It has never been the case with those who are self-employed in service businesses such as mental health professionals who own their own small business.

> **Private Practice Principle Number 20:** Although you may receive consultation from others, the responsibility for your retirement planning remains with you, the private practitioner.

Howard and Meltzer (2001) advocated the position that the number one investment priority should be on funding your own retirement:

> You can't rely on the traditional vehicles that may have helped your parents' or grandparents' retirement. Their generations had a strong Social Security system and pension plans that were fully funded by their employers. Today's working Americans will get only a small portion of the funds they need from Social Security. . . . Without the government or a paternalistic corporation to fall back on, you have to be much smarter and more aggressive in planning for your retirement. (p. 37)

According to Howard and Meltzer (2001), people are generally undersaving for their retirement.

Retirement investing is done for the long term. Investments are placed in specialized retirement funds that are not targeted for withdrawal until retirement age, generally beginning after age $59\frac{1}{2}$ and before age 70. Farrell (2000) contended the deck is stacked in favor of the long-term investor. She pointed out that although there are down times in the stock market, the long-term trend has historically been up. She advised to start investing early to take advantage of compounding interest. Farrell defined compounding as "the process of interest earning interest" (p. 34).

The value of compounding interest may be seen in the Rule of 72. The Rule of 72 tells you the number of years required to double money at a given interest rate. If you divide the interest rate into 72, the answer will be how many years it will take for the investment to be worth twice as much. For example, an investment of $1,000 at 6% interest will become $2,000 in 12 years. An investment of $1,000 receiving 12% interest will become $2,000 in 6 years. Therefore, money invested at relatively low interest rates that are found in savings accounts will generally not be productive. Because of compounding interest, the earlier money is invested, the greater the value at the time of retirement. Farrell (2000) provided an example of someone who starts saving $10,000 per year in his or her retirement fund at age 21, compared with someone who starts this rate of savings at age 30. If both retire at the age of 65 and receive an average annual return of 10% on their investments, the difference between these amounts is staggering. The person starting 9 years later would have accumulated wealth in the amount of $2.7 million, whereas the person starting 9 years earlier would have accumulated wealth in the amount of $6.5 million.

Private practitioners have several types of retirement accounts available to them. Each has its own set of rules and restrictions and its own benefits and liabilities.

KEOGH PLANS

A Keogh plan is a self-employed retirement plan. When employees have a retirement plan through their organization, the employer may match the employees' contributions. For example, the employee may contribute 10% of his or her salary to the retirement plan and the company may match that investment with another 5% to 10%. This money is then invested in a stock account on behalf of the employee.

In private practice there are no employers to match contributions. According to Tyson (2006), a Keogh is a "tax-deductible retirement savings plan available to self-employed individuals" (p. 434). The paperwork involved in setting this plan up is minimal. A similar plan, called a Simplified Employee Pension (SEP) plan, requires less paperwork. However, more money can be set aside each year in the Keogh than in the SEP plan. The limits change from year to year and are generally a percentage of income up to an upper dollar limit.

In Keogh plans the amount invested is tax deductible for that year. In other words, if you invest $10,000 in a Keogh plan then this same amount is deducted from your gross annual income. For example, if you earn $100,000 per year and contribute $10,000 to the Keogh plan then you will be paying taxes on only $90,000. The money you put in the Keogh plan will then grow (one hopes) through wise investments. However, when you withdraw this money from the plan at retirement, you will have to pay taxes on the amount taken out of the account on the basis of your tax bracket at the time of withdrawal.

With a Keogh or SEP there are penalties (with some exceptions) for early withdrawal (before age 59½). In addition to the penalties on withdrawal, taxes also have to be paid on these monies. For this combined reason (penalty plus taxes) most people try to not make early withdrawals from their account.

ROTH IRA

A Roth individual retirement account (IRA) differs from a Keogh in that the limits on what one can contribute to an account each year are lower. The annual limits for a Roth IRA are set at a dollar amount and are not based on a percentage of income with an upper limit of contribution. In addition, the Roth IRA differs from a Keogh Plan in relation to taxes. The contributions to a Roth IRA are taxable. However, the investments grow tax-free and when withdrawn no taxes are paid on these monies. However, Keoghs are considered tax-deferred accounts.

Buildings as Investments

In chapter 4 (see Exhibit 4.3, pp. 76–77) we highlighted an interview with Barrie Alexander and Nancy McGarrah. These individuals knew they wanted to set roots in the community and find a practice setting in which they could stay for a long time. As part of this process, and because they were committed to living in the community, they decided to buy and renovate a house for use as an office. Thanks to the rise in the Atlanta housing market over the 22 years they have been owners, this investment has turned out to be positive. This investment has come with costs (renovations, all of the repairs and upkeep that accompany owning a house), but in this instance the costs have outweighed the gains.

As such, for those knowing they want to practice long-term in a location, purchasing an office may be a key financial investment. Dr. Tammy

Martin-Causey, a psychologist and coach in Phoenix, Arizona (http://www.drmartincausey.com), recently went this route. She generously agreed to share her experience (see Exhibit 11.1). It is clear from this interview that there are challenges to be overcome, but she believes the long-term benefits will be well worth the investment.

EXHIBIT 11.1

Building Your Own Building: An Interview With Tammy Martin-Causey, Psychologist and Coach, Phoenix, Arizona

---

What had been your office arrangement before you built a place of your own?

I have leased office space either as the only leaser or as a subletter. When I first moved to Arizona, I was not clear on what direction my practice would take and I knew little about the geographic area. So I started renting an office 1 day a week from another psychologist. Then I rented from another psychologist 1 day a week in a different location. That allowed me to get a better idea of the community, traffic patterns, and desirable office locations. When my practice grew enough to need 3 days a week, I noticed that it was more cost-efficient to secure a full-time office rather than rent part-time for 3 days. Going from 2 to 3 days seemed to be the magic tipping point. I signed a full-time lease in one location but was still not sure if that was the best location. Being somewhat of a risk-taker, I decided to sign a second full-time lease and rent out both offices on the days I was not at that particular location. The net result was that the rental income covered over three fourths of the lease amounts. That is when I started to discover that my practice was a "business" and that there are many ways to generate income.

What was the impetus for moving in this direction?

As my lease expiration date started to approach, I knew it was time to reevaluate my office situation. I applied the same logic to the office that I would for home buying. Most of us will agree that it is a better investment to own a home rather than rent for many years. A home is an asset that appreciates over time. It becomes an investment. The same can be said about offices. For most people, it does not make sense to lease for many years. Another impetus was my dissatisfaction with my "retirement package" as a self-employed independent practitioner. I knew I needed to take large steps to be in the position I wanted to be in when I'm old enough to not want to work so many hours a week.

How did you go about planning and implementing the project?

The first step was to be clear about where I wanted to own an office. I did this by leasing in different locations. Location and local markets are critical to the success of your business. Understanding that fit is imperative before making a purchase. Another important consideration with location is the value of real estate in a particular area. Not only are you focusing on where your clientele are located but also on real estate values in various locations. Even though it is your office, it is an investment and you want to make sure the property will appreciate.

The second step I took was to find a commercial realtor. I had no prior knowledge or skills in purchasing commercial real estate. At this juncture, home-buying and commercial-building-buying skill sets part ways. The process is entirely different. My realtor explained everything I needed to know about timelines and what happens in the purchase process and I absorbed about half of it. It is similar to when an undergraduate psychology student is explained the process of the steps involved in obtaining a doctoral degree and licensure for becoming a practicing psychologist. It all sounds good and exciting, but the student will likely fail to grasp

(Continued)

EXHIBIT 11.1 (*Continued*)

the enormity and details of the steps involved. But it didn't matter because unbeknownst to me, I had just hired the first person on my team of people who would help comanage the process with me.

How did you go about financing the project?

I chose a Small Business Administration (SBA) loan for the building and equipment and a conventional business line of credit for working capital. It was a difficult decision to make. The most viable options were as follows:

- **Medical financing.** The banking industry considers psychologists in the same category as physicians. Therefore, we qualify for medical financing loans. These loans have some of the lowest default rates, so lenders are more willing to assume risk. What that means is that you may qualify for 0%, 5%, or 10% down at a rate that is much more below prime than conventional business loan rates. To qualify for 0% to 10% down, you have to show a strong financial history with your business. This is a good option for the experienced practitioner who has several years of financial records to show stability of the practice. If you can qualify for this, it is a huge investment opportunity. If you do not qualify, there are still other options.
- **Conventional business loan.** A standard business loan will typically require 20% down and have a rate that is between the medical financing and SBA rates. If you have the down payment and still have adequate cash flow, this is probably a good option.
- **SBA.** If you are an early career psychologist with little money saved but have a good business plan, good ideas, and common sense, an SBA loan can get you into office ownership. The primary focus of the SBA is not to finance buildings but to finance small businesses. However, owning a building is considered a reasonable business expense. The SBA's interest rates and fees are usually higher than any of the above options, but they do not require you to have a long financial and business track record before you apply. Also, you only have to put 10% down and it can come from about anywhere. SBA has a few options within its lending program. For example, you can choose to pay a higher interest rate with no prepayment penalties after 3 years or you can choose a lower interest rate with a prepayment penalty before about 20 years. I chose a higher interest rate to have the option of refinancing in 3 years when I knew the business would be so successful that I would have more negotiating power with lenders.

Did you have any fears about moving in this direction?

Of course! And I still do. It's a huge jump to increase what I pay for office space by about $5,000 a month. But I kept putting one foot in front of the other and remembered that I have a business plan, a budget, and monthly projections for 3 years that were attainable. That little bit of pressure pushed me to reach my goals. Before I purchased an office, my perspective was a little different. I would know my monthly bills and would know about how much work I needed to do to cover those bills (including my paycheck). I also had a small plan for growth. But growth really didn't happen much more than in incremental raises. That's not much different from working for someone else. The purchase of an office required me to think on a much larger scale. My payables were going to increase drastically so I knew I needed to think about receivables much differently. I had to dream bigger, think bigger, and recruit a team of consultants. My team included my realtor, accountant, attorney, marketing firm, and business coach. These people allowed me to see what was possible based on their areas of expertise. My world and dreams suddenly grew!

EXHIBIT 11.1 (*Continued*)

What do you believe will be the short-term costs and benefits for you in owning as opposed to renting?

Short-term costs include many up-front expenses that you might not be aware of at the start unless you are an experienced commercial real estate investor. That is why adequate cash flow is so important. If you don't have a reserve to tap into for necessary expenses, I would recommend SBA because that type of working capital can be built into the loan. And if you don't use the money, you can return it. An example of an expense that I didn't count on was my security system. It was not included in my contractor's fees but was required as a condition from the lender. You can't say toward the end that you'll forgo it if you run out of money. Another short-term cost involves your time. If building out, you will devote many hours to the process and your practice business may suffer temporarily. Even though I had people tell me how many hours a week they spent on the process, I thought I could do it faster. I was wrong. Listen to those people and build the time into your schedule.

Short-term benefits include having an office that is tailored specifically to your practice needs and is designed the way you choose. Another benefit is that it requires you to focus on developing a business plan, a budget, and monthly projections.

What do you believe will be the long-term costs and benefits for you in owning as opposed to renting?

Well, I don't see too many long-term costs other than maintenance and repairs. Long-term costs would be similar to home ownership. The greatest benefit is that you've owned an appreciating asset for a period. Another benefit is the potential for retirement income. You could sell or lease at retirement. You may choose one or the other depending on your retirement goals. Leasing will give you steady, monthly income. Selling will give you a sum of money to invest in other income-producing ventures.

What, if any, surprises were there for you in the building process?

The complexity and time involved in completing the project was more than I expected. I underestimated what it would take. I think that was due in part to having obtained a doctoral degree and license. I said to myself that if I could accomplish those milestones, this would be easy. Wrong!

I was totally surprised at the paperwork, oversight, and at times disorganization involved with an SBA loan versus a conventional loan. If you go with SBA, you have to put it in perspective and sit back and relax. It is a government agency and contains the same amount of bureaucracy as any government agency. This can be frustrating to an entrepreneur. But if SBA is the best option for you, prepare yourself for the process and keep your eyes on the goal instead of on the minutiae in the process.

A good surprise was how building an office totally changed the way I do business. It opened my mind to new ideas for what I could accomplish. Building an office forced me to focus on the numbers in a way I had not previously. Once I did that, I could see possibilities and ways to implement new practice ideas. The office project basically reshaped and expanded my practice in new ways. Another good surprise was that the building placed me in direct contact with other professions and many interesting people. Sometimes we psychologists tend to interact only with other psychologists and our clients. I acquired and maintained business connections that will help my business grow for years to come.

It was also surprising how much I needed and benefited from having a team of people working with me in this project. The main players were the realtor, attorney, accountant, personal

(*Continued*)

EXHIBIT 11.1 (*Continued*)

banker, architect, contractor, project manager, and coach. I learned to trust and rely on others' expertise in ways I had never done before because of the fast pace at which decisions needed to be made. There was no time to hear data, research, evaluate, and then make a decision when I was absolutely sure. In the building process, I had to hear the data, listen to recommendations, make a decision, and move forward without looking back. It was an opportunity to grow personally in ways that allowed me to take more risks and expand the business in new ways.

Do you have any advice for those considering such a project for themselves?
The advice most often given to me was to make sure there was adequate cash flow. I didn't know why that was so important for a building at first. But as I got into the project, there were many intangible and unpredicted expenses. The process also leads you into thinking about your business in a new way that could add to your expense. For example, you may realize you have extra space that will allow you to do some area of practice that you were not doing before. So now a building has suddenly led to the purchase of new equipment, materials, or even staff. You want to be able to accommodate those growth ideas. That is why I went with an SBA loan even though it was more expensive.

Another piece of advice is that once you've made your decision to build, move forward and realize you'll have doubts, fears, and your share of second-guessing. These reactions are all normal when you start a new endeavor or take a new risk. You are building more than an office. You are building a business with a new vision. You are growing personally and professionally in new ways. Enjoy the ride and keep your eyes on the goal. It is one of the most enriching professional experiences you will have!

How Much Money Do I Need to Retire?

This is the $64,000 question or, more likely, the $1, $2, or $3 million question. The answer to this question may depend on your life circumstances, your health, your values, and how you want to live in your retirement (e.g., travel the world or stay at home and rock grandchildren on the front porch).

Every one of the financial magazines mentioned earlier addresses these issues at some point during the year. A retirement calculator (which you can find on the Internet) will help you determine how much you may need to save to live in a way that you would like to during your retirement years. It may also make suggestions regarding the age at which you can retire and live at a certain income level. We actively encourage you to make such calculations so you can plan as early as possible to reach your retirement goals. To maintain their standard of living in retirement Tyson (2006) suggested that people need to generate a dividend and investment income of 70% to 80% percent of their preretirement income. These figures may vary depending on whether your home is owned free of debt and if you want to increase or decrease your amount of preretirement spending.

Conclusion

We have tried to make the point that mental health professionals in private practice can earn an excellent income. However, the responsibility for managing and growing this money also falls to the clinician as well. We have attempted to highlight several forms of investments but we are sure there are many others of which we are not aware. Clinicians should consult with financial management professionals to possibly increase their rate of return as well as to become aware of all investment options open to them. As Private Practice Principle Number 20 indicates, clinicians in private practice are responsible for their own retirement planning and funding. With proper planning and attention to this matter, a high quality of life is possible during your retirement years. But without proper planning and attention, your retirement years may be jeopardized despite your having earned an excellent income for many years of successful clinical practice.

Closing Your Practice
Financial Implications and Options

12

T he operation of this particular small business will one day come to an end. Reasons for this could include relocation, poor health or disability, retirement, or death. Cantor (2005) pointed out that she has known very few psychotherapists to retire from practicing their craft. Rather, they continue to practice, though at a slower pace than when they were in full-time practice. She noted that psychotherapists are fortunate because there is no mandatory retirement age. Private practitioners can continue to practice for as long as they are healthy and effective as clinicians.

Closing a practice for any reason is accompanied by a host of emotional reactions and practical decisions, along with ethical and legal obligations, that must receive attention. We address each area in this chapter, along with issues related to the possible sale of a practice.

Leaving a Practice

Steve Walfish has closed two full-time practices because he relocated to new cities. He notes it is an enormous task. There are personal issues for the clinician, client reactions to hearing the news, and then a host of practical details that cannot be overlooked.

Koocher (2003) suggested that ideally this transition (or retirement) can be carefully planned. If the transition is planned, the clinician can personally inform clients he or she will be leaving and develop termination and continuing care plans to meet the needs of each of them. He further added that effective planning is key with respect to ethical practice and risk management. Barnett (1997a) elaborated on this concept by stating, "Regardless of the circumstance each clinician's primary concern should be the welfare of his or her patients" (p. 182). Barnett cited the ethics codes of several disciplines in pointing out clinicians have an obligation not to abandon clients. "It seems clear that the legal and ethical burden rests squarely on the provider's shoulders to focus on the patient's treatment needs and to take all reasonable steps to ensure that these needs are met" (Barnett, 1997a, p. 183).

The "Ethical Principles of Psychologists and Code of Conduct" of the American Psychological Association (2002) has three standards of direct relevance to this obligation. Ethical Standard 3.12, Interruption of Psychological Services, stresses that psychologists must plan in advance for smooth transitions should they be unable to continue working with their clients. This standard provides examples such as "the psychologist's illness, death, unavailability, relocation, or retirement or by the client's/patient's relocation or financial limitations" (p. 1066). Ethical Standard 10.09, Interruption of Therapy, shares each psychologist's obligation to address such issues "when entering into employment or contractual relationships" (p. 1073) so that clients' treatment needs are appropriately addressed even if a job or contract comes to an end. Finally, Ethical Standard 10.10, Terminating Therapy, addresses the circumstances under which termination should occur such as when the client is no longer benefiting from treatment, and when termination may occur such as when a psychologist is "threatened or otherwise endangered by the client/patient" (p. 1073) or by an individual associated with the client. This standard stresses the need to provide pretermination counseling before ending treatment and make referrals if ongoing treatment is still needed unless this is prevented by actions by the client or other parties. These standards are consistent with standards from the ethics codes of other mental health professions including social workers and counselors. All mental health professionals have the ethical obligation to appropriately attend to these issues.

One issue that has both clinical and financial implications is when to tell clients that you will be leaving the practice. This decision has clinical implications because clients are likely to have transference reactions to hearing this news. McGee (2003) provided excellent examples of transference reactions that clients may have to hearing from their psychotherapist that he or she is going to retire. He also presented counter-transference reactions the psychotherapist may have as a result of leaving his or her clients and, in the case of retirement, no longer having the work identity of being a clinician. No set guidelines exist for when to inform clients of the impending closing of one's practice so clinicians will need to use their best judgment on this issue. Most likely clients in long-term psychodynamic psychotherapy will need to be told sooner than will clients in cognitive–behavioral psychotherapy. This is because the latter tends to be shorter term in nature than the former, and clients' reactions may be less a focus of treatment in cognitive–behavioral treatments.

The decision regarding when to announce the closing of a practice has financial implications, and possibly a countertransference reaction related to income, for the mental health professional. Recall that clinicians do not get paid if they do not provide a service. They cannot cash in unused vacation or sick leave benefits from an employer when leaving a position. Therefore, when one winds down a practice, the income winds down as well. Depending on the financial standing of the psychotherapist, this may create a financial hardship. When Steve Walfish closed both of his practices he gave clients a 1-month notice that he was leaving. He also decided to stop accepting new clients 2 months before moving. He primarily practices short-term cognitive–behavioral psychotherapy, with most of his clients completing therapy in fewer than eight sessions. When he did receive a referral of a new client that he believed would need longer term treatment, he referred the person to another clinician, indicating that he was not accepting new clients at the time. However, he was also aware that he needed to earn fees to (a) finance the cross-country moves he was paying for on his own and (b) have an income buffer as he knew it would take a while before he would see income from the new practice that he was starting. Fortunately, he has both psychotherapy and psychological evaluation components to his practice. When his psychotherapy practice was winding down he was able to concurrently increase his evaluation practice. The last month of his Seattle practice he was completing 25 Social Security Disability evaluations each week. This work was especially helpful financially as he had terminated with most of his psychotherapy clients and saw only five his last week in practice. The point we are trying to make is that clinicians have to be aware of the reduction of income that may come from the closing of a practice and to take this into consideration in their planning process. If they do not do so they may be at risk of having a negative countertransference reaction to this financial loss. If a negative reaction occurs, a smooth termination with clients may be jeopardized because the best interests of the client may not be fully taken into consideration (e.g., inadequate notice of the practice closing being given for fear clients will terminate prematurely, seeing clients more frequently than is clinically necessary).

Emotional Issues

Cantor (2005) suggested that decisions about retirement should be made only after much planning. She presented two reasons for this being the case. First, if this decision is made in one's 50s the clinician will have time to decide if this path is suitable. Second, it will allow for trying to determine how the clinician is going to spend his or her time when he or she is no longer busy with a private practice.

Cantor (2005) pointed to the need for self-examination to identify the gratifications that accompany working in a private practice and as a mental health professional. For example, she noted that her practice provides her with a purpose and goals. The question to be explored then becomes what other ways might be available to obtain this same level of gratification. She suggested that because of the demands on one's career, other goals and interests may have needed to be put aside and the retirement years may afford the time to pursue these interests.

Cantor (2005) urged clinicians to best suit their own retirement desires and expectations and not be concerned with the expectations of others. Harrington and Steinberg (2007), citing the work of psychologist Nancy Schlossberg, pointed to five approaches to retirement. *Continuers* do similar activities but in a new context. *Adventurers* start down a completely different path, learning a completely new skill. *Searchers* try out many different plans hoping to find the right fit for them. *Easy gliders* just go with the flow and are happy being with others or by themselves. Finally, *retreaters* break away from their past and withdraw from many life activities. In discussing retirement from the profession McGee (2003) insightfully elaborated,

> Psychologists are not immune from experiencing a range of deep feelings around transitions, losses, and the giving up of important attachments, and retirement is an event that has the capacity to stimulate such feelings. (p. 392)

McGee pointed to the need to have self-insight into the retirement process as well as issues to understand and resolve to have a gratifying retirement. He also suggested that it is important to understand the impact retirement may have on the family system and support network of the mental health professional.

Practical Issues

Barnett, MacGlashan, and Clarke (2000) pointed out the need for psychotherapists to take steps to ensure patients' treatment needs are met and continuity of care is provided regardless of the reason for termination. Failure to do so, according to these authors, may lead to claims of abandonment by the client.

Several steps have been identified as essential to take when closing a practice. McGee (2003) discussed the need to have a proper termination process. This process includes informing clients of the ending of the psychotherapeutic relationship, processing this information with the clients over a number of sessions, and making an appropriate referral if further treatment is warranted. McGee indicated that any referral for continuing care should be made with the best interest of the client at the forefront. McGee suggested that the introduction to a new psychotherapist is best done in person. However, with the client's permission a treatment summary would suffice. McGee (2003) advised that it might be helpful to seek clinical consultation when arranging therapeutic transfers for difficult or complicated clients.

Koocher (2003) indicated that when possible, recent past clients also need to be notified that the clinician is closing the practice. This notification may be accomplished by mailing letters to former clients; some jurisdictions require the posting of the closing in the legal announcement sections of local newspapers.

McGee also discussed matters related to the maintenance and storage of client records. There are state regulations the clinician should adhere to when making these decisions. When Steve Walfish moved from Seattle to Atlanta, the moving van included 12 boxes of client files that according to state law needed to be maintained for 5 years. Most state statutes also have special rules related to the records of children and adolescents.

As discussed in chapter 8 it is important that clinicians remain covered by malpractice insurance when they retire. Koocher (2003) pointed out that not all insurance carriers are licensed in every state, which might result in a coverage problem. Therefore, it is important for clinicians who do not have occurrence malpractice insurance to purchase a tail from their carrier (or a carrier in the new state) to cover any claims that may be made against them for past acts.

McGee (2003) also pointed to the need for clinicians to develop a professional will. In it one designates an executor who will carry out the continued wishes and responsibilities of the mental health professional in the event of death or incapacitation. Take the unfortunate example of a private practitioner retiring and then 4 years later passing away. There is likely a legal obligation to maintain client records for 5 or 7 years after the termination of treatment. Who will control the records after the death of the clinician is important to plan for as there may be requests for the records. If this process is not handled appropriately the estate of the deceased clinician may be held liable for not complying with state law regarding maintenance of records. Ballard (2005) and Pope and Vasquez (2005) provided guidelines for the development of a professional will for private practitioners. See http://www.kspope.com/therapistas/will.php for a helpful overview of Pope and Vasquez's recommendations for creating a professional will.

Selling a Practice

Mental health professionals may deal with these emotional and practical issues and opt to simply just close their business. As an alternative they may opt to attempt to receive compensation for their hard work and entrepreneurship by selling their business to someone who wants to purchase part or all of their practice. If this option is chosen, one must be aware of the ethical and practical aspects of selling a mental health practice.

ETHICS ISSUES

As noted earlier, psychotherapists are obligated to take steps to ensure patients' treatment needs are met and continuity of care is provided regardless of the reason for termination; furthermore, the primary concern should be the welfare of the client (Barnett, 1997a; Barnett et al., 2000). Koocher (2003) indicated that if a selling clinician is to have access to a current practice owner's records, consent should be sought from the client. Clinicians cannot simply turn over all of their client records and solely refer all of their clients to the buying clinician. Some states have specific regulations regarding the sale of a practice. For example, on the basis of statutory and regulatory provisions, the New York State Office of the Professions (n.d.) stated the following regarding psychologists selling their practice:

> Psychologists who are planning to terminate a practice may consider selling the practice. The tangible assets of a practice may be sold, but the patient's/client's names and records may not be sold. Psychologists who wish to transfer patient/client records to another practitioner's care could do so by following the recommended process for making this kind of transfer, which includes patient/client consent for both the release of their name to the other practitioner, as well as consent for the other practitioner to view their records.

Controls must be put in place so that any referral for continuing care is in the best interest of the client and not in the financial best interests of the individuals buying and selling the practice.

PRACTICAL ISSUES

The sale of a practice takes great planning. R. Woody (1997) pointed out that it is faulty to assume that the process (and value) of selling a mental health practice is similar to the sale of other professional practices such as medicine, dentistry, or law. He noted, "Psychologist-client relationships tend to be more idiosyncratic (e.g., predicated on highly emotionalized reasons) than certain other professional relationships" (p. 78).

In doing research for this chapter, Ms. Aubree Lundie, a student who works with Steve Walfish, conducted interviews with individuals who had advertised their practice being for sale in the American Psychological Association publication *Monitor on Psychology*. It is instructive to briefly review some of their experiences. The first person interviewed had been in solo psychotherapy practice in a major city. She was unsuccessful in selling her practice. During the interview she indicated:

> I built a successful practice that had been in existence for 25 years. I wanted compensation for all of the hard work that I put into the practice. I thought it would be a shame to walk away from everything I had built. Since I had seen ads for years I had assumed that a process of selling a practice existed. I felt very prepared to sell the practice but I was wrong. I received very little response from either my ad or the business broker that I also worked with to try and sell the practice.

This individual clearly had a negative experience and although she thought she was prepared for the sale of her practice, she was not.

The second person interviewed, a psychologist in a moderate-sized city in the Southeast, did not feel very knowledgeable about what was entailed in selling a practice. He also felt unaware of the tax implications of selling a practice. The person who at the time of the interview was in the process of buying the psychologist's practice was not a mental health professional but rather a speech pathologist. A previous sale to a psychologist fell through. When asked what he would have liked to have known before putting his practice up for sale, the interviewee replied:

> How complex the process has been. It involved hiring an attorney to protect me during the sale and it just dragged on for a long time. I was not prepared for the length of time involved with selling the practice. It has just been months of phone calls, and offers, and waiting.

This individual's experience points to the need for patience on the part of the seller. Imagine how frustrating it must have been for him when the sale to the psychologist fell through. Yet such an outcome is not unusual for the sale of any business, so the mental health professional is advised to be cautiously optimistic when it seems a sale is imminent and to save exuberance for when it actually is consummated. In addition, this individual creatively went outside of traditional sources to find a buyer, which suggests that casting a wide, rather than a narrow, net may be advantageous in locating a buyer.

The third person, a psychologist in a moderate-sized city in the Northeast, was not successful in selling his practice. The practice included three to six master's-level psychotherapists who were going to continue in the practice. He had a particular area of specialization and was going to remain in the practice for 1 year to help build the practice and train the person in the specialty area. He set the asking price such that the buyer could recoup his or her investment in 3 to 5 years. His accountant told him,

> It is difficult to sell a practice, especially since much of it is intangible. Every potential buyer had a different opinion as to what was valuable and how, and what they were looking for in a practice.

When asked what he would have liked to have known before placing his practice up for sale, he replied:

> Knowing what the audience is like out there—it was overwhelmingly disappointing. I entertained no less than 15 people who showed interest in purchasing the practice. None of them led to a successful offer or sale. There is a difference in opinions among buyers as to how a practice is valued. I received offers as low as $41,000 to $400,000. In every case regardless of the number, I tried to work with their number, their assessment of the value of his practice, and did my best to reason with them. However, it still resulted in failure to sell the practice. I also learned that there are some vicious people out there.

With his consultants this psychologist determined the financial value of his practice. However, what he learned through this negative experience is that although clinicians may place a certain dollar value on their practice, market forces and perceived value on the part of the potential buyer may not live up to these valuations.

The last person, a psychologist in Florida, could not complete a full interview. However, she indicated that she was unable to sell her clinical practice but was able to sell the building in which the practice was housed. This sale reinforces the decisions described by Barrie Alexander and Nancy McGarrah in Exhibit 4.3 (pp. 76–77) and Tammy Martin-Causey in Exhibit 11.1 (pp. 223–226) to purchase their buildings as part of a long-term financial strategy.

Placing a financial value, a specific dollar amount, on a private practice is a difficult task. It is likely the mental health professional, who has put in years of building the practice, is not the most objective person to do this. Koocher (2003) pointed out that other than tangible property such as real estate or office equipment and furniture, most practices have little, if any, tangible assets. Rather, as Koocher pointed out, the main value is likely to be intangible—for instance, the reputation of the practice. R. Woody (1997), in an important paper on valuing practices, wrote the following:

> There is neither a circumspect list of factors to be evaluated nor a
> formula to apply to the factors that are relevant to a particular
> practice. . . . The challenge is, therefore, to define the factors that
> are inherent to a particular practice and determine a valuation
> method that is reasonable and appropriate. (pp. 77–78)

Woody sees value in established contracts remaining with the business,
in employees and practitioners currently in the practice remaining, and
the current owner of the practice remaining, at least for a time.

Established contracts can be a valuable asset. For example, the practice may have a contract to provide employee assistance programs to a
number of companies. These help maintain a consistent flow of clients
into the practice, especially if the companies are large. Some practices
have signed capitation agreements with health maintenance organizations (HMOs) to provide their mental health services. (To avoid hiring
its own mental health staff the HMO may carve out this benefit to a particular large group practice.) This arrangement also guarantees a steady
flow of clients. A practice may have a contract with a hospital to provide psychological testing services. These are all examples of contracts
that have an economic value if they remain with the practice.

If the current employees and the principal owner remain with the
practice, there will likely be little disruption in the community perception of the practice. If the practice has several clinicians, who either pay
a monthly fee for renting space and office services or pay a percentage
of their gross income to the practice, there will be little disruption in
cash flow to the practice. If support staff employees (e.g., reception,
billing) remain, there will be no additional costs in hiring and training
new personnel. These features should be attractive to a prospective
buyer.

Weitz (1983) described his experience as the seller of his practice to
Samuels (1983), who described his experience as the purchaser. They
agreed to a 2-year transition period in which the owner of the practice
agreed to stay on as a partner and help integrate the new owner into
the practice and into the community. In many ways, this arrangement
appears to be ideal as the good will (e.g., positive reputation of the clinician in the community) of the practice likely remained intact while
the new owner developed an identity in the community.

Many questions need to be asked when considering purchasing a
practice. Henry Harlow is a licensed mental health counselor who also
coaches clinicians in practice development issues. He has advised clinicians regarding the purchase and sale of practices. Exhibit 12.1 presents
his list of questions to consider when buying a practice. Potential sellers
should also pay attention to these questions as positive answers would
increase the attractiveness of their practice to potential purchasers.

EXHIBIT 12.1

A Few Quick Business Questions to Ask When Considering Buying a Practice by Henry Harlow (http://www.Law-Firm-Marketing-Coach.com)

1. Is this practice a personality-based practice or a systems-based practice? See *The E-Myth Revisited* by Michael Gerber (1995). If it is personality based then you don't have much value to buy because much if not all of the business will go away when the personality goes away. Also, there are no written systems on the business because the owner is running it randomly by his or her personality so, unlike say a McDonald's, it is hard to replicate.

2. What types of records does the practice have on its marketing systems that you can review and how well do these marketing systems deliver clients to the practice? Will this level be sustainable with or without the owner? See *Get Clients Now! Second Edition* by C. J. Hayden (2007).

3. What is the "brand" and does that brand have value? How do you know the brand has value? Is the name of the practice a brand name or tied to the owner's name in some way? Can you use the name if it is tied to the owner or will you have to change the name?

4. How long will the owner stay with the practice during the transition phase? What will the owner do to ensure the clients stay with you long term? Will there be a separate charge for this service or is it included in the sales price?

5. If a team of employees is in place, will they remain in place after the owner departs? How do you know that?

6. Ask yourself: If you were to start your own practice within a few miles of this practice, how much time and money would it take for you to build this new practice to the level you think you will retain once the buyer is gone? If you think you can build a practice like the one you are considering buying relatively easily and fast, why buy the practice? If not, then maybe the practice has real value to you. The question to be asked and answered is, How much?

7. Ask yourself whether you are a technician, manager, or entrepreneur type (see Gerber, 1995, again). Most professionals are technician oriented. Do you really, really want to be a manager and entrepreneur? If you don't have the skill set and knowledge to be a manager and entrepreneur, how will you get it?

8. If you are buying the practice, what are you buying? Are you buying a sole proprietorship, corporation, or the assets of the practice? The general wisdom is that it is best to buy the assets of the practice and not the legal entity that owns those assets because that minimizes your possible liabilities. You almost certainly want an attorney to be involved in the buying process on your side.

9. Will the sale include a noncompete agreement with the seller? You certainly don't want the seller to open up again near your practice, at least for a reasonable period of time. This is another reason to have an attorney involved in the process.

10. The value of a service business or practice can be from 40% to 100% of the annual gross revenues. If the practice is personality based with not very good or no marketing systems in place and little to no brand, then the value is closer to 40% or even less. If the practice is on the systems side, then maybe the value is 100%. Some might say the value of a practice is three times the net of the practice. That being said, the value and price is all really negotiable. There are other methods of calculating the value of a business (market-based, earnings-based, and value-based) used by different professionals who do value businesses (appraisers, accountants, business brokers, etc.) so you might want to get an independent appraisal of the practice if the seller has not already done it. The owner generally tends to overvalue a practice, and the buyer tends to undervalue the practice. Thus the two need to negotiate.

A Closing Note

One approach we advocate is for private practitioners to take a long-term perspective in planning to eventually sell their practice. In his interview Henry Harlow noted the work of Gerber (1995), who differentiated between a personality-based and a systems-based small business. The latter is more attractive to a buyer than the former. In a personality-based private practice the success is based on you, the small-business owner—your clinical skills, social skills, and business network. However, in making the sale you are disengaging from the practice. Thus, when losing the personality or key player that made the practice a success, the purchaser would be losing the key asset. When positioning yourself to make a sale of the practice, ask yourself what the purchaser would be buying. A systems-based private practice would be more attractive to a buyer because financial success would not depend on your clinical skills and reputation in the community.

Practices can then be developed and structured in a planned manner with this overarching goal as a guide. As previously noted, the purchase of real estate, a tangible asset, would be one strategy consistent with this goal. New associates can be brought into the practice not specifically to fill empty space but rather with a purpose in mind regarding what value they add to the practice (new specialties, ability to attract new referral sources). The practice can be structured to provide incentives for people to remain in the practice and help it to grow. We are aware of one group practice of psychologists with entrepreneurial spirit who took such a stance. With four psychologists as partners, they grew the practice to have 32 clinicians working within their system. They had contracts with several companies to provide employee assistance programs. They had agreements with HMOs to provide all of their mental health services. They had contracts to provide screening of public safety personnel (e.g., police, firefighters). They became a profitable company and eventually had a national health care company approach them for purchase. They negotiated a favorable price, stayed on for 2 years to help the new owners with the transition into the practice, and then each partner left with a significant nest egg. Considerable time, energy, and sacrifice went into building the practice into one that would be attractive to a buyer. We are aware this level of practice will not be the norm for most mental health professionals. However, keeping these principles, along with the suggestions of Harlow in Exhibit 12.1, in mind will increase the likelihood that a practice will be attractive for a potential buyer. Build a system that can be profitable for someone else (not just yourself) and most likely there will be a buyer to reward you for what you have built.

References

Ackley, D. (1997). *Breaking free of managed care.* New York: Guilford Press.

Alleman, J. (2001). Personal, practical and professional issues in providing managed mental health care: A discussion for new psychotherapists. *Ethics and Behavior, 11,* 413–429.

American Association for Marriage and Family Therapy. (n.d.). *What MFTs get paid.* Retrieved July 7, 2007, from http://www.aamft.org/resources/Career_PracticeInformation/MFTSalaries.asp

American Psychiatric Association. (1994). *Diagnostic and statistical manual of mental disorders* (4th ed.). Washington, DC: Author.

American Psychological Association. (2002). Ethical principles of psychologists and code of conduct. *American Psychologist, 57,* 1060–1073.

American Psychological Association Insurance Trust. (n.d.). *Trust Income Protection Insurance—Plan detail.* Retrieved July 7, 2007, from http://www.apait.org/apait/products/incomeprotection/detail.aspx

Ames, M., & Runco, M. (2005). Predicting entrepreneurship from ideation and divergent thinking. *Creativity and Innovation Management, 14,* 311–315.

Anderson, J., & Barrett, B. (2001). *Ethics in HIV-related psychotherapy: Clinical decision making in complex cases.* Washington, DC: American Psychological Association.

Anderson, P., Zimand, E., Hodges, L., & Rothbaum, B. (2005). Cognitive behavioral therapy for public-speaking anxiety using virtual reality for exposure. *Depression and Anxiety, 22,* 156–158.

Archer, R., Buffington-Vollum, K., Stredny, R., & Handel, R. (2006). A survey of psychological test use patterns among forensic psychologists. *Journal of Personality Assessment, 87,* 84–94.

Ballard, D. (2005). Planning ahead to close or sell your practice. In J. E. Barnett & M. Gallardo (Eds.), *Handbook for success in independent practice* (pp. 165–172). Phoenix, AZ: Psychologists in Independent Practice.

Barker, R. (1982). *The business of psychotherapy.* New York: Columbia University Press.

Barker, K., & Kohout, J. (2003). Contemporary employment in psychology and future trends. In M. J. Prinstein & M. Patterson (Eds.), *The portable mentor: Expert guide to a successful career in psychology* (pp. 309–332). New York: Kluwer Academic/Plenum Publishers.

Barnett, J. E. (1993). Ethical practice within a managed care environment. *The Independent Practitioner, 13,* 160–162.

Barnett, J. E. (1996). How to avoid malpractice. *Psychotherapy Bulletin, 31*(3), 46–51.

Barnett, J. E. (1997a). Leaving a practice: Ethical and legal issues and dilemmas. In L. VandeCreek, S. Knapp, & T. Jackson (Eds.), *Innovations in clinical practice* (pp. 181–188). Sarasota, FL: Professional Resource Press.

Barnett, J. E. (1997b). Why managed care? *Psychotherapy in Private Practice, 16,* 1–14.

Barnett, J. E. (1998). Confidentiality in the age of managed care. *The Clinical Psychologist, 51*(1), 30–33.

Barnett, J. E., & Henshaw, E. A. (2002). Ethical, clinical, and risk management issues in rural practice. In L. VandeCreek & T. Jackson (Eds.), *Innovations in clinical practice* (pp. 411–422). Sarasota, FL: Professional Resource Press.

Barnett, J. E., & Henshaw, E. A. (2003). Training to begin a private practice. In M. Prinstein & M. Patterson (Eds.), *The portable mentor: Expert guide to a successful career in psychology* (pp. 145–156). New York: Kluwer Academic/Plenum Publishers.

Barnett, J. E., & Johnson, W. B. (2008). *Ethics desk reference for psychologists.* Washington, DC: American Psychological Association.

Barnett, J. E., MacGlashan, S., & Clarke, A. J. (2000). Risk management and ethical issues regarding termination and abandonment. In L. VandeCreek & T. Jackson (Eds.), *Innovations in clinical practice* (pp. 231–246). Sarasota, FL: Professional Resource Press.

Barnett, J. E., & Porter, J. E. (1998). The suicidal patient: Clinical, ethical, and risk management strategies. In L. VandeCreek, S. Knapp, & T. Jackson (Eds.), *Innovations in clinical practice* (pp. 95–107). Sarasota, FL: Professional Resource Press.

Barnett, J. E., & Sanzone, M. (1997). Termination: Ethical and legal issues. *The Clinical Psychologist, 50*(1), 9–13.

Barnett, J. E., & Scheetz, K. (2003). Technological advances and telehealth: Ethics, law, and the practice of psychology. *Psychotherapy: Theory, Research, Practice, Training, 40,* 86–93.

Baron, R. (2002). OB and entrepreneurship: The reciprocal benefits of closer conceptual links. In B. M. Staw & R. Kramer (Eds.), *Research in organizational behavior* (pp. 225–269). Greenwich, CT: JAI Press.

Baron, R., & Shane, S. (2008). *Entrepreneurship: A process perspective.* New York: Thomson-South-Western.

Barth, F. D. (2001). Money as a tool for negotiating separateness and connectedness in the therapeutic relationship. *Clinical Social Work Journal, 29,* 79–93.

Bennett, B. E., Bricklin, P. M., Harris, E., Knapp, S., VandeCreek, L., & Younggren, J. N. (2006). *Assessing and managing risk in psychological practice: An individualized approach.* Rockville, MD: The Trust.

Berman, B. (2005). How to delight your customers. *California Management Review, 48,* 129–151.

Bernay, T. (1983). Making a practice: Overcoming passivity and masochism. *Psychotherapy in Private Practice, 1,* 25–29.

Blanchard, E., Hickling, E., Taylor, A., Loos, W., & Gerardi, R. (1994). Psychological morbidity associated with motor vehicle accidents. *Behaviour Research and Therapy, 32,* 283–290.

Blau, T., & Alberts, F. (2004). *The forensic documentation sourcebook: The complete paperwork resource for forensic mental health practice.* New York: Wiley.

Bogo, M., Michalsk, J., Raphael, D., & Roberts, R. (1995). Practice interests and self-identification among social work students: Changes over the course of graduate social work education. *Journal of Social Work Education, 31,* 228–246.

Boice, R., & Myers, P. (1987). Which setting is happier, academe or private practice? *Professional Psychology: Research and Practice, 18,* 526–529.

Bookkeeping. (n.d.). In *Dictionary.com's online dictionary*. Retrieved from http://www.dictionary.com

Broskowski, A. (1984). Organizational controls and leadership. *Professional Psychology: Research and Practice, 15*, 645–663.

Broskowski, A. (1991). Current mental health environments: Why managed care is necessary. *Professional Psychology: Research and Practice, 22*, 6–14.

Bush, S., Connell, M., & Denny, R. (2006). *Ethical practice in forensic psychology: A systematic model for decision making*. Washington, DC: American Psychological Association.

Camara, W., Nathan, J., & Puente, A. (2000). Psychological test usage: Implications in professional psychology. *Professional Psychology: Research and Practice, 31*, 141–154.

Cantor, D. (1983). Independent practice: Minding your own business. *Psychotherapy in Private Practice, 1*, 19–24.

Cantor, D. (2005). Do I ever want to retire? Making a well-planned decision. In J. E. Barnett & M. Gallardo (Eds.), *Handbook for success in independent practice* (pp. 161–165). Phoenix, AZ: Psychologists in Independent Practice.

Cashel, L. (2002). Child and adolescent psychological assessment: Current clinical practices and the impact of managed care. *Professional Psychology: Research and Practice, 33*, 446–453.

Cheeseman, H. (2005). *The legal environment of business and online commerce*. Upper Saddle River, NJ: Prentice Hall.

Clay, R. (1998, July). More clinical psychologists move into organizational consulting realm. *Monitor on Psychology, 29*, 28–29.

Cohen, J., Maracek, J., & Gillham, J. (2007). Is three a crowd? Clients, clinicians, and managed care. *American Journal of Orthopsychiatry, 76*, 251–259.

Comas-Diaz, L. (2006). The present and future of clinical psychology in private practice. *Clinical Psychology: Science and Practice, 13*, 273–277.

Community Hospital Group, Inc. v. More, 183 N.J. 36, 869 A.2d 884 (N.J. S. Ct. 2005).

Company Corporation, The. (2001). *Incorporating your business for dummies*. Hoboken, NJ: Wiley.

Comprehensive Psychological System, P.C. v. Prince, 867 A.2d 1187, 1189 (N.J. Super. Ct. App. Div. 2005).

Connor, R., & Davidson, J. (2001). *Marketing your consulting and professional services*. New York: Wiley.

Cowen, E. (1982). Help is where you find it: Four informal helping groups. *American Psychologist, 37*, 385–395.

Crosby, L., & Johnson, S. (2006, July/August). Make it memorable. *Marketing Management, 15*(4), 12–13.

Customer. (n.d.-a). In *Dictionary.com's online dictionary*. Retrieved February 21, 2008, from http://dictionary.reference.com/search?r=2&q=customer

Customer. (n.d.-b). In *Merriam-Webster's online dictionary*. Retrieved February 21, 2008, from http://www.merriam-webster.com/dictionary/customer

DeSalvo, D., Koch, E., & Kennon, J. (2006). *The complete idiot's guide to investing*. New York: Alpha Books.

Dixon, K., Keefe, F., Scipio, C., Perri, L., & Abernathy, A. (2007). Psychological interventions for arthritis pain management in adults: A meta-analysis. *Health Psychology, 26*, 241–250.

Doak, C., Doak, L., & Root, J. (1996). *Teaching patients with low literacy skills*. Philadelphia: Lippincott Williams & Wilkins.

Dwore, R. B. (1993). Managing hospital quality performance in two related areas: Patient care and customer service. *Hospital Topics, 71*(2), 29–34.

D'Zurilla, T. J., & Goldfried, M. R. (1971). Problem solving and behavior modification. *Journal of Abnormal Psychology, 78*, 107–126.

Elhai, J., Gray, M., Kashdan, T., & Franklin, L. (2005). Which instruments are most commonly used to assess traumatic event exposure and posttraumatic effects? A survey of traumatic stress professionals. *Journal of Traumatic Stress, 18*, 541–545.

Epstein, L. (2006). *Bookkeeping for dummies*. Hoboken, NJ: Wiley.

Falender, C. A., & Shafranske, E. P. (2004). *Clinical supervision: A competency-based approach*. Washington, DC: American Psychological Association.

Farrell, M. (2000). *Beyond the basics: How to invest your money now that you know a thing or two*. New York: Simon & Schuster.

Finlay, S. (1999, June). Survey returns to dealership roots—J.D. Power and Associates customer service index—Editorial. *Ward's Dealer Business, 33*. Retrieved March 13, 2007, from http://www.findarticles.com/p/articles/mi_m0FJN/is_10_33/ai_55174517

Ford, W. (2003). Communication practices of professional service providers: Predicting customer satisfaction and loyalty. *Journal of Applied Communications Research, 31*, 189–211.

Fox, R. (1995). The rape of psychotherapy. *Professional Psychology: Research and Practice, 26*, 147–155.

Frager, S. (2002). *Successful private practice strategies: Winning strategies for mental health professionals*. New York: Wiley.

Fuhriman, A., & Burlingame, G. (1994). *Handbook of group psychotherapy: An empirical and clinical synthesis.* New York: Wiley.

Gaglio, C., & Katz, J. (2001). The psychological basis of opportunity identification: Entrepreneurial alertness. *Small Business Economics, 16,* 95–111.

Gelhert, S., & Browne, T. (2006). *Handbook of health social work.* New York: Wiley.

Gelso, C., & Hayes, J. (2001). Countertransference management. *Psychotherapy: Theory, Research, and Practice, 80,* 418–422.

Gentile, S., Asamen, J., Harmell, P., & Weathers, R. (2002). The stalking of psychologists by their clients. *Professional Psychology: Research and Practice, 33,* 490–494.

Gerber, M. (1995). *The e-myth revisited: Why most small businesses don't work and what to do about it.* New York: HarperCollins.

Gibelman, M., & Schervish, P. (1996). The private practice of social work: Current trends and projected scenarios in a managed care environment. *Clinical Social Work Journal, 24,* 323–338.

Glazer, J., & Merris, K. (2004, March). When customer service and patient care collide. *Family Practice Management, 11*(3), 16–17.

Grand, L. (2002). *The therapist's advertising and marketing kit.* New York: Wiley.

Grodzki, L. (2004). Making peace with money: The social worker as entrepreneur. *Social Work Today, 4,* 18–20.

Haley, W., McDaniel, S., Bray, J., Frank, R., Heldring, M., Johnson, S., et al. (1998). Psychological practice in primary care: Practical tips for clinicians. *Professional Psychology: Research and Practice, 29,* 237–244.

Handelsman, M. (2001). Learning to become ethical. In S. Walfish & A. K. Hess (Eds.), *Succeeding in graduate school: The career guide for psychology students* (pp. 189–202). Mahwah, NJ: Erlbaum.

Handelsman, M., Martinez, A., Geisendorfer, S., Jordan, L., Wagner, L., Daniel, P., & Davis, S. (1995). Does legally mandated consent to psychotherapy ensure ethical appropriateness? The Colorado experience. *Ethics and Behavior, 5,* 119–129.

Hanson, S., Kerkhoff, T., & Bush, S. (2004). *Health care ethics for psychologists: A casebook.* Washington, DC: American Psychological Association.

Harrington, J. (2002). *The everything start your own business book* (2nd ed.). Avon, MA: Adams Media.

Harrington, J., & Steinberg, S. (2007). *The everything retirement planning book.* Avon, MA: Adams Media.

Hayden, C. J. (2007). *Get clients now: A 28-day marketing program for professionals, consultants and coaches* (2nd ed.). New York: Amacom Books.

Hellstrom, K., Fellenius, J., & Ost, L.-G. (1996). One versus five sessions of applied tension in the treatment of blood phobia. *Behaviour Research and Therapy, 34,* 101–112.

Hendricks, M. (2004, February). What not to do: A seasoned entrepreneur reveals the 17 most common mistakes start-ups make and how to avoid them—plus, the 5 things you must do to ensure success. *Entrepreneur.* Retrieved February 25, 2007, from http://findarticles.com/p/articles/mi_m0DTI/is_2_32/ai_n6040833/pg_1

Herron, W. (1995).Visible and invisible psychotherapy fees. *Psychotherapy in Private Practice, 14,* 7–17.

Hersch, L. (1995). Adapting to health care reform and managed care: Three strategies for survival and growth. *Professional Psychology: Research and Practice, 26,* 16–26.

Hess, A. K. (1980). *Psychotherapy supervision: Theory, research and practice.* New York: Wiley.

Hess, A. K. (1998). Accepting forensic case referrals: Ethical and professional considerations. *Professional Psychology: Research and Practice, 29,* 109–114.

Hess, A. K. (2005). Practicing principled forensic psychology: Legal, ethical, and moral considerations. In I. Weiner & A. K. Hess (Eds.), *The handbook of forensic psychology* (3rd ed., pp. 321–358). New York: Wiley.

Hess, A. K., Hess, K., & Hess, T. (2008). *Handbook of psychotherapy supervision.* New York: Wiley.

Hochhauser, M. (2005, December). Unhealthy communications: Health care bills make patients sicker. *The Receivables Report,* 6–7.

Hogan, J., Lemon, K., & Libai, B. (2003). What is the true value of a lost customer? *Journal of Service Research, 5,* 196–208.

Houts, A., Berman, J., & Abramson, H. (1994). Effectiveness of psychological and pharmacological treatments for nocturnal enuresis. *Journal of Consulting and Clinical Psychology, 62,* 737–745.

Howard, C., & Meltzer, M. (2001). *Get Clark smart: The ultimate guide to getting rich from America's money-saving expert.* New York: Hyperion.

Internal Revenue Service. (2006). Deducting business expenses. Chap. 1 in *Publication 535.* Retrieved March 17, 2008, from http://www.irs.gov/publications/p535/ch01.html#d0e272

Kainz, K. (2002). Barriers and enhancements to physician-psychologist collaboration. *Professional Psychology: Research and Practice, 33,* 169–175.

Kano, N. (1984). Attractive quality and must-quality. *Journal of the Japanese Society for Quality Control, 14,* 39–48.

Karon, B. (1995). Provision of psychotherapy under managed health care: A growing crisis and national nightmare. *Professional Psychology: Research and Practice, 26,* 5–9.

Kase, L. (2005). *The successful therapist*. New York: Wiley.

Kennon, J. (n.d.). *Before you open a brokerage account*. Retrieved July 8, 2007, from http://beginnersinvest.about.com/od/choosingabroker/a/brokeraccount.htm

Kielbasa, A., Pomerantz, A., Krohn, E., & Sullivan, B. (2004). How does client method of payment influence psychologist's diagnostic decisions. *Ethics and Behavior, 14,* 187–195.

Kilburg, R. (2000). *Executive coaching: Developing managerial wisdom in a world of chaos*. Washington, DC: American Psychological Association.

Kilburg, R. (2006). *Executive wisdom: Coaching and the emergence of virtuous leaders*. Washington, DC: American Psychological Association.

Kiyosaki, R. (1997). *Rich dad, poor dad*. Scottsdale, AZ: Tech Press.

Knapp, S. J., & VandeCreek, L. (2006). *Practical ethics for psychologists: A positive approach*. Washington, DC: American Psychological Association.

Koeske, G., Lichtenwalter, S., & Koeske, R. (2005). Social workers' current and desired involvement in various practice activities: Explorations and implications. *Administration in Social Work, 29,* 63–84.

Kolt, L. (1999). *How to build a thriving fee-for-service practice*. San Diego, CA: Academic Press.

Koocher, G. (2003). Ethical and legal issues in professional practice transitions. *Professional Psychology: Research and Practice, 34,* 383–387.

Korn, J. (2001). Developing teaching skills. In S. Walfish & A. K. Hess (Eds.), *Succeeding in graduate school: The career guide for psychology students* (pp. 221–232). Mahwah, NJ: Erlbaum.

Kotler, P., Hayes, T., & Bloom, P. (2002). *Marketing professional services* (Rev. ed.). New York: Prentice Hall.

Kremer, T., & Gesten, E. (1998). Confidentiality limits of managed care and clients' willingness to self-disclose. *Professional Psychology: Research and Practice, 29,* 553–558.

Lally, S. (2003). What tests are acceptable for use in forensic evaluations? A survey of experts. *Professional Psychology: Research and Practice, 34,* 491–498.

Lambert, M. J., & Ogles, B. M. (2004). The efficacy and effectiveness of psychotherapy. In M. J. Lambert (Ed.), *Bergin and Garfield's handbook of psychotherapy and behavior change* (pp. 139–193). New York: Wiley.

Lawless, L. (1997). *How to build and market your mental health practice*. New York: Wiley.

Le, J., & Walfish, S. (2007, August). *Clinical practice strategies outside the realm of managed care: An update*. Paper presented at the annual meeting of the American Psychological Association, San Francisco, CA.

Levine, M., Perkins, D., & Perkins, D. (2004). *Principles of community psychology: Perspectives and applications* (3rd ed.). New York: Oxford University Press.

Lish, R., McMinn, M., Fitzsimmons, C., & Root, A. (2003). Clergy interest in innovative collaboration with psychologists. *Journal of Psychology and Christianity, 22,* 294–298.

Lorion, R. P., & Hightower, A. D. (2001). Community intervention: Applying psychological skills in the real world. In S. Walfish & A. K. Hess (Eds.), *Succeeding in graduate school: The career guide for psychology students* (pp. 369–384). Mahwah, NJ: Erlbaum.

Lowman, R. (1998). *The ethical practice of psychology in organizations.* Washington, DC: American Psychological Association.

Lowman, R. (2006). *The ethical practice of psychology in organizations* (2nd ed.). Washington, DC: American Psychological Association.

Maddock, J. (n.d.). *Business telephone systems: Buying tips.* Retrieved June 7, 2007, from http://ezinearticles.com/?Business-Telephone-Systems:-Buying-Tips&id=297813

Magellan Health Services. (2007). *Join the network.* Retrieved July 1, 2007, from http://www.magellanprovider.com/MHS/MGL/provnet/join_network/index.asp

Mallen, M., Vogel, D., & Rochlen, A. (2005). The practical aspects of online counseling. *Counseling Psychologist, 33,* 776–818.

Markman, G., Baron, R., & Balkin, S. (2005). Are perseverance and self-efficacy costless? Assessing entrepreneur's regretful thinking. *Journal of Organizational Behavior, 26,* 1–19.

Mart, E. (2006). *Getting started in forensic psychology practice.* New York: Wiley.

Martin-Causey, T. (2005). Building your dream practice from the ground up. In J. E. Barnett & M. Gallardo (Eds.), *Handbook for success in independent practice* (pp. 59–65). Phoenix, AZ: Psychologists in Independent Practice.

Martini, R. (n.d.). *Five tips for choosing a phone system.* Retrieved June 7, 2007, from http://technology.inc.com/telecom/articles/200608/fivephones.html

McGee, T. (2003). Observations on the retirement of professional psychologists. *Professional Psychology: Research and Practice, 34,* 388–395.

McKeachie, W. (1999). *Teaching tips: Strategies, research and theory for college and university teachers* (10th ed.). Boston: Houghton Mifflin.

McMinn, M., Aikins, D., & Lish, R. (2003). Basic and advanced competence in collaborating with clergy. *Professional Psychology: Research and Practice, 34,* 197–202.

McMinn, M., Runner, S., Fairchild, J., Lefler, J., & Suntay, R. (2005). Factors affecting clergy-psychologist referral patterns. *Journal of Psychology and Theology, 33,* 299–309.

Miller, W. R., & Rollnick, S. (2002). *Motivational interviewing: Preparing people to change.* New York: Guilford Press.

Nagy, T. (2005). *Ethics in plain English: An illustrative casebook for psychologists* (2nd ed.). Washington, DC: American Psychological Association.

Nash, J., Norcross, J., & Prochaska, J. (1984). Satisfactions and stresses of independent practice. *Psychotherapy in Private Practice, 2,* 39–48.

National Association of Social Workers Practice Research Network. (2002). *Issue 6.* Retrieved March 23, 2008, from http://search.social workers.org/naswprn/surveyOne/income2.pdf

New York State Office of the Professions. (n.d.). *Practice alerts and guidelines: When practices cease temporarily or permanently.* Retrieved July 12, 2007, from http://www.op.nysed.gov/psychcease.htm

Norcross, J., Hedges, M., & Castle, P. (2002). Psychologists conducting psychotherapy in 2001: A study of the Division 29 membership. *Psychotherapy: Theory, Research, Practice, Training, 39,* 97–102.

Norcross, J., Karpiak, C., & Santoro, S. (2005). Clinical psychologists across the years: The Division of Clinical Psychology from 1960 to 2003. *Journal of Clinical Psychology, 61,* 1467–1483.

Norcross, J., Prochaska, J., & Farber, J. (1993). Psychologists conducting psychotherapy: New findings and historical comparison on the Psychotherapy Division Membership. *Psychotherapy: Theory, Research, Practice, Training, 30,* 692–697.

Norris, F. (1992). Epidemiology of trauma: Frequency and impact of different potentially traumatic events on different demographic groups. *Journal of Consulting and Clinical Psychology, 60,* 409–418.

O'Neill, P. (2005). The ethics of problem definition. *Canadian Psychology, 46,* 13–22.

Orman, S. (1998). *Financial freedom: Creating true wealth now.* [Workbook that accompanies S. Orman's (1997) *The 9 steps to financial freedom.*] New York: Crown House Publishing.

Orman, S. (1999). *The courage to be rich.* New York: Riverhead Books.

Paasche-Orlow, M., Taylor, H., & Brancati, F. (2003). Readability standards for informed consent forms as compared with actual readability. *New England Journal of Medicine, 348,* 721–726.

Palmiter, D., & Renjilian, D. (2003). Clinical Web pages: Do they meet expectations? *Professional Psychology: Research and Practice, 34,* 164–169.

Perlman, B., McCann, L., & McFadden, S. (1999). *Lessons learned: Practical advice for the teaching of psychology.* Washington, DC: American Psychological Association.

Perrott, L. (1998). Business psychology: A new specialty. *The Independent Practitioner, 8,* 30–33.

Phelps, R., Eisman, E., & Kohout, J. (1998). Psychological practice and managed care: Results of the CAPP practitioner survey. *Professional Psychology: Research and Practice, 29,* 31–36.

Plante, T. (1996). Ten principles of success for psychology trainees embarking on their careers. *Professional Psychology: Research and Practice, 27,* 304–307.

Pomerantz, A., & Segrist, D. (2006). The influence of payment method on psychologists' diagnostic decisions regarding minimally impaired clients. *Ethics and Behavior, 16,* 253–263.

Pope, K., & Vasquez, M. (2005). *How to survive and thrive as a therapist: Information, ideas, and resources for psychologists in practice.* Washington, DC: American Psychological Association.

Pope, K., & Vasquez, M. (2007). *Ethics in psychotherapy and counseling: A practical guide* (3rd ed.). San Francisco: Jossey-Bass.

Princeton Review. (n.d.). *Top 10 most popular psychology majors.* Retrieved July 1, 2007, from http://www.princetonreview.com/college/research/articles/majors/popular.asp

Prochaska, J., & Norcross, J. (1983a). Contemporary psychotherapists: A national survey of characteristics, practices, orientations, and attitudes. *Psychotherapy: Theory, Research, Practice, and Training, 20,* 161–173.

Prochaska, J., & Norcross, J. (1983b). Psychotherapists in independent practice: Some findings and issues. *Professional Psychology: Research and Practice, 14,* 869–881.

Pruitt, S., Klapow, J., Epping-Jordan, J., & Dresselhaus, T. (1998). Moving behavioral medicine to the front line: A model for the integration of behavioral and medical sciences in primary care. *Professional Psychology: Research and Practice, 29,* 230–236.

Rabin, L., Barr, W., & Burton, L. (2005). Assessment practices of clinical neuropsychologists in the United States and Canada: A survey of INS, NAN, and APA Division 40 members. *Archives of Clinical Neuropsychology, 20,* 33–65.

Ralston, R. (2003). The effects of customer service, branding, and price on the perceived value of local telephone service. *Journal of Business Research, 56,* 201–213.

Reamer, F. (1995). Malpractice claims against social workers: First facts. *Social Work, 40,* 595–601.

Reamer, F. (2006). *Social work values and ethics* (3rd ed.). New York: Columbia University Press.

Rodino, E. (2005). It's about you: Money and your psychodynamics. In J. E. Barnett & M. Gallardo (Eds.), *Handbook for success in independent practice* (pp. 54–58). Phoenix, AZ: Psychologists in Independent Practice.

Rodino, E., Haber, S., & Lipner, I. (2001). *Saying goodbye to managed care.* New York: Springer Publishing Company.

Rosenberg, T., & Pace, M. (2006). Burnout among mental health professionals: Special considerations for the marriage and family therapist. *Journal of Marital and Family Therapy, 32,* 87–99.

Rothbaum, P., Bernstein, D., Haller, O., Phelps, R., & Kohout, J. (1998). New Jersey psychologist's report on managed mental health care. *Professional Psychology: Research and Practice, 29,* 37–42.

Rupert, P., & Morgan, D. (2005). Work settings and burnout among professional psychologists. *Professional Psychology: Research and Practice, 36,* 544–550.

Sacco, J. (n.d.-a). *Choosing a multi-line phone system.* Retrieved June 7, 2007, from http://businessweek.buyerzone.com/telecom_equipment/phone_systems/multi-line-phone-system.html

Sacco, J. (n.d.-b). *Is copier leasing the right choice for you?* Retrieved June 9, 2007, from http://www.buyerzone.com/office_equipment/copiers digital/copier-leasing.html

Salovey, P., & Grewal, D. (2005). The science of emotional intelligence. *Current Directions in Psychological Science, 14,* 281–285.

Samuels, R. (1983). I bought his private practice. *Psychotherapy in Private Practice, 1,* 104–107.

Sarason, S. (1974). *The creation of settings and the future societies.* San Francisco: Jossey-Bass.

Sarason, S. (1981). An asocial psychology and a misdirected clinical psychology. *American Psychologist, 36,* 827–836.

Schank, J., & Skovholt, T. (2005). *Ethical practice in small communities: Challenges and rewards for psychologists.* Washington, DC: American Psychological Association.

Schlosser, B. (1989). Practitioner-computer fit. *Independent Practitioner, 9,* 7–9.

Schlosser, B. (1990). Rats, cheese and choices. *Independent Practitioner, 10,* 8–10.

Schlosser, B. (1993). Something has happened to me. It's probably temporary. *Independent Practitioner, 13,* 146–147.

Schultz, G. (n.d.). *Financing start-up & break-away practices.* Retrieved June 16, 2007, from http://www.physiciansnews.com/business/999schultz.html

Schurenberg, E. (2007). The off-ramp to riches. *Money Magazine, 36,* 16.

Sharfstein, S., Towery, O., & Milowe, I. (1980). Accuracy of diagnostic information submitted to an insurance company. *American Journal of Psychiatry, 137,* 70–73.

Simono, R., & Wachiowiak, D. (1983). Career patterns in college counseling centers: Counseling psychologists report on their present, past and future. *Professional Psychology: Research and Practice, 14,* 142–148.

Singleton, D., Tate, A., & Randall, G. (2003). *Salaries in Psychology 2001: Report of the 2001 APA Salary Survey.* Retrieved July 7, 2007, from http://research.apa.org/01salary

Snyder, T. A., & Barnett, J. E. (2006). Informed consent and the psychotherapy process. *Psychotherapy Bulletin, 41*(1), 37–42.

Stanley, T., & Danko, W. (1996). *The millionaire next door.* New York: Pocket Books.

Stout, C., & Grand, L. (2005). *Getting started in private practice.* Hoboken, NJ: Wiley.

Stout, C., Levant, R., Reed, G., & Murphy, M. (2001). Contracts: A primer for psychologists. *Professional Psychology: Research and Practice, 32,* 88–91.

Stromberg, C., & Schuetze, J. (1997). Beyond flying solo: A guide to options in structuring the practice. *The Psychologist's Legal Update.* Washington, DC: National Register of Health Service Providers in Psychology.

Strom-Gottfried, K. (1998). Is ethical managed care an oxymoron? *Families in Society, 79,* 297–307.

Strom-Gottfried, K. (1999). Professional boundaries: An analysis of violations by social workers. *Families in Society, 80,* 439–449.

Tovian, S. (2006). Interdisciplinary collaboration in outpatient practice. *Professional Psychology: Research and Practice, 37,* 268–272.

Trachtman, R. (1999). The money taboo: Its effects in everyday life and in the practice of psychotherapy. *Clinical Social Work Journal, 27,* 275–288.

Tracy, J. (2005). *Accounting for dummies.* Hoboken, NJ: Wiley.

Tryon, G. (1983). Full-time private practice in the United States: Results of a national survey. *Professional Psychology: Research and Practice, 14,* 685–696.

Twomey, D. P., & Jennings, M. M. (2007). *Anderson's business law and the legal environment, comprehensive volume* (20th ed.). Mason, OH: South-Western College/West.

Tyson, E. (2006). *Personal finance for dummies.* Hoboken, NJ: Wiley.

United Behavioral Health. (2007). Join our clinician network. Retrieved July 1, 2007, from http://www.ubhonline.com/cred/credmenu.jsp? State=GA+StateName=Georgia

Vogel, D., Wade, N., & Haake, S. (2006). Measuring the self-stigma associated with seeking psychological help. *Journal of Counseling Psychology, 53,* 325–337.

Walfish, S. (2001a). Developing a career in psychology. In S. Walfish & A. K. Hess (Eds.), *Succeeding in graduate school: The career guide for psychology students* (pp. 385–400). Mahwah, NJ: Erlbaum.

Walfish, S. (2001b, August). *Clinical practice strategies outside the realm of managed care.* Paper presented at the annual meeting of the American Psychological Association, San Francisco, CA.

Walfish, S., & Coovert, D. (1989). Beginning and maintaining an independent practice: A Delphi poll. *Professional Psychology: Research and Practice, 20,* 54–55.

Walfish, S., & Coovert, D. (1990). Career as business. In N. E. Margenau (Ed.), *The encyclopedic handbook of private practice* (pp. 431–441). New York: Gardner Press.

Walfish, S., & Ducey, B. (2007). Readability level of HIPAA notices of privacy practices utilized by psychologists in clinical practice. *Professional Psychology: Research and Practice, 38,* 203–207.

Walfish, S., & Jannsen, L. (1988). Financing outpatient mental health care: How much will insurance actually help? *American Journal of Orthopsychiatry, 58,* 470–472.

Walfish, S., Keenan, N., & Tecala, M. (2008a). Career satisfaction of clinical social in private practice. Manuscript submitted for publication.

Walfish, S., Keenan, N., & Tecala, M. (2008b). Clinical social workers practicing outside of managed care. Manuscript submitted for publication.

Walfish, S., McAllister, B., O'Connell, P., & Lambert, M. (2007). *Are all therapists from Lake Wobegon?: An investigation of self-assessment bias in mental health providers.* Manuscript submitted for publication.

Walfish, S., & O'Donnell, P. (in press). Satisfaction and stresses in private practice. *The Independent Practitioner.*

Walfish, S., & Walraven, S. (2005). Career satisfaction of psychologists in independent practice. *Counseling and Clinical Psychology Journal, 2,* 124–133.

Ware, M. (2001). Pursuing a career with a bachelor's degree in psychology. In S. Walfish & A. K. Hess (Eds.), *Succeeding in graduate school: The career guide for psychology students* (pp. 11–30). Mahwah, NJ: Erlbaum.

Watkins, E. (1997). *Handbook of psychotherapy supervision.* New York: Wiley.

Weitz, R. (1983). I sold my private practice. *Psychotherapy in Private Practice, 1,* 101–107.

Whitaker, T., Weismiller, T., & Clark, E. (2006). *Assuring the sufficiency of a frontline workforce: A national study of licensed social workers.* [Executive summary.] Washington, DC: National Association of Social Workers.

Woody, J., & Woody, R. (2001). *Ethics in marriage and family therapy.* Washington, DC: American Association for Marriage and Family Therapy.

Woody, R. (1988). *Protecting your mental health practice: How to minimize legal and financial risk.* San Francisco: Jossey-Bass.

Woody, R. (1989). *Business success in mental health practice.* San Francisco: Jossey-Bass.

Woody, R. (1997). Valuing a psychological practice. *Professional Psychology: Research and Practice, 28,* 77–80.

Woody, R. (1998). Bartering for psychological services. *Professional Psychology: Research and Practice, 29,* 174–178.

Young, J., & Weishaar, M. (1997). Psychologists in private practice. In R. Sternberg (Ed.), *Career paths in psychology: Where your degree can take you* (pp. 71–92). Washington, DC: American Psychological Association.

Young, S. (2002). *Great failures of the extremely successful: Mistakes, adversity, failure and other stepping stones to success.* Beverly Hills, CA: Tallfellow Press.

Zevnik, R. (2004). *The complete book of insurance.* Naperville, IL: Sphinx.

Index

About the Authors

Steven Walfish, PhD, is a licensed psychologist in independent practice in Atlanta, Georgia. He is the associate editor of the *Independent Practitioner* and has served on the editorial boards of several journals. He has published in the areas of substance abuse, weight loss surgery, and professional training and practice. He received the American Psychological Association Division of Consulting Psychology Award for Outstanding Research in Consulting Psychology and the Walter Barton Award for Outstanding Research in Mental Health Administration from the American College of Mental Health Administration. His first book (coedited with Allen Hess, 2001) was *Succeeding in Graduate School: The Career Guide for Psychology Students.* He received his PhD in clinical/community psychology from the University of South Florida and has been a visiting professor at Kennesaw State University and Georgia State University. He is currently a clinical assistant professor in the Department of Psychiatry and Behavioral Sciences at the Emory University School of Medicine.

Jeffrey E. Barnett, PsyD, ABPP, is a licensed psychologist in independent practice in Arnold, Maryland, and a professor on the affiliate faculty in the Department of Psychology at Loyola College in Maryland. He is a diplomate of the American Board of Professional Psychology in clinical psychology and in clinical child and adolescent psychology and is a Distinguished Practitioner in Psychology of the National Academies of Practice. Dr. Barnett is a fellow of seven divisions of the American Psychological Association (APA) and has served on the APA Ethics Committee. He is an associate editor of the journal *Professional Psychology: Research and Practice* and editor of its "Focus on Ethics" section. Dr. Barnett has presented and published widely on issues relevant to ethical, legal, and professional practice issues in psychology. His recent book (coauthored with W. Brad Johnson, 2008), *Ethics Desk Reference for Psychologists,* is published by APA Books. He is active in leadership positions in the profession of psychology and has served as president of the Maryland Psychological Association and three APA divisions.